# Forbidden Universe

# Forbidden Universe

## Mysteries of the Psychic World

### Leo Talamonti

Preface by
WILLIAM MACKENZIE

Translated by
PAUL STEVENSON

STEIN AND DAY/*Publishers*/New York

First published in the United States of America, 1975
Copyright © 1974 by Sugar Editore
All rights reserved
Printed in the United States of America
Stein and Day/*Publishers*/Scarborough House
Briarcliff Manor, N.Y. 10510


*Library of Congress Cataloging in Publication Data*

Talamonti, Leo.
Forbidden universe.

(The Prehistory and ancient science library)
Translation of Universo proibito.
Includes bibliographical references and index.
1.   Psychical research.   2.   Occult sciences.
I. Title.
BF1034.T313   1975        133.8        74-23121
ISBN 0-8128-1767-2

# CONTENTS

## PART VI: THE DIFFUSION OF MIND

## TRANSLATOR'S NOTE

Foreign language works cited in the Notes and elsewhere are generally referred to in English versions when these exist. On the other hand, quotations from works originally written in English are generally back-translated from the Italian.

Additional references, especially to works in Italian, will be found in the Notes to the Italian edition.

In bibliographical references, the absence of a place of publication usually signifies that the work was published in London (if in English) or Paris (if in French).

P.S.

# Forbidden Universe

# PREFACE

Before discussing this useful and timely book, I would mention one or two instances from my own experience of the obstinacy with which some authors refuse to admit the existence of facts that are based on abundant evidence although they have not been accepted by 'official' science.

As long ago as 1912, together with respected scientists from several countries, I witnessed the performance of the celebrated 'calculating horses' at Elberfeld in Germany. All my colleagues without exception agreed in writing with the conclusion that I and others had reached, viz. that the horses' 'answers' to the questions put to them were in no way prompted by their master or anyone else; yet the 'scientific editor' of a well-known Italian review not long ago wrote in his column that 'as everybody knows', the reverse was the case.

Again, in the science column of a popular weekly I read, not long ago, the confident statement that ghosts did not exist and that belief in them was a mere superstition. Of course anyone is entitled to disbelieve in ghosts, but he should do so with a measure of philosophic doubt. For my part, I have seen, heard and touched a number of ghosts, or rather been touched by them, under rigorous control conditions and without my emotions being in any way engaged. This took place in Warsaw in 1923, at the second International Congress of Psychic Research, of which I had the honour to be chairman. In a prolonged séance with a medium named Guzik, who entered into a trance with myself and a doctor friend holding each of his hands, a succession of luminous phantoms appeared with the utmost clarity. These male and female figures, materialized as far down as the waist, hovered about my head, whispered words of greeting in my ear and even kissed my forehead. A closely similar record of apparitions in Mexico was made by

7

Gutierre Tibón, as readers will see in a Chapter 14 of this book.

In general we may expect 'popular science' writers to respect and encourage popular prejudices, especially in an age which idolizes science without properly understanding its aims, limitations and possibilities. I am all the more glad, therefore, to welcome Sig. Talamonti's book, which does justice to neglected aspects of nature and shows up the errors of scepticism and prejudice. The author is a journalist who has made a long study of paranormal phenomena, and he has done an excellent job of making its results and problems clear to the general reader. While the work is fresh and popular in style, it is full of the seriousness that befits a student of science and a philosopher, with a clear view of the unity of the sensible world with that which lies beyond the senses. Such a view is necessary if science is ever to comprehend the universe as a whole. The opposing attitude, which we may call 'neo-Aristotelianism', tends to deny certain aspects of reality or to rule them out as inaccessible to science. Sig. Talamonti joins issue with this restrictive and outdated viewpoint, and in so doing renders a service not only to the general reader but to specialists in parapsychology and the philosophy of science, not least by the stimulating connections he suggests between fields of knowledge that are generally kept apart.

The subject is of course beset by difficulties of method and verification; but it would be a sad thing if scientists were deterred by these, or if the whole subject were discredited because certain mediums have been shown to be fraudulent. It is in fact human nature to be shy of occult phenomena: primitive man was afraid of them for supersitious reasons, modern man because they threaten his tidy and reassuring view of a perfectly regular and predictable universe. But every scientist knows that human knowledge is surrounded by a vast *terra incognita* and that the attempt to extend its boundaries is a never-ending one. This being so, there is no excuse for refusing to accept evidence of the unknown or for restricting the area of research on a *priori* grounds.

The present book gives a clear picture of those aspects of nature for which official science has at present no room, but it eschews arbitrary or fanatical judgements. The author leaves the field open to various hypotheses, all of which he discusses fairly and objectively, while suggesting a theory of his own which would reduce the phenomena to a single pattern. The basis of this theory is that paranormal phenomena can all be brought under the common denominator of 'oneiric' or dream-like mental states, thanks to which individuals are able to mobilize their latent faculties and enter into direct touch with a world that underlies our everyday perceptions. As the book shows in detail, there are many cases of interaction between this wider world and the everyday one, and the supersession of the latter's laws by the former.

We have still to discover the nature of the basic world to which only our subconscious mind has access, and the author of this book approaches the problem with the aid of hypotheses and intuitions of many kinds, ranging from psychology to physics and mathematics, but with the overriding aim of reducing the evidence to a metaphysical unity. He is at pains to note every possible link between the results of parapsychic observation and the most daring speculations of modern physics, which have liberated scientific thought from the strait-jacket of Cartesian rationalism. It may well be that parapsychology will not take its place as an official science until that liberation is complete, and in that sense it is a science of tomorrow rather than of today. But it is all the more important to lay its foundations properly and not allow ourselves to be trammelled by an outworn conception of human knowledge. Science in all ages has owed much to unorthodox thought, and every open-minded person must hope and believe that parapsychology will be no exception to this rule.

The present work combines balance of view with boldness of speculation, and among its many valuable hypotheses is one shared by eminent psychologists and psychiatrists, viz. that the unconscious has a 'luminous polarity' of its own, the nature and properties of which have yet to be explored. Related to this is the view that instead of paranormal faculties being, as is generally thought today, a relic of primitive and atavistic powers, they may represent Nature's attempt to raise mankind on to a higher evolutionary plane. On this view, which I think deserves serious consideration, the effect of evolution may be to achieve a more stable degree of co-ordination between our two kinds of cognitive faculty, the primeval intuitive one and the rational one which is of later date. It may be thought that the first intimation of this effect is to be seen in those exceptional individuals who can exercise at will

9

the ordinary powers of consciousness and the super-rational faculties of the unconscious. Other intriguing hypotheses are that of a biological function of psychokinesis (the power to affect matter at a distance) as a natural though almost imperceptible component of every manifestation of the will; and the suggestion of a unity embracing all aspects of 'contact with the past', from retrospective dreams to psychometry, from spiritualistic manifestations to what has been called the 'extravasation of mind and personality'.

I will stop at this point so that the reader may have the pleasure of making his own discoveries. He will not, I believe, have wasted his time if the work inclines him to suspect, if not to conclude with certainty, that official science does not have the answer to everything, and that mankind is surrounded by a wider realm of mystery than is generally supposed.

William Mackenzie,
former Lecturer in the Philosophy of Biology
at the University of Geneva, and Honorary
President of the Italian Society of
Parapsychology.

# INTRODUCTION

*The unknown dimension of reality*

> Science tells us what we can know, but
> what we can know is little, and if we
> forget how much we cannot know we become
> insensitive to many things of very great
> importance.
>
> Bertrand Russell,
> History of Western
> Philosophy.

This book is based on a series of critical observations of the rich and varied world of clairvoyants, mediums and persons gifted with supernormal sensory powers — a world of which the ordinary public is only aware in a superficial and distorted manner. Do these abnormal individuals, or do they not, possess the power to cause phenomena that seem contrary to the laws of nature? In answering this question we must avoid two extremes; that of over-credulity, which has been sufficiently emphasized, and the risk of thwarting a legitimate and fruitful curiosity. At a time when we seem more in danger of stifling freedom of thought than of believing too much, the aim of the present work is to show that a thorough study of paranormal phenomena may enable us to explore a whole new dimension of reality and obtain a better understanding of life, mankind and the universe. But before we can advance in this direction we must overcome the weight of preconceptions and prejudices based on the sceptical, rationalistic trend of our civilization.

Up to now we have been justly proud of the philosophic doubt which enabled modern science to shake off the bonds of antiquity, but perhaps it is time to look at the other side of the medal and count the cost of our victorious advance. Scepticism was a creative factor at the outset of our progress, but it can become a destructive force, undermining the bases of knowledge. The present work is therefore also an attack on disbelief, of the restless, neurotic kind which never calls itself in question. Modern psychology has taught us to be mistrustful of this kind of doubt, exposing it as a quest for 'absolute certainty' which, as Gide pointed out, is the antithesis of a love for truth. Only if the reader accepts this viewpoint will he derive profit from the following pages. My thanks go to all those who have enriched the work by their suggestions, and especially to my wife, whose spiritual and practical resources have made it possible for our joint efforts to be accomplished.

# PART I

## Frontiers of the mind

# CHAPTER 1

## In the beginning was the dream

*Two types of consciousness*

From time immemorial, the basic questions that Man has put to himself are: Who and what am I? What is the essence of human personality, what are its limitations, and in what kind of universe do we live? Many answers have been given to these problems, including the answer that they are insoluble; and still the enquiry goes on. But the nature of the answer depends in every case on the type of consciousness that it presupposes.

If, for instance, we are thinking in terms of our daytime self, then we are three-dimensional beings who depend on our senses for information about the outside world; we are subject to the restrictions of space and the inexorable flow of time. But there is a different form of consciousness that comes to light in certain dreams, in which we are freed from the bondage of time and space, logic and sense perception. Such states of mind are subjective, but not necessarily illusory, for at times they prove to be correlated to external reality, as many examples show.

If we reserve the term 'reality' for our daytime existence, what are we to call the events that occur in dreams? If these too are reality, what relation do they bear to the other sort? Many, of course, regard the dream-world as a thing of darkness, unconsciousness and, literally, absence of mind; but this is an inadequate view. Psychogists, philosophers and doctors are well aware that the conscious mind is only part of our psyche: the unconscious is prior and more fundamental, or so many believe, and when we are asleep it resumes its rights. As the psychoanalyst Erich Froom puts it, 'Our daytime world is just as unconscious in relation to our dream world as the latter is in relation to the former. They are simply different mental states relating to different modes of existence.[1]

15

This is an important point, but the only evidence we have on which to assess the value of our night-time world consists in our dreams, or rather the small portion of them that we remember. And, to all appearances, most of the dreams we recall signify very little: a thread of more or less fantastic 'story', vague reminiscences of waking experience, and an absence of critical control by the mind. Dreams of this sort may be of interest to the specialists who know how to interpret them; but we are concerned here with dreams of a much rarer type which impress us by their unusual character and especially, as Titus Burckhardt puts it, by 'the loftiness of their formal language, purged of everything that is turbid and chaotic'. These are what Macrobius in his *Commentarii* called 'great dreams'; they seem to reveal unsuspected capabilities and powers of comprehension belonging, we may think, to a kind of psychic nucleus hidden somewhere in the recesses of the self.

Among these are precognitive dreams, which in some inexplicable way foretell the future. For centuries it has been known that sad or gay events announce themselves through dream-images which may be either symbolic or highly realistic. We read of these in religious texts and the records of scholarly investigators,[2, 3] and they are attested by popular tradition and belief. The volume of evidence, and the critical examination it has been subjected to, should suffice to rebut suspicions of error, bad faith or coincidence. As is well known, President Lincoln dreamt of his own imminent death; and Gaetano Dall'Oglio, a young seminary instructor at Bologna, had a dream predicting the death of Pope Benedict XV in 1922 and the election of Cardinal Achille Ratti to succeed him. We shall describe in a later chapter the many instances of dreams predicting disasters, especially large-scale ones: the frequency of these may be due to the fact that the events themselves naturally make a profound impression on individual and collective memory.

As regards fortunate events, we may recall that on 4 April 1917, when things were going badly for the Allies in the first world war, Sir Arthur Conan Doyle dreamt that a turn in the fortunes of war would be somehow connected with the small Italian river Piave. He informed the Society for Psychical Research of his dream, which, as we know, came true.

An Italian lady, Dr B., informed the present author that

16

before she was engaged or had met her future husband, she dreamt that she was married to a rich young man with a country villa: this, as she saw in her dream, had a terrace and an outdoor flight of steps built in a particular way. Later she met a young man whom she married, and who turned out to have a villa exactly like the one in the dream. Professor George Zorab of The Hague has collected many examples of dreams like this one, predicting marriages or wealth or indicating means of making money. He relates, for instance, that a citizen of Venlo dreamt one night of the numbers 3, 6, 8 and 4 and heard a mysterious voice telling him they would win in the lottery; twice he awoke and went to sleep again, when the dream recurred. He obtained a ticket No. 3684 from Groningen and won a large sum.[4]

A few years ago a girl living at Bredore (Bergamo) dreamt that she was on her way to the government lottery office with a casket of jewels and a bundle of gold rods. In her dream she met a certain Canon who had died the year before: he took away two rods and said: 'In 1990 this gold would be worth 41 million lire.' The people of Predore put this omen to good effect by betting on numbers 2, 41 and 90 at the Genoa lottery (chosen because the Canon's name began with the letters GEN), and their total winnings amounted to 25 million lire.

At Macerata, a few years ago, a lady dreamt that her dead father was standing on a threshing-machine and saying to her: 'The crop is better this year than last, it is 70 quintals instead of 60. As we have harvested 66, that leaves 4.' Using these figures the lady won 16 million lire in the lottery. Many similar cases could be quoted, from a study on this subject by the well-known psychiatrist Cesare Lombroso.

### Night does away with the time-barrier

Before considering the theory of precognition we may note that 'great dreams' do not necessarily relate to great events, or to such as are of major importance to the dreamer. Trintzius, for example, describes an incident that happened to the philosopher Schopenhauer. One morning he overturned an inkwell by accident, and the maid whom he called to wipe the floor said that she had dreamt, the night before, of wiping off an inkstain from that very spot. Her master was doubtful of this until another maid who slept in the same room declared that the first maid had related her dream to her in the small hours of the morning. Trintzius suggests that this minor incident may have led to some of Schopenhauer's most interesting speculations on chance, freedom and destiny.[5]

The examples we have considered show that dreams may correspond precisely with the objective reality, subject only to time-displacement, and are therefore not so hopelessly subjective as is sometimes thought. They deserve, in fact, more serious attention than orthodox science has so far given them. The first person in modern times to make a systematic study of precognitive dreams was J.W. Dunne, an aeronautical engineer by profession, whose *Experiment with Time* was published in 1927. Dunne evolved a technique of recording his dreams first thing every morning and identifying those which turned out to foretell events; he also got his friends and relations to take part in the experiment, subject to strict controls from the point of view of method and evaluation. After accumulating a large quantity of data he evolved a theory of precognition which has not been refuted and is to some extent confirmed by more recent research.

One of his main points was that nocturnal precognitive activity is of a continuous and normal character and is unrelated to the importance of the events in question. We all dream of future events, however minor, but few of us remember them. This is partly because our waking self is determined to erase the memory of dreams, and partly because the dreamer's mind distorts and misinterprets what it perceives, and confuses elements from past experience with those that relate to the future. It may be added that what Fromm calls the 'existential modality' of dreams enables us to enter a wider world whose physical laws are different and more basic than those of the universe we know. This is also illustrated by the type of dream which conveys information about events happening at a distance.

### Dreams of far-off events

The distinctive characteristic of 'great dreams' is that they are extremely vivid, reflecting a kind of hyper-vigilance in some part of the mind, and that they impress the dreamer so strongly as to impel him or her to take some action, or at least impart the dream to others.

Boutet tells the story of a French boy aged six, sleeping in his parents' bedroom, who woke at eleven o'clock screaming: 'La Hêtraye is on fire!' (This was the name of a property where the family had spent several holidays). They made him go back to sleep, but he kept on waking and screaming in the same manner until five o'clock. Next day a telegram came to say that the country house had indeed been destroyed by a fire, which had lasted from eleven till five and could not be extinguished because the water in the pipes had frozen during the night.[6]

On 19 March 1852 Garibaldi, who was crossing the Pacific *en route* for Asia, dreamt that he was present at his mother's funeral; it turned out that she had in fact died that day. Giuseppina Perlasco, another patriot of the *risorgimento,* learnt in a dream of the execution of her lover Luigi Dottesio, who had been under arrest for conspiring against the Austrian empire. She awoke at dawn on 11 October 1851 crying that Luigi had been killed: the execution had in fact just taken place, though the family had hoped till the last that he would be pardoned.

Some years ago the Italian press told the story of Alfonsina C., an old lady who had a nightmare concerning the death of her daughter, aged 58. She rose at dawn, made her way to Sampierdarena where the daughter lived, entered the house with the aid of the police and found her lying with her wrists cut (as the dream had foretold), lying on the floor of the gas-filled kitchen where she had committed suicide.

At Miami in 1961, a Mrs James A. Young dreamt that she saw her husband's body lying on the street and 'knew' that he had been murdered, which proved to be the case. These and many other examples show that dreams can overleap the barriers of space as well as time. The explanation of telepathy fits well enough in many cases; but there are others where no individual 'sender' can be identified, and we are bound to conclude that the secret self has some mysterious power of perceiving events at a distance. We shall revert to this in chapters 2 and 6.

*Collective dreams*

Among the most remarkable dream-stories are those in which two people, usually linked by some special bond of affection, simultaneously dream of the same event, real or fictitious.

In 1916, during the first world war, a boy of seven named Jetti Brand dreamt vividly that his father was very thirsty and called for some beer, which the boy fetched. He told his mother of the dream next morning. A few days later a letter came from his father, who was at the front, saying that he had suffered acute thirst owing to a breakdown in the water supply, but his thirst had disappeared after a curious dream in which he had returned home and been given a glass of beer by his son. The case is the subject of a detailed account by G. Schmeidler and E. Frommer, which shows how closely the two dreams agreed together. It hardly seems that they can be fully explained by telepathy.

The sharing of dream experiences appears, at all events, to refute the view that human beings can only communicate by means of language, spoken or written. Perhaps Charles Richet is right when he says that 'we are in mysterious communion with all other human beings', or G.N.M. Tyrrell when he maintains that certain states of consciousness can be shared or, as we would rather say, experienced in common. These include certain kinds of waking dream, as we shall see in the further course of this study.

Other collective dreams have been reported by F.H. Myers and Professor Cesare Biondi. The latter published in 1930 the fact that Giovanni Pascoli and his sister Mariu had, one night, an identical dream in which each of them was holding a small bird in their left hand and a repulsive insect in the right. They told each other of the dream next day, and thought it so extraordinary that they made a formal record then and there.

A Piedmontese lady, an artist who is known outside Italy, has given me details of dreams that she has shared with her cook, who has been with her for many years and who, like her, appears unusually sensitive to this type of experience. It would seem from all the evidence that dreams, or some dreams, belong to a sphere of reality which, though non-material, is objective in its own way, and which might be referred to as the 'dream dimension' if it were not that the word 'dream' is tainted by a suggestion of unreality.

Professor Hornell Hart of Duke University, North Carolina, believes that shared dreams are more frequent than our scanty evidence suggests.[8] He puts this down to the fact that people remember barely one per cent of their dreams, so that there is at best one chance in ten thousand that two people who have shared a dream will be aware of the fact next day. In short, not only do we forget our dreams, as Dunne and others have pointed out, but we are not in a position to assess the importance of those we remember, on account of the curtain which separates our diurnal from our nocturnal existence. The curtain, of course, has its uses, but it prevents us from attaining a complete understanding of ourselves.

*Warnings in dreans*

In ancient times dreams were reverenced as the means chosen by the gods to communicate with human minds and impart instructions to them, couched in symbolic language that was often hard to interpret. As Aristotle put it, it was when the human mind and will are unable to function that the gods chose to exercise the power of direction in a visible manner. There is thus an antithesis, or perhaps we should say an apparent conflict, between the processes of the conscious mind and those that can only operate when the former is, so to speak, reduced to its lowest terms. Marcus Aurelius urged men to be thankful to the gods for the aid received in dreams; and the neo-Platonist Iamblichus wrote: 'An invisible spirit watches over sleeping men to protect them from mental and bodily suffering, and sometimes, when we experience a "heaven-sent" dream, we hear a faint voice telling us how we should act.'[9]

Coming to the present day, the following incident was reported in the Italian press in October 1961. A student named Luigi D., aged 18, was awoken at five in the morning by faint but insistent cries for help. He got up reluctantly, walked about the house but found nothing unusual. He would have gone back to bed, but an inexplicable sense of anxiety prompted him, instead, to lie down on a sofa in the next room. Suddenly there was a crash: the ceiling in his own room had collapsed, burying the bed and furniture under a heap of rubble. We may wonder whether, if Luigi D. had been fully awake and in possession of his faculties, he would have obeyed the mysterious warning to which he owed his life.

Man, in fact, is governed by two forces which are potentially complementary but which are difficult to harmonize: the

21

waking, conscious mind with its critical faculty and powers of volition, of which he is so proud, and another, obscurer force which guides him unawares. Socrates, as Plato tells us in the *Theaetetus*, had a secret counsellor which he called his *daimon* and which advised him from time to time in practical matters when his rational judgement would have led him astray.[10] In actual fact every man has his own *daimon*, which speaks to him clearly and intelligibly provided it is allowed to do so by the conscious ego; but the latter is often too assertive for the *daimon's* voice to be heard. It should be realized, moreover, that this secret self is an integral part of human nature, though it may seem to partake of what is normally thought of as superhuman — Maeterlinck, for example, called it the *numen*, and Jung has emphasised the ambiguous and disquieting aspect of its formidable powers. It is the dark side of the ego, the self that responds to hidden influences and inexplicable inspirations, and to it belong the paranormal forms of awareness that occur in certain dreams. We shall understand its nature better as we continue to explore its enigmatic feats and capabilities.

## Dreams of past events

Another mysterious type of dream is that which brings to light past events, not only in the dreamer's own life but in that of others. For instance, Violet Tweedale relates how Lady Cromartie had a dream revealing the hiding-place of a casket of jewels in the library of her home at Tarbat. [11] Not long ago, at Oppido Mamertina, a certain Vittorio F. dreamt that his dead father had told him 'to dig a foot below the walnut tree', and when he did so he found a tin box containing two thousand 500-lire coins, which he had been seeking ever since the old man died.

In some cases of this sort the dream may represent facts that we have known and forgotten, or result from unconscious cerebration on the basis of knowledge acquired in the ordinary way; but this can hardly be the explanation in all instances. Myers relates the story of a Mrs Anna Simpson of Perth, who dreamt repeatedly of an old country woman who asked her to find a Catholic priest to pay a debt of three shillings and sixpence which she, on dying, had left undischarged. Enquiries proved that the debt did in fact exist.

A case of greater importance to the world is that of the last thirteen cantos of Dante's *Divine Comedy*, which were missing for years until the poet's son Jacopo had a dream in which he was told of their whereabouts, apparently by the spirit of his dead father. This is related in Boccaccio's *In laude di Dante*, and seems to be confirmed by recent historical and literary research.

Paul Brunton states in *The Quest of the Overself* that he spent a night inside the Great Pyramid and saw visions of a dream-like character which revealed to him the solution of important problems in Egyptology, the results being confirmed by later research on the part of others. He also relates how Professor Hermann V. Hilprecht of Pennsylvania University had a dream which revealed to him the exact origin of two fragments of agate from the ruins of Nippur, the first Babylonian capital. This information enabled the Professor to amend the proofs of an article in which he had advanced a different hypothesis, on the basis of drawings of the fragments which were all he then possessed. When he was able to examine the actual stones in the Museum at Constantinople, he realized that the dream-solution was the correct one. Hilprecht, it should be mentioned, was the first scholar to discover large quantities of clay tablets inscribed in Babylonian cuneiform and to make significant progress towards decyphering them. The form of his dreams was reminiscent of Jacopo Alighieri's: a 'tall, lean priest of ancient Nippur' led him into the treasury of the temple and explained at length the story of the two pieces of agate.

Different theories have been advanced to explain dreams of this type, Ania Teillard describes them as 'the invasion of our world by another, or the opening by ourselves of a window on to other worlds.' According to others, the objects or figures that appear in dreams are symbols called into being by our secret self in order to convey a message in the terms most acceptable to the conscious mind. This hypothesis is wide enough to account for the most frequent type of retrospective dream, in which the communicating agent does not take the form of an individual human figure; but clearly the matter is still at a highly speculative stage.

23

As Aeschylus said long ago, dreamers have penetrating eyes. Science, it is true, does not pay much attention to poetic aphorisms of this sort; but, as Huizinga has remarked, 'when life transcends logic, as we must admit it sometimes does, then we must look to the poets to interpret it.' To resolve some problems we need the help of both poets and scholars, and of folklore as well. Ever since the Age of Enlightenment dreams have been at a discount; yet popular wisdom still tells us that if we are baffled by a problem we should sleep on it.

Elias Howe — the inventor of the sewing machine, which he patented in 1846 — had been grappling with the problem for some time previously, until he had a nightmare in which he was pursued by savages. Lying in his path was a large nail, upright in the ground, and after trying in vain to remove it he hit on the idea of drilling a hole in one end, inserting a piece of string and pulling on it. The nail may suggest to us a phallic image; but this was before the days of psychoanalysis, and Howe interpreted the message more or less literally, with the simplicity that is allied to genius. His subconscious mind had in fact presented him with the basic principle of his invention: an upright, moving needle with a hole near the point, into which the thread was inserted.

Many discoveries can be said in this way to have been inspired by a dream, or by the peculiar state of lucidity that occurs in certain dreams. Instances are to be found in the careers of two Nobel prizewinners: the Danish physicist Niels Bohr and the Canadian physician, Sir Frederick Grant Banting. Thanks to a dream of a planetary system evolving in a certain way, Niels Bohr understood what modifications were necessary to make Rutherford's model of the atom conform to the quantum theory. The resulting 'Bohr theory' of atomic structure holds the field to this day. Banting discovered in a dream the laboratory procedure for the production of insulin, which until a few years ago was the only effective remedy against diabetes.

Otto Loewi, the Austrian pharmacologist and co-winner of the Nobel prize for physiology and medicine in 1936, had a dream on two successive nights indicating the complex method of producing a certain drug. Immediately after the first dream he awoke and took notes, but in the morning they were undecypherable. On the next night he got up at once, went to his laboratory and carried out the process indicated by the dream. Other scientists who received information of this sort in dreams were the mathematicians Condorcet and William Lamberton, the naturalist Louis Agassiz and many more.

These and other instances suggest that our subconscious mind continues working at each and every problem that has baffled us during the day, even though in many cases we are unaware, on awaking, that this cerebration has taken place. The result may be that our conscious mind takes the credit for the successful endeavours of our subconscious. As Jung has put it: 'I have no doubt that all the mental activities of consciousness may also be present in the subconscious.'[12] We may add that hypnopaedia, or instruction during sleep, is based on a similar principle, though in this case cerebration is imposed on the subconscious by a decision of the conscious mind.

Dreams, of course, are also a source of artistic and literary inspiration. Stevenson's character Dr Jekyll owes his existence to a recurrent dream, and so does Andersen's story *The Emporor's New Clothes*. During an afternoon nap Wagner dreamt that he was being swept along by a mighty river, and the sound of its waves was finally transmuted into the *Rheingold* prelude. Another composer, Tartini, is said to have had a dream in which he challenged the Devil to play the violin, whereupon the latter executed a solo which inspired the 'Devil's Trill' in the sonata of that name.

*Dreams that serve a practical purpose*

The examples just mentioned relate to exceptional men, but experience shows that the hidden founts of knowledge are also open to ordinary people. This raises a point that should be borne in mind throughout the rest of this work. Some scholars tend on principle to reject the evidence of mediums and 'sensitives', but in doing so they are behaving like people who want to know how a war is progressing but will only listen to official communiqués. It is surely worth while hearing, in addition, what soldiers back from the front have to say, though it may require discounting in the light of other knowledge. The mediums are in the front line as far as exploration of the unknown is concerned, and we shall do well to pay attention to their evidence, albeit with a critical mind and without necessarily accepting their interpretation of the phen-

25

omena in which they are involved.

The following incident is quoted from the autobiography of Elizabeth d'Espérance, a famous medium whom we shall encounter again in these pages and whose *Shadow Land* appeared in London in 1897. At the age of thirteen she was set an essay to write which her schoolmates found fairly easy but which seemed to be beyond her powers. On the evening before it was due to be handed in she scribbled a few sentences in her exercise book and then went to bed in despair. She slept soundly, and on awakening was amazed to find that the book had been filled in with an essay in her handwriting, far superior to anything she could have composed from her own knowledge, so that the teachers were understandably suspicious when she handed it in. This incident seems to suggest that our minds contain secret powers that can be mobilized in case of emergency, in some kind of a dream-like state and under the direction, as it were, of what we have called the *daimon*. At the time of her experience, Elizabeth was a sleep-walker, and we know that people in this condition may perform actions and court physical dangers of which they remember nothing next day. But it would seem that even those who do not walk in their sleep have a nocturnal life full of significant mental experiences, although communication between the two planes of our existence is so imperfect that very little of these survives in the waking memory, and that in a confused state.

Two more incidents may be related, and some may treat them with more credence because of the authorities that vouch for them. Jung (op. cit.) tells the story of a commercial expert who had spent some days vainly trying to unravel a case of fraudulent bankruptcy. One night, having gone to bed at twelve, he awoke at three and went to his study, where his wife followed him. He sat at his desk writing notes for a quarter of an hour and then went back to bed. Next morning he remembered nothing of this, but the notes proved to contain the solution of his problem.

Myers tells a similar story of an accountant who got up one night and took notes in the dark which enabled him, next day, to clear up a professional error that had taken place months before. [13] These cases, and others like them, show that sleep can help us to solve the problems, great or small, of our waking life, endowing us with increased intellectual efficiency and knowledge that we do not normally possess. How this happens we can only conjecture. Perhaps the mind, liberated from daily circumstances, is in a better condition to focus on refractory problems, a state of hyper-vigilance *vis à vis* some special aspect of reality. At all events, we must recognize that the unconscious does not consist merely of instinctive elements but is also capable of filling gaps in our conscious intellectual processes, to an extent far exceeding our normal powers.

## Dreams and psychology

We are thus led to review the various opinions that have been expressed about dreams in general, both by psychologists and by students of other disciplines. According to Freudian doctrine, a dream is an attempt to compensate in unreal terms for the frustrations of everyday life: it is a flight from reality and a regression to an archaic, pre-logical state of mind, as witness the fact that it consists of images. This, however, takes no account of those dreams in which our secret self prepares the way for our waking thoughts and actions: dreams that are a seed-bed of future choices, through the medium of suggestions and conditioned reflexes that guide our daytime self without its knowledge, like an individual who has been given orders while in a hypnotic trance. Apart from dreams that solve practical difficulties or tell us where to find lost objects, there are those which guide young people towards a future vocation that seems highly improbable yet which comes true in a more or less remote future. Aldous Huxley drew attention to the fact that dreams, or the unconscious without the aid of dreams, can supply us with fresh sources of life and wisdom. This is a much more profitable approach for our purpose, as is the observation of Jung that 'dreams often anticipate the future', or of Adler that 'dreams are the point where the present and the future meet': this may not be true of all dreams, but it certainly is of some.

This being so, it is difficult to argue that dreams are the opposite of reality, and, as we shall see, there are many ways in which they can affect everyday life and make it conform to the rules of a dream-universe — a simpler universe than the daytime one, but also more basic and richer in possibilities. Baudouin, although a Freudian, is aware of this, and has compared dreams to orchestral music in which one or another instrument may predominate at different times. We may attend to any of these, and our theory of dreams will vary in consequence, but we must not forget the orchestra as a whole. The Jungian school has heeded this advice, and its representative Ernst Aeppli says that dreams 'appear to contain infinite knowledge of all events and possibilities.' They are able, as Jung observed, to put us in touch with a 'transcendental source' which transcends individual being and the categories of space and time; they speak to us in terms of antique wisdom, traditional symbols or 'archetypes' of whose significance the dreamer is often unaware.[14]

### The evidence of neuro-physiology

According to Aeppli, dreams are 'the language of the unconscious, speaking to us during our sleep'. There are two parties to the dialogue, and these are the facets or planes of our own personality, the conscious and the unconscious mind — the dialogue involving, as we saw, not only instinct but also intelligence and will. Collaboration between two parts of our mind is indispensable and fundamental: it is a unique aspect of human personality and one, perhaps, which evolution will one day make perfect.

In recent years neuro-physiology has enhanced our understanding by observations that can be made the subject of laboratory tests, like the brilliant research of Kleitman and Dement on the nature of sleep. These show that dreams are a universal psychic and physiological need, and take place in all of us, whether we remember them or not, according to a regular, unalterable rhythm; however, only a small part of our dreams ever reaches the level of consciousness.[15] Mankind needs to dream no less than to sleep, and, according to French investigators, the most evolved living creatures are those in which the need to dream is greatest — a sufficient refutation of the early modern psychologists and others who dismiss dreams as regressive and primitive.

Unfortunately science cannot unlock the mystery of what lies behind 'dreamless sleep', a condition which, the neuro-physiologists tell us, alternates regularly with the dreaming state whose existence can be objectively recorded. From a simplistic and anthropocentric point of view, we might regard dreamless sleep as a complete absence or suspension of the psyche; but, on the other hand, it may represent a mode of existence which, although impenetrable to us, is none the less an attribute of the human soul. This tends to be confirmed by the observation of some forms of trance (which was once called 'deep magnetic sleep') and by ancient Oriental experience.[16]

It is much to be hoped that dreaming in all its manifestations, not only nocturnal ones, can be made the subject of objective analysis. But care must be taken not to rule out any form of explanation in advance, or to insist that psychological phenomena, including dreams, can only be the product (or by-product, as was once said) of neuro-physiological forces. Such a view denies the autonomous reality of the psyche on premises that are futed by the very phenomena we are considering. It is in fact an eighteenth-century attitude, proper to those who have not yet realized that, as Huizinga puts it, 'the science of the past is mere fable'; or, as the same author says, 'categories of thought that were useful a short while ago seem to dissolve; boundaries are abolished, and contraries merge together.'[17] Such contraries, in the present context, are mind and matter, which may prove to be no more fundamentally distinct than modern physics have shown matter and energy to be. The distinction is a convenient one in practice, but if the two are really opposed to each other, then paranormal phenomena suggest strongly that it is a matter which depends on mind and not the other way about. As Jung puts it, 'The unconscious is sometimes regarded, if not as a kind of rubbish-dump beneath conscious level, at all events as something purely animal. But in fact its nature and scope are, by definition, indeterminate, and it is an idle prejudice either to exaggerate or to belittle its value.'[18]

## Dream-messages in daytime

We may now take a small but important step forward in the argument. If dreams are regarded as a dialogue or 'collaboration' between the two parts of our mind, we must extend the enquiry to cover all mental states in which our deeper or inner self tends to gain the upper hand over the ordinary ego, taking advantage of some relaxation of the latter's vigilance which it may itself have contrived to bring about. Waking dreams of this kind have not been fully investigated,

29

but Kleitman, for instance, has shown that during the day our conscious awareness relaxes at regular intervals, exactly as we alternate at night between deep and light sleep. According to John Pfeiffer, we are in a state of 'full conscious vigilance' for not more than a minute or two in every hour.

Non-physiologists such as Myers and Brunton had already noticed that a certain dream-like activity persists during the waking state, though it may be only latent, and moreover that it is an essential factor in mental creativity. We are all familiar with waking states in which we 'switch off' from the external world in order to reflect or to allow our minds to wander, so that the dream-world takes possession of our consciousness and imposes, for better or worse, its own emotions, fantasies and awareness. If this habit were to be stigmatized, whenever it occurs, as a sign of regression or dissociation, the whole human race would have to be regarded as mentally abnormal.

At eleven in the morning on 13 March 1814 Napoleon, who was talking to General Bertrand, suddenly began to weep for no reason that he or others could understand. It turned out that at that moment Josephine de Beauharnais was dying at the Malmaison. Although the secret knowledge did not break through the barrier of consciousness, it managed to trouble the Emperor's mind in the form of what may be called a visceral echo. A similar story is related of the Italian philosopher and psychiatrist Sante De Sanctis (1862-1935), who was at his books one evening when he felt an increasing conviction that his brother was in danger of death by fire at the Costanzi theatre in Rome, where he was attending a gala performance. At midnight his brother came home and said a fire had indeed started in the theatre and caused a panic. This time the warning took the form of a mental image as well as a state of mind: both, of course, are typical of dreams, which ought to be called primeval rather than primitive. We see in these examples how the dream-consciousness, in rare cases, succeeds in forcing a 'dialogue' on the other: this will be more or less vivid according to the solidity at a given moment of the barrier of which we spoke, which may be identified with the Freudian 'censor.' If it is true, as will be argued in the last part of this book, that animals are genuine somnambulists, it must be admitted that we share in this aspect of their nature and that there is a force within us that is ready to

30

challenge the supremacy of our daytime consciousness whenever anything happens to reduce the latter's vigilance.

The story is reported of a housewife at Salerno named Rosa P. who, one day, suddenly dropped her household chores, hired a car and drove to Teggiano in the same province, where she found her son lying dead in the gutter, having had an accident on his motor-cycle. This took place on Christmas Eve, 1955; the mother had had a waking dream in which she heard her son crying for help and telling her where his body was to be found. Also in 1955, a solderer in Boston dropped his work and told his mates that he was needed in another part of the city: he felt this urgently though he did not know why. He walked about for some time like a somnambulist or a homing animal, until he came to a mineshaft: entering it, he found the body, half-buried by a landslide, of an employer who had befriended him in the past, and he was luckily in time to save the man's life. A report of this case by Fraser and Betty Nichol appeared in 1958 in the journal of the American Society for Psychical Research.

## The multiplicity of dream-states

None of the people mentioned above, including Napoleon and De Sanctis, could be technically described as abnormal, and yet they provide instances of the 'somnambulism' that lurks in human nature, though the snobbery of the conscious ego has caused its existence to be neglected. Apart from invasions of the conscious mind by the unconscious, there are waking states in which the former's vigilance is dimmed to the point at which a creative or recreative dialogue can take place between the two. These have been examined in an interesting work by Dr Nicola Gentile, the pioneer of psychoanalysis in Italy. Gentile, for instance, defines 'artistic contemplation' as a hypnoid state 'that teaches us to dream, withdrawing from the external world without an effort of the will'. We may recall that Goethe's *Werther* was written in a sort of semi-trance: as the poet afterwards told a friend, 'I wrote the book almost unconsciously, like a somnambulist, and was amazed when I realized what I had done.'[19]

From the psychiatric point of view one may speak of 'dissociation' or split personality in some cases of this sort, but we cannot write all artists off as lunatics. D.H. Lawrence,

31

it appears, wrote all his novels in an almost perfect state of trance during which he lost contact with the outside world. Dialogues with the secret self can be of an extremely compelling nature. Kekule von Stradonitz, the German chemist (1829-96), was led by 'visions' to his most interesting discoveries, and to this context belong the phenomenal powers of mental arithmetic displayed by Lidoreau, Shakuntala Devi and others whom we shall discuss presently.

In ancient Greece, the Pythagoreans possessed the secret of ecstatic meditation leading to the acquisition of abstruse knowledge; and we know that Socrates used to relapse for hours into a kind of trance which inspired him with 'dream-like wisdom' (Plato, *Symposium*, 175). Another example is Archimedes, whose absorption in mathematical calculations cost him his life. There is, it will be seen, a parallelism between the great 'dreams' that occur at night and those of the day-time, which are no less powerful to unleash the creative powers of our innermost consciousness. Gentile distinguishes such states as meditation, concentration and self-hypnosis; but we should also take account of other varieties of hallucination, hypnotic trance and waking dream, including the mediumistic experience which, in a very few cases, exalts the creative power of the dream to its highest level. It was in a state of this kind that Victor Hugo composed a short poem of more than average interest, and, as we shall see, there are novels and pictures that have been created by untaught artists in a condition of semi-trance.

Unfortunately, although we can classify dream-states, we cannot say that we understand much more about them in the light of psychology or neuro-physiology, except perhaps in the case of hypnotism, which is becoming respectable again after fifty years' ostracism. This is probably the fault of modern science, which shows a distaste for 'subjective' and therefore supposedly unverifiable phenomena. In point of fact, researchers in various countries have applied modern laboratory techniques to states of trance and semi-trance, with results of which we shall give some account.

### The strange dream-world of mediums

Some people believe that there is something pathological about mediums and clairvoyance, but they should remember

32

that we are all to some extent clairvoyant, at any rate unconsciously and at night, if Dunne's observations and theories are to be believed. As Chauvin-Duval says,[20] the medium's universe has much in common with that of dreams; he is able, as E. Osty puts it, to suspend the operation of his waking mind for a short time in order to experience such hallucinations as are met with in sleep. The applicability of these descriptions will appear as we proceed, but one or two typical cases may be cited meanwhile.

The present writer was acquainted at Rome with a gifted clairvoyante named I.R., who made such frequent use of her power to suspend consciousness that eventually her lapses into the dream-world became involuntary. They related, as a rule, to impending catastrophes on a large scale, of which she was aware two or three days before they happened and which not only affected her cognitive faculty but produced in her lively feelings of distress. By way of experiment I asked her to telephone me on such occasions, and she did so in three instances separated by quite long intervals. The first was a mining disaster in a distant place: she did not know where, however, and although her description was realistic enough it did not rule out in my mind the possibility of a coincidence. On the second occasion she spoke of an explosion in the sky followed by an outbreak of fire: it was, not, she said, an atomic bomb, but there would be 'many orphans'. Two days later a large aircraft exploded over Switzerland and the burning fragments destroyed a whole village in which, according to the press, there were unusually many children. Even this did not strike me as an irrefutable case of clairvoyance, but I was convinced on the third occasion. Having tried to reach me by telephone several times during the day, the lady in question finally got through and repeated her story, which she had meanwhile told to a member of my family. From five till eight that morning she had lain in a kind of trance witnessing a horrific scene, the memory of whch made her voice tremble as she spoke to me. First she thought a mountain was crashing into the sea, but then she realized it was a lake, the waters of which splashed out all around, causing fearful damage. Two days after this dream — it was in 1963 — came the news of the tragedy at Vaiont, when a high dam in the Piave valley collapsed and 2,000 villagers were killed.

The Vaiont disaster had already been the subject of a

precognitive dream by Maria Lambertini, a clairvoyante at Bologna. In the record of a seance attested by several signatures we read of 'a hugh cauldron, or tub full of water . . . on a flat space at the top of five or six very high steps': the cauldron overturned, and although in literal terms there was nothing frightful in this, the medium was filled with terror. Immediately afterwards she had a realistic vision of men and women weeping at a spot where rows of coffins had been freshly buried.[21]

Such is the power of the mediumistic gift to transcend the barriers of space and time, and also the barrier which the conscious mind, like a Freudian censor, erects in order to protect its own functions against invasion from the super-sensory world.

### The secret ego in the dream dimension

We can now perhaps see a little more clearly what these facts imply as regards the nature of human personality. Although we tend to regard the conscious mind as the pure self, there exists beneath it a whole unknown area subject to the secret self, or *daimon* as we have called it. This hidden self is a sort of counterpart to the conscious mind, and displays its powers in the realm of dreams, whether sleeping or waking. Its rules and processes are too unlike those of the conscious mind to fit into ordinary rational categories. As Maeterlinck says, 'it takes no account of time and space, those formidable yet illusory walls that prevent our reason from straying: it knows no difference of near or far, present or future, nor is it affected by the resistance of matter.'[22]

The term 'unconscious' is not a satisfactory one to denote the hidden self: it has a deorgatory sound, whereas the faculty we are speaking of is one of luminous creativity and may convey messages not only for the individual but for the future of our species. Maeterlinck, the great modern apologist of the secret self, called it our 'unknown guest'. Other names are 'transcendent ego' (Novalis), 'subliminal ego' (Myers), 'intimate, almost divine self' (Paul Brunton), 'intrinsic, real self' (A.G. Bennett) and 'integral subconscious personality' (Bozzano). In Hindu philosophy, as expounded by G. Tucci, the secret self may be identified with the cosmic consciousness from which all things derive and to which they ultimately return.

The reason we find it difficult to explore the secret self is that it only functions perceptibly in dream-like states, when the ordinary light of consciousness is withdrawn. Preoccupied with the universe of sense, we are only fleetingly aware of the wider, more basic powers of our second self, far-ranging as it is; and the two selves only achieve a precarious contact in our recollections of dreams. When dreams are especially vivid it is as though the secret self were overpowering the conscious mind and giving us an insight into what is as yet an unknown universe. We cannot tell how far that universe is in fact knowable, but philosophers and psychologists in their different ways have given us an inkling of its laws. William James, for instance, postulates a continuum of cosmic awareness, that is to say a universe based on mind rather than matter — an hypothesis also favoured by many eminent physicists, mathematicians and biologists. Occultists use the term *akasha* (a Sanskrit word sometimes translated 'ether') to bridge the gulf between space and mind: this, according to T. Burckhardt, is an element in which we live as fish do in the sea, and which we perceive as little as a fish perceives water. Or we may speak of a psychic universe[23] or dream-dimension. To borrow an image from the *Mahabharata,* the hidden universe is like an ocean in which the life of the individual is a single wave, and the crest of that wave has no suspicion of the depths which lie beneath.

Dreams tell us something of the unseen world, but it may well be that the most important truths about it are concealed from us by the barrier of so-called dreamless sleep. The reader may draw his own conclusions about this in the light of the experiences described in this book, all of which are dreamlike in character even though they may have occurred in a waking state. We shall see how the mind can wander outside the body's control, how the 'dreams' of children and young people can affect inanimate objects, how mental calculation can achieve miraculous results and how some people appear capable of establishing a relationship, however imperfect, between psychokinesis and the conscious mind. We shall also study the momentous dreams concerned with life beyond the grave, and the ecstatic visions that have brought some minds into touch with the Unknown.

Voltaire once said that life is a succession of dreams from

which we must one day awaken; and a character in H.G. Wells speaks of 'dreams containing dreams, until we come at last, maybe, to the Dreamer of all dreams, the Being who is all beings.'

# CHAPTER 2

---

## Excursions of the mind

*Diagnosis at a distance*

When I first encountered the clairvoyante Pasqualina Pezzola she was kneeling on the floor of her house at Civitanova Marche, with her eyes closed and her left hand raised; her head was stretched forward as though she were looking intently at an object just in front of her. A man sitting in the corner watched her anxiously: he was a *carabiniere* officer in plain clothes who had come to consult the medium, and had kindly allowed me to be present.

From the opposite corner of the room my photographer took one flashlight picture after another, but Pasqualina paid no attention. The person she was concentrating on was the officer's sick father-in-law, then in hospital at Fabriano. From the movement of her lips she seemed to be conducting a silent conversation: from time to time she would smile and nod, or appear to ask a question or listen to a reply. If I had not read reliable accounts of her performance I might have thought it a piece of second-rate deception, but as it was I knew that the process had a specific meaning. After a time she rose to her feet, bowed slightly and sat down with a deep sigh. For a minute or two longer she rubbed her leg in a rhythmic fashion with her right hand. Then she opened her eyes: they were clear and serene, but her face wore a serious expression as she told the officer: 'I'm sorry, but the news is bad. Your father-in-law's liver is in a very bad state: it's as big as this . . . The doctors want to operate, but it won't do any good, he can't live long. Do you know that he only weighs 45 kilograms (about 7 stone), when he used to weigh over 100? I'm so sorry!'

At this point the photographer and I went into the next room, where a dozen more applicants were waiting. Outside the house were several cars, including one with a Marseilles number-plate. When the officer reappeared I asked him to let me know what happened, and a few days later he wrote to say that both the diagnosis and the prognosis had been correct.

Two years afterwards I returned to see Pasqualina with three friends of mine: one had a chronic abdominal illness, the second was his physician and the third was Federico Fellini, the film director. The medium went through the same process as before, then called for a pencil and paper and drew the exact spot where the trouble was located; she answered the doctor's questions with precision, and he was obliged to admit that this simple, unassuming peasant woman had extraordinary powers. They were in fact the subject of two scientific studies: one, over twenty years ago, by Dr Giuseppina Mancini of the Scientific Committee of the Italian Society of Parapsychology, and the other by Dr Piero Cassoli, former president of the Centre for Parapsychological Studies at Bologna. From 1953 onwards Dr Cassoli and his colleague Dr Enrico Marabini subjected Pasqualina to a series of tests, the results of which were published in a scientific review. The studies showed beyond reasonable doubt that this woman of scant education was able to achieve mental contact with distant patients and 'see' their diseased organs, which she described with precision though in everyday language.

Dr Cassoli relates, for instance, that in 1948 a youth named Erminio B. was discharged from hospital at Milan with a diagnosis of malignant osteosarcoma and the prediction that he had not long to live. His parents consulted Pasqualina, who emerged from her trance smiling and told them that the boy had nothing wrong with him and would soon get better, as in fact he did. It was this case which led Dr Cassoli to make a systematic study of Pasqualina, whom he subjected first to medical and psychological tests that showed her to be perfectly normal. Meurisse's 'doodle' test showed her to be rather say and diffident, while under a Rorschach test she interpreted every stain or blot in terms of human anatomy, healthy or pathological.

The routine of Pasqualina's 'telediagnosis' was as follows. She would ask for a sheet of paper with the patient's address and then sit down, close her eyes and go through the ritual movement described above. Then the trance would begin, and she would give a running account of her 'journey', conversations and so on, at times going through the motions of walking up or down stairs. Once, during a trance, Dr Cassoli pricked her leg unexpectedly to make sure she was not shamming; but she paid no attention, and there was no flow of blood or other physical symptom. The trance, though not deep, was clearly a real one.

Cassoli and Marabini began by making Pasqualina 'visit' patients of their own at Bologna, and the results, with the doctor's comments in brackets, are appended. 'Signora Margherita A. is not very old and not badly ill.' (Correct). 'No tumour or grave disease' (correct). 'She had a temperature until a few days ago, but not now.' (Correct, although neither of us knew this, as we had last seen the patient, two days earlier, at a critical stage of bronchial pneumonia). 'Her illness was here' (pointing to the base of the lung). 'She is breathing with difficulty' (probably). 'Her arterial pressure seems to be about 150-160' (correct, although a day or two before it had been about 190-200). 'She is a little depressed, but not badly so' (correct). 'She told me she gets bad headaches' (correct).

From another report: 'I found the patient in bed and in great pain' (correct). 'Her mind is confused, her heart is in bad shape, she has difficulty in breathing' (correct). 'I can see knots in her inside' (she had undergone a hysterectomy at 30 years of age, and there were adhesions and scars). 'She cannot be cured' (correct). 'She has been ill for many years' (actually 26). 'There was a youngish woman also visiting her' (this would be the person who had attended the patient throughout her illness). It should be mentioned that none of the people, patients or others, whom Pasqualina met in the course of her 'visits' were in any way aware of her. If she met them subsequently in the ordinary way she knew who they were, but none of them even recognized her.

In order to make sure that Pasqualina's statements could not be put down to telepathy between her and the doctors, the latter devised another experiment. They telephoned from Porta Civitanova to a clinic in Bologna and asked whether a certain bed in the gynaecological ward, of which they gave the number, was occupied; they asked no questions about the patient, of whom they knew nothing. Receiving an affirmative answer, they sent Pasqualina on a 'visit' and she reported as follows.

'It is a woman of average figure, with a pleasant expression, but in pain. There is nothing seriously wrong with her, only an inflammation of the abdomen. Her reproductive organs are normal and she can have children.' Next day these details were checked and found to be correct. Dr Mancini performed a similar experiment by making Pasqualina 'examine' patients suffering from various diseases — nervous ailments, renal calculus, gastric ulcers, cancer — before she did so herself. She found that Pasqualina's diagnoses were always correct within the limits of her knowledge, which was remarkably wide. 'I was particularly struck by her detailed description of internal organs and their interrelations, such as only a doctor could appreciate. She does not use technical terms, but her meaning is perfectly clear, and if one uses such terms oneself she understands them.'

Pasqualina's extraordinary gifts are a challenge to the common-sense belief that our self can only be located where our body is, and that we can only see with our eyes — not at an unlimited distance, and not through intervening matter. Pasqualina's visual sense did operate in this way, and she was even able to measure blood-pressure at a distance and without any apparatus. When 'absurdities' of this kind happen, it must mean that our scientific preconceptions are wrong.

Confronted by the fact that mental processes can take place independently of their normal basis, materialists tend to deny the existence of such phenomena or to assume that they will be explained by some future development of physical science. But this is an act of faith on their part, the more so as modern science has come a long way from Cartesian logic and 'common-sense' answers to the problems of the universe.

If, on the other hand, we part company with the 'physicalists' and admit that mind can be independent of the cerebral and nervous system, the alleged absurdity of psychic phenomena disappears. This is the position adopted by such philosophers and psychologists as Bergson and William James, and by contemporary Catholic thinkers such as Gabriel Marcel and Father Raphael Sanzio Bastiani. Bergson held that the mind has unlimited cognitive powers independent of the senses or of space-time categories, and that the function of the brain is to act as a filter to prevent our receiving an excessive number of impressions, especially such as would interfere with our normal three-dimensional existence. William James believed that we live in a sort of psychic ocean, a continuum of the universal mind, from which every individual receives a share of intellectual and sensitive capacity — cf. the 'wave' metaphor referred to in the previous chapter. According to this view, which many others have adopted though with varying terminology, on the unconscious level there is no absolute distinction between one individual and another. Gabriel Marcel, writing as a Catholic existentialist and a follower of Bergson, declares that the term '*my* unconscious self' is meaningless; and Professor Nicola Pende speaks of paranormal phenomena as 'unconscious inter-human relationships'.[1]

However such ideas may be derided by traditionalists,[2] it cannot be denied that they have a certain heuristic value. For instance, Bergson's idea of a 'filter' serves to explain how people could 'converse' with Pasqualina yet retain no knowledge of the fact. And, if we hold with Marcel, Broad and others that the self is not located in space, there is no difficulty in believing that a person's mind may be detached from his body, or appear to function in two places at once. Father Bastiani maintains that 'the association between thought and the brain is in no sense absolute, and the two can be completely detached; while Boris Noyer says that 'the time has come for man to look at himself and the universe in a new way. He may then see that all he regards as "real", including space and time by which he is imprisoned, is part of a limitless ocean in which the only reality is probably something resembling his own spirit.'[3]

*Wanderers in the unknown dimension*

We have described Pasqualina's case at some length, because recent examples of extraordinary powers of this type are well attested and more apt to carry conviction than older ones; but the latter should not be neglected either. For example, Aulus Gellius relates that on the day in 48 B.C. when Caesar's army defeated Pompey at Pharsalus, a priest named Cornelius at Patavium (Padua) 'followed' the course of the battle and described it in detail. In 1571 Pope Pius V in Rome 'saw' the defeat of the Turkish fleet at Lepanto, and ordered a Te Deum before receiving the official news of the victory. The philosopher Kant tells us that Emanuel Swedenborg, among other visions, was clearly aware of a fire taking place at Stockholm, hundreds of miles away.[4]

In Swedenborg's case the power to see visions did not interfere with his awareness of the ordinary world, as though the
secret self were functioning alongside the everyday one. This
is unusual: clairvoyance generally requires a state of trance,
though this may be so shallow as to be almost unperceived:
the ordinary self relaxes its vigilance and we have what
Bastiani calls a 'state of liberated consciousness'.[5]

During the last century a Paris clairvoyant, Alexis Didier,
was consulted by a M. Prévost, who had been robbed of
200,000 francs. After a brief semi-trance the medium told
him that the thief was at that moment in a certain hotel at
Brussels, and later that he was squandering the money at the
Spa casino: the police caught up with him there, and found
that he had indeed lost all the money at the tables.[6]

At that time 'animal magnetism' was much in vogue, i.e.
the use of hypnotic techniques to induce the required state of
trance. Dr Charpignon tells the story of a Mlle Céline, a
patient of his at Orleans, who took mental trips to the town
of Meung and brought back news which proved to be accurate.[7] A similar feat is related of Molly Fancher, a bed-ridden
girl in Brooklyn, whose powers were vouched for in a well-
documented book by a family friend, Judge Dailey.[8]

The British Society for Psychical Research investigated
many such cases in the first few years of its activity, and
rigorous experiments were carried out by Sir William Barrett,
professor of physics at Dublin and a Fellow of the Royal
Society. Pierre Janet, the eminent French psychologist,
carried out similar research, and would doubtless have done
so for longer if it had not been for academic hostility. On one
occasion he hypnotized a Norman peasant woman named
Léonie (whose powers were also studied by Ochorowicz) and
told her to go on a 'visit' to Professor Richet in Paris. Léonie
obeyed, and suddenly shouted: 'There's a fire!' Janet calmed
her down and she fell back into a trance, but awoke from it
again crying 'Fire!', and sure enough it proved that at that
moment a fire had broken out in Richet's laboratory.

In *Beyond Telepathy* (New York, 1962) Dr Andrija
Puharich tells of a patient of his, a business man of 44 named
Bob Rame, who had elaborate 'dreams' of distant events
under the influence of ether, to which he was addicted and
which apparently released his paranormal faculties. Many
hallucinogenic drugs have this effect, though they cannot

confer the power of 'second sight' on someone who has not got it. In Mexico the priests of some Mixtec tribes use 'sacred mushrooms' for the same purpose,[9] as do shamans in the extreme north of Asia. There have been cases of powers of this sort being used for espionage: for instance, during the Indo-Chinese was a bonze named Fo-Satu is reported to have eavesdropped on a meeting of the French general staff at which a new offensive was decided on.[10] In 1936-7 the Italian command, operating against rebels in East Africa, made use of a Sergeant-Major Luigi Andalini, a faith-healer who, it appears, was able on two or three occasions to divine the movements of the rebel forces at a distance.

As we have already seen, some of the most significant revelations take place in dreams, when, as some primitives declare, 'the soul quits the body and flits to and fro like a butterfly, seeking adventure.' A lady of our acquaintance named M.C.F., who was in hospital in Rome in 1940-3, dreamt for three nights in succession of the Allied preparations for the invasion of Sicily, and described what she had 'seen' in full detail to the other patients in her ward and to the doctor and nurse. This recalls the suggestion advanced by J.B. Rhine in an article in 1957, that paranormal gifts might be put to use by the military to spy out enemy plans and prevent an aggressor enjoying the advantage of surprise;[11] but there is considerable room for doubt whether this would be effective in the present state of our knowledge.

## Specialized clairvoyance

It should be noted that while a medium such as Pasqualina Pezzola is gifted with the power to perceive medical facts, this is a faculty which has manifested itself of its own accord and not in obedience to the conscious will. When Pasqualina tried to apply her gift, under the supervision of Dr Mancini, to discerning the numbers on lottery cards in the room next to her own, she was unable to do so. Dr Mancini tried the experiment of asking Pasqualina to tell her what a certain person was thinking about at a given moment, but this too was a failure. On emerging from her trance Pasqualina said that the man 'had not allowed her to look inside his head', but she had seen his body and noticed that the intestine was contracted by a violent purge he had just taken — which Dr

43

Mancini found to be true.

Another specialized gift was that of Adèle Maginot, a subject hypnotized by Alphonse Cahagnet and studied by Dr Lecocq, who was able to trace the whereabouts of people who had migrated overseas: she held conversation with them while in a trance, and could repeat their replies on awakening. Then checked, the information turned out to be accurate. Asked how it was that the people in question were not aware they had talked to her, she replied: 'I talk to them inside; their outside knows nothing about it.'

On the whole, however, the examples of medical clairvoyance are the most striking. Vincent N. Turvey, a rich and cultivated man and a gifted medium, performed remarkable feats of diagnosis at a distance.[12] Edgar Cayce, a photographer who died in 1945, showed similar powers to those of Pasqualina Pezzola, and in addition was able to prescribe cures for the sufferers.[13] An American rustic named Andrew Jackson Davis, born in 1826, is also said to have been able to 'look inside' human bodies and, as his biographer puts it, to 'suck knowledge' out of other people's minds, so that at the age of sixty he was able, without having read any books, to qualify as a doctor.[14]

In all cases of this kind it would seem that the subject's personality is organized towards a highly specialized form of perception, achieved by means of a trance or semi-trance, that is to say a kind of dream in which, as in other dreams, the twin aspects of our being confront each other: the waking, Euclidean or Cartesian self, and the hidden self with its infinite possibilities of cognition. The dialogue between the two selves takes place in the only universal human language, that of fundamental symbols or archetypes. In Pasqualina's case, for instance, the recurrent archetypes are those of a journey, talk or visit, but, as we shall see, there are other possibilities.

*Outdistancing evolution*

The secret of the clairvoyant's power may consist in the fact that he or she is able to effect a momentary fusion or collaboration between the conscious mind and the secret self; and some believe that this power, exceptional as it is today, may, as evolution progresses, become a normal human faculty and present itself in a more stable, regular guise. This view is

44

encouraged by the types of mediumship that confer special-ized knowledge and skills, and which seem to belong to a supra-rational rather than a primitive mode of consciousness.

Those who hold that, on the contrary, clairvoyance is a form of atavistic regression point to the fact that it is chiefly found among less developed peoples. But there is a confusion here between biological evolution and the development of civilization, and it is clear that from the former point of view a shaman in some Tungus tribe is no less evolved than a European. Certain manifestations of the 'ancestral psyche' may tend to become unusual as the conscious, reasoning side of human personality gains the upper hand; but it may well be that nature has in store for us a fusion or co-ordination of the archaic but fundamental aspects of our being with the other, ratiocinative aspects that now seem opposed to them.[15] Thus Teilhard de Chardin believed that humanity might be due to cross some 'threshold of higher consciousness' and take a decisive step forward. [16] The nuclear physicist, Campbell, a keen student of these problems, speaks of para-normal powers as 'weapons for tomorrow's man', while Boris Noyer writes that 'the descendants of modern man may enjoy forms of consciousness of which he has no idea.' We must realize, however, that this evolution may take ages to come about. It has taken Nature millions of years to bring us to our present state, and it might be millions more before mankind as a whole can reach the higher, freer stage of development to which only a few individuals have so far attained.

# CHAPTER 3

===

## Divination of the past

*Objects that speak*

In 1952-5 a lady named Luisa A.G. paid several visits to the
Centre for Parapsychological Studies at Bologna, where she
underwent a carefully-controlled series of experiments pre-
sided over by Dr Piero Cassoli. The procedure was as follows.
Luisa would sit in the middle of a circle formed by the committee of observers and gaze at a distant point, then close
her eyes and fall into a trance, denoted by heavy breathing.
She would then rise to her feet and walk about slowly,
answering questions concerning objects that were handed
to her one by one.[1]

On 29 March 1953, in the presence of twelve people, she
was handed a crucifix that Padre Pio of Pietralcina had given
to an old woman twenty years before. Luisa, who was in a
trance with her eyes closed, at once declared: 'I feel as if a
hand were stroking my head. . . . A tall, bearded priest,
weakened by suffering.' At this point she began to speak as
though she herself were the sufferer. 'I sweat a great deal.
At times I feel quite exhausted. I feel like a white cloud,
a scented cloud, . . . I feel sometimes as if I could enter into
other people.' Here Dr Cassoli intervened and asked her about
the second owner of the crucifix. Luisa got up slowly and
walked towards him saying: 'I think it's your —'; then, cor-
recting herself and addressing Signora Cassoli, 'No, *your*
grandmother. She was very fond of you. I feel as if she were
beside you. . . . She looks transparent, as though she were
dead.' The old lady had in fact died five months before.

On 15 March 1952 Luisa was given a pair of spectacles
with tortoiseshell rims. As soon as she touched them her face
expressed disgust and horror. She then threw herself on the
floor and remained motionless, with her legs almost straight
and her right arm bent over her head — symbolizing, and per-

haps imitating, the tragic end of the woman who had owned the spectacles, and who had jumped to her death from a third-floor window.

In the relevant literature this power to divine by means of objects is called psychometry: it includes, as we have seen, the faculty of re-living past episodes connected with the objects and experiencing the joy or grief that accompanied them. The psychometric subject nearly always identifies with the person involved and may imitate the latter's gestures and attitudes. Sometimes this effect is so strong that the subject's own personality appears to be submerged for the time being, thus recalling the disquieting phenomena of possession and split personality.[2]

### Fragments of history

On 29 March 1953 Luisa A.G. was handed an old, yellowing letter and spoke as follows: 'It feels like a much-folded sheet of paper . . . as though all sorts of people had handled it at different times. I feel as if I was running behind a horse, and could hear bugles. I am breathless — goodness, what a race! I can see a whole expanse of poppy-red, but it's people; they seem to have travelled a long way.' They had indeed: the letter was by Garibaldi, and the people in the vision were his red-shirted followers.

Two of the first explorers of this way of investigating the past were Dr Joseph Rhodes Buchanan, the physiologist, in 1849 and William Denton, the geologist, in 1854.[3] Buchanan held that inanimate objects possessed a soul and a memory, and that these enabled clairvoyants to discern their past; while Denton believed that objects were 'steeped in images', and declared that 'a pebble from the streets of Jerusalem is a library containing the history of the whole Jewish nation.' Denton's exaggeration was excusable in the light of his wife Elizabeth's psychometric prowess,[4] but things are not quite so simple as he supposed: psychometry is a function of the medium's powers and not of the properties of objects. Here the 'oceanic' theory comes to our aid again, as do the speculations of William James, Geley, Osty and others on the subject of a Cosmic Mind preserving the memory of all past events. Others again believe that the past does not cease to exist but has a real, imperishable being of its own, though

47

human minds are incapable of grasping how this is so. This view tends to be popular with mathematicians such as Dunne, Ouspensky and Fantappiè; it has been fervently defended by the Orientalist Pietro Silvio Rivetta, better known by his pseudonym of Toddi, in a book entitled 'The Geometry of Reality'. Such great thinkers as Henri Poincaré, Bertrand Russell and Max Planck have reminded us more than once that, however paradoxical these opinions may seem, the test of a theory is not whether it offends 'common sense' but whether it serves to explain phenomena that would otherwise be incomprehensible.[5]

If, then, the past truly exists, it must be located in the infinite dimension of time in which the whole universe is enclosed; and we must imagine the mind of the clairvoyant following a 'chronotopic' line in the space-time continuum, representing the succession of moments and events in which a given material object has been involved. This more up-to-date interpretation of psychometry is not necessarily at variance with philosophical and psychological theories: it probably complements them and serves to deepen our understanding of multiform reality, which need not be any means be thought of as essentially physical.

### A woman who explored the past

María Reyes de Z. was the daughter of General Epifanio de Reyes, governor of the Mexican state of Michoacán. Under the supervision of Dr Gustav Pagenstecher, an émigré German surgeon and gynaecologist, she performed psychometric feats of a vivid and detailed character.[6]

On one occasion she was handed a farewell letter which the victim of a shipwreck had written and placed in a bottle many years before. Although she knew nothing of the event, she at once identified with the writer of the letter and described the sinking of the passenger ship by a German torpedo in the Atlantic in 1917: the frantic efforts of the officers and sailors, the explosion of the boilers, the writer's despair and last thoughts of his wife and family . . . A cufflink that had belonged to the emperor Maximilian inspired her to describe the festivities with which he and his consort had been received in Mexico City in 1863. Given a small piece of marble from the Roman Forum, near the temple of Castor and Pollux, she responded with an exact description of the ruins in question, and every time the same fragment was produced it aroused an identical reaction.

In each of these cases María Reyes was in a trance with her eyes closed, so that she did not even see the object. Dr Pagenstecher did his utmost to check her testimony and always found it accurate, at least in broad lines. In any case, although a woman of good family, she was an ordinary housewife of no special erudition and could not have invented or remembered, in the normal way, the detailed information contained in her statements.

On 29 October 1919 she was presented, while in a trance, with a small obsidian knife from the Archaelogical Museum, and at once gave a vivid description of an Aztec sacrifice. 'I see two or three hundred Mexican Indians, crowded together in a large open space — perhaps for a ceremony. Now four Indians are dragging along a fifth, who is struggling. He is being stretched out on a round, flat stone, dark-grey in colour, about a yard high and a yard across. A tall, strong man approaches.' The description continued with horrific details, and at its climax the medium was overcome by convulsions. Dr Pagenstecher took the knife away and tried, by post-hypnotic suggestion, to make her forget the experience; but she awoke weeping frantically, and for some time afterwards was afflicted by a nervous tremor of the right arm.

In a deep trance, the medium's self-identification with victims of disaster or peril may be very strong, and he or she is exposed in consequence to violent emotional shocks. On one occasion Maria Reyes identified with an aerolith and felt as though she were plunging with increased speed into an abyss. Another time, a fragment of lava caused her to 'witness' a volcanic eruption that must have taken place ages before. She saw the advancing river of fire, heard the desperate cries of the victims and felt choked by the fumes; moreover she had the frightening sensation of being rooted to the spot. All this she described afterwards to the doctor, insisting that it was not a vision but an actual experience.

### Jung's retrospective dream

These examples confirm what we have said about the 'existential reality' of such dreams and their independence of

49

personal memory and the nervous system. The clairvoyant's power to identify with individuals who have lived in the past is analogous to that of the spiritualistic medium. At the same time, there have been instances of retrocognition on the part of people who were not conscious of possessing any special powers, and who did not go into a trance for the purpose. Jung relates in his posthumous work *Memories, Dreams, Reflections* (London, 1963) that one night in 1924, when sleeping alone in the 'Tower' — his house at Bollingen near Zurich — he was awakened by a sound of light footsteps followed by music that seemed to be coming closer, and the noise of people talking and laughing. He looked out of the window, but could see nothing. He went back to sleep and was again awakened by laughter and song and the playing of an accordion. Again he looked out, but there was no one to be seen. The auditory hallucination was so clear that he suspected it to have some connection with the past, and on investigating he found that in the Middle Ages the locality had been a meeting-place, every spring, for young mountaineers who came to say farewell to their homeland before enlisting as mercenaries in Italy. It appears that Jung inherited from his mother a degree of sensitivity to perceptions of this kind.

Elizabeth d'Espérance relates in her autobiography[7] that when she was thirteen her father took her on a cruise in the merchant vessel which he commanded, her parents hoping that this might cure her of the 'strange fancies' which took the form of seeing ghosts and so forth. One day she ran up on deck in pursuit of the ship's pet (a monkey), and suddenly stopped in amazement: she had seen a large ship in full sail, on a course converging with their own. A tall man stood on the bridge with his arms folded, while a ragged crew, like galley-slaves, could be seen on the lower decks. The child cried out in alarm, as she thought the strange vessel was about to ram her father's ship; but the young officer of the watch could see nothing. Elizabeth buried her head in terror against the officer's chest, but when she raised her eyes again she saw the sailing-ship on the opposite bow, as though it had passed through their own without touching it. We may call it a ghost-ship if we will, but it is simpler to think of a visual message from a remote part of the great panorama of time which our ordinary consciousness can only perceive successively; or again, we may compare the effect of super-imposing photographs of the same place at two different times.

## A visit to the court of Marie Antoinette

An analogous case, well known in England, is that of Annie Moberly and Eleanor Jourdain, both of St Hugh's College, Oxford, who, on 10 August 1901, were walking in the garden of the Petit Trianon at Versailles when they felt a sense of oppression and began to notice something uncanny about the landscape. Instead of a noisy twentieth-century crowd they encountered men and women in wigs and eighteenth-century costume: however, these people did not exhibit the calm we associate with the period before 1789, but seemed inexplicably agitated. One of them was a dark pock-marked man of repulsive appearance. Then they heard the sound of running and noticed a tall handsome man with curling black hair and large dark eyes: he was wearing a big hat and dark cloak, and looked like an old picture. He urged them excitedly to walk in a different direction, as they were 'in danger'. They followed him along a line of trees and came to a square building (the Petit Trianon) next to a meadow. Here, in the garden, they came upon a blonde, distinguished-looking lady drawing in water-colours: she was not in her first youth and appeared tense and weary. Through a window of the building the two English ladies heard a tune being played which was unfamiliar to them.

After the visions had disappeared, the two ladies (whose ages at the time were 56 and 38) both felt that they had been living for a short period in the eighteenth century. Their impression became a certainty within a year or two of their experience, after they had consulted historical memoirs, visited museums, examined old prints and musical scores etc. They found maps of the gardens and paths which differed from the present-day layout but which they remembered from their walk; they identified the mysterious tune and discovered that the unknown lady's features were those of Queen Marie Antoinette in a painting by Wertmüller. The date of their 'vision', moreover, was the anniversary of the sacking of the Tuileries and the massacre of the Swiss guards.

The two women wrote a detailed account of their ex-

51

perience and investigations, which they published under assumed names in 1911 under the title *An Adventure*. It aroused lively interest in the press and was the subject of a long analysis by Professor Hyslop of the Society for Psychical Research. The case, which is still controversial, has given rise to recent studies by Pierre Devaux, G.W. Lambert and Serge Hutin, all of whom recognize its importance and the good faith of the protagonists.[8]

In general there is no lack of testimony to the possibility of retrocognition, but apart from scepticism there is a tendency to divide up the evidence into watertight compartments such as psychometry, ghosts, spiritualism etc., whereas all these are part of a single phenomenon, as Jung correctly observed. There is no essential difference between the experiences of Luisa A.G. and María Reyes de Z., on the one hand, and minor feats of psychometry by subjects who are able to suspend their ordinary consciousness to the necessary degree without actually going into a trance. Such people are able to listen to the 'voice' of their secret self, a term which is not purely metaphorical: Pascal Fortuny, a noted clairvoyant studied by Geley and Osty, maintained that he heard a 'soft voice' telling him what to say. Another psychometrist, Sandra Bajetto of Rome, speaks of 'voices' and 'images from the depths', and an accountant named C.M. also speaks of images representing persons unknown to him. In short, the phenomenon assumes different forms with different mediums, but in all cases it is of a dream-like quality, either realistic or symbolical, and is touched off by a specific object or by something propitious in the atmosphere. Apropos of objects, we may recall what Guy de Maupassant says in one of his stories: 'It seems as though walls retain something of the people who have lived within them: their habits, their speech and lineaments.'

## The 'personality' of objects

Psychometry is one of the best-known and most frequently studied of paranormal phenomena, as may be judged from the number of books describing it. This may be because, as Maeterlinck observed,[9] psychometric phenomena are the easiest to check and verify, as they can be repeated more or less at will, and a number of well-known mediums are ready to do so at any time; they relate solely to the things of this world and are emanations of our own living but unconscious self. Some scholars have made use of psychometry as an aid to their own science: e.g. Dr Wood the Egyptologist, in his excavations at Karnak in 1955, used the powers of a Miss J. Beaumont, known as Rosemary, to obtain information on the phonetics of ancient Egyptian and court life under the Pharaohs,[10] and María Reyes de Z. has aided scientists in a similar way.[11]

One puzzle presented by these phenomena is why the mind, in its wanderings through space and time, should fasten on one past event more than another . It may be that this is determined by the strength of the emotional 'charge' adhering to the event from the seer's point of view, but this is only a conjecture. Mediums themselves speak of 'vibrations' or 'fluids', and we may use such terms for convenience provided we realize that they are metaphors of uncertain content. What is certain is that an object or atmosphere is required to trigger off the experience, but, once this has happened — as Osty showed in a celebrated experiment — the psychometric process will continue even if the object is destroyed by fire. In other words, the mind makes use of the object but does not depend on it; and it is also known that the mind may deviate at any moment from the course suggested by the object, in order to follow some more interesting line that suggests itself meanwhile.

It has been noted that if the same object is shown to two psychometrists their reactions may be diverse or complementary, but they never contradict one another. The present author made this experiment with a small Ethiopian Gospel, written on parchment with vegetable ink and bound roughly in wood: it was generally kept in a leather case, and the outside gave no indication of what it was. The accountant C.M. was given it to handle in 1949 and declared: 'It is an object possessing some kind of authority; perhaps sacred; I think it is often kissed. I see a man of darkish skin, with close-fitting trousers or breeches, who seems to have worked on it for a long time.' Thirteen years later the Gospel, still in its case, was handed to Sandra Bajetto, who at once identified with its former owner. Her face took on a grave expression and she declared: 'I feel as though I ought to kneel and beg forgiveness for my sins. I have done penance, but not enough . . . I see a

53

round building with a great white dome, and I am approaching it on my knees with other penitents. It is a hot country and I don't know the language. The people are in white, and the women hold on to each other's clothes as they walk along.' Anyone who knows Ethiopian ways will appreciate the probability of these complementary accounts. The Gospel had belonged to a hermit named Saladingil Woldesadig, who lived in the eucalyptus forests outside Addis Ababa; I know nothing, however, of what sins he had to expiate or how often he had kissed the little volume.

Signora Bajetto once gave me an interesting account of the 'personality' of objects. Some, like crucifixes or religious medallions, were good and soothing, others bad and painful; some were 'open' or expansive, others closed or uncommunicative. Among the former was an antique medallion which brought to mind loving words spoken by a woman who had owned it long ago, and caused the medium to pronounce the name of Olga, which had been that of the woman's grandmother.

Professor Francesco Egidi, when president of the Italian Society for Psychical Research, inherited a small antique piece of furniture, the door of which was closed by a padlock with an alphabetical combination. He had tried to open it in vain, but as soon as Signora Bajetto touched it she uttered the English name Mary, which proved to be the key.

Signora Bajetto also relates that 'Professor Egidi once handed me a small silk handkerchief, and as soon as I touched it I felt sick and shivery. It had been used for a moment to cover the face of a woman killed in a car crash . . . Another time, a visiting card gave me an electric shock, and I found out afterwards that it belonged to a woman who was being given electro-therapy. But the strangest object of all was a wallet that would not let me touch it at all — I kept putting my hand out, but felt as though prevented by a superior force. Perhaps it had belonged to a miserly and suspicious person who was convinced that someone would try to steal it.' Thus, like dream-images, the objects that inspire psychometrists speak a universal, symbolic language.

# CHAPTER 4

———

## Exploration of the future

*Exploration of the future*

To quote Signora Bajetto once again: 'There was one occasion on which my clairvoyance led to my being so frightened and upset that I wished I had never become aware of it. In February 1954 I was visited in Rome by Professor Hans Dannert, a German student of rhabdomancy [use of the divining-rod] well known in his own country and in South Africa, where he had lived for a long time and employed his gifts in the search for mineral ore. We did not speak each other's language, but he brought a friend, Mr. Koch, as an interpreter and we had quite a long conversation, in the course of which he asked whether I would advise him to continue his work in South Africa.

'I was somewhat taken aback since, as you know, my own form of psychometry deals with recalling the past; but sometimes the future does reveal itself to me, and I thought I should try and meet his wishes. So I touched his hand to have some sort of guidance, and the moment I did so I felt that *there was no future of any kind in store for him.* I had never before had such a sensation and was greatly startled, but collected myself and told the Professor I thought he had better not return to South Africa. I also told Mr Koch what I had actually felt, but begged him to keep it a secret. Alas, the Professor died a month later, though I do not know exactly in what circumstances.'

This incident is one of many that go to confirm Dunne's theory that every human mind is capable of directly perceiving the remote past or the future, albeit in a fragmentary way. In the present chapter we shall discuss further cases of precognition, a faculty that appears most frequently and in a more spectacular way among those whose unconscious mind is 'freer', to use Maeterlinck's expression.[1] In our dreams, perhaps, we are all capable of divining the future, but in our waking hours it is rare for the secret self to break through the barrier of consciousness. None the less it happens with some people, such as Sir Arthur Eggar, a former RAF officer, whose story was reported some years ago in the *Sunday Express.*

Shortly after the first world war Eggar, then a young officer, received orders to join his squadron in Burma. The day before leaving London to embark on the SS *Patricia,* he had a confused but strong presentiment that something would happen to the ship before it reached Aden. In the past he had had other such forebodings that had turned out to be justified, and so this time he informed his parents and a few fellow-passengers. He did not cancel his passage, however, and as the ship entered the Red Sea he was able to add that the accident would take place 400 miles from Aden but would not be serious. Sure enough, a night or two later the ship ran aground on a small island and was not able to continue its journey until next morning.

### Predictions of war

Osty and Richet are among the scientists who, after much hesitation and doubt, eventually came to accept the evidence that precognition is a fact. Richet himself relates the following instance. In 1984, when he was a young man, an election took place to the French Presidency: neither Richet nor his fellow-student Gallet were much interested in the outcome, but Gallet suddenly took a notebook and wrote, almost casually: 'Casimir-Périer elected by 451 votes.' This came true, including the number of votes, although Casimir-Périer had not been thought of as a likely winner of the election.

We should mention here the work of Louisa Rhine, wife of Professor J.B. Rhine, who before publishing her *Hidden Channels of the Mind* (1962) collected thousands of instances of paranormal events, many of them precognitive. Some of these are dramatic or tragic, others happy, and others, as in the case of Richet's friend, of no special interest to the percipient.

Professor Soal, a British mathematician, and his colleague F. Bateman also collected extensive data of this kind, including the case of a nurse who heard a conversation between

Dr. Lawrence Bendit and some friends an hour before it took place. Eileen Garrett, a well-known Irish medium and president of the Parapsychology Foundation, relates in her autobiography that she used from time to time to 'hear' scraps of conversation on subjects of no particular interest to her, and a few days later the conversation would occur in real life. In 1934 Signora S.A. of Turin used to hear the clatter of typewriters in her house every night, although there were none until the building was turned into an office some years later.

Although precognition is, as Richet says, one of the best-attested paranormal phenomena, it is one which the ordinary mind has the greatest difficulty in accepting. Jan Ehrenwald, a New York psychiatrist who investigates these phenomena, admits that the idea of it being possible to know the future, which 'does not yet exist', is especially repugnant to his Western mind. Confronted with undoubted instances of per-cognition, however, we are more inclined to believe with Sir Arthur Eggar that future events are, so to speak, already there and waiting for us as we move towards them, generally at an immutable pace but with occasional glimpses of special insight.

If official science were ever to take serious account of pre-cognition it would have to re-examine many aspects of its conception of reality, including the principle of causation. If a future event is non-existent at the present time, how can it bring about a perception of itself? This, however, is an imaginary difficulty, as the study of further examples may show.

Ernesto Bozzano quotes the instance of an Anglican clergy-man staying in the house of some friends, who went into a dark room and saw, as he thought, a girl sleeping: she was a handsome brunette, with a perfect oval face and well-shaped hands.[2] Five years later, when a missionary in India, he en-tered into correspondence with an English girl whom he had not then met, but whom he eventually married: she proved to have the same features as the vision in the darkened room.

Violet Tweedale, whom we have already mentioned, was sitting alone in her London flat one afternoon when she saw her friend Lord Colin Campbell come into the room, accom-panied by his dog and holding a large bunch of strongly-scented lilac. She thought it strange that he had not been announced, but was about to welcome him when the vision disappeared. She feared that this was a presage of misfortune, but an hour later Lord Colin in fact arrived, complete with the bunch of lilac and his dog: he explained that he had meant to come an hour before but had been held up unexpectedly.

Some people might call this precognitive telepathy, others a telepathic hallucination; but distinctions of this kind are probably too subtle and tend to obscure the fundamental unity of the phenomenon whereby the mind is liberated, as in 'great dreams', from the barriers of space and time. The state of hypnotic trance which enables certain subjects to look into the past may, in other cases, be favourable to precognition, but we do not have abundant evidence on this. However, in 1898 the British *Metaphysical Magazine* published an account of experiments by a Professor Harry Brown, who hypnotized five students and told them to direct their minds to a football match that was to take place a week later. The students, who were all keen on football, gave, independently of one another, a running commentary on the match which proved, in the event, to be largely accurate.[3]

Another instance of precognition took place under the somewhat different circumstances of a mediumistic trance. During the Russo-Polish wars of 1920 a Polish medium named Przybylska uttered a series of messages that were 'transcribed' and forwarded to the Warsaw Society for Psychical Research and to Dr Gustave Geley, then president of the Institut métapsychique in Paris. On July 12 the message ran: 'You will soon have to abandon the right bank of the Vistula. There will be catastrophe all this month, and a wave of invaders, but do not fear: the disaster will only be on the right bank, and everything will change for the better.' The messages went on this way, correctly predicting the course of events including the final Polish victory.[4]

### Knucklebones of destiny

The story of actual or attempted precognition is as old as human history, and augurs and oracles played an important part in classical religion and society. Were these always fraudulent? As Professor B. Brocchieri writes: 'It may seem highly scientific to reduce a miraculous tale to mythical symbolism, but in fact it rests on a dogmatic assumption that the supernatural cannot happen.' De Cressac, after calculating that the budget of the oracle at Delphi was, in relative terms, roughly equivalent to the whole of the French state budget in modern times, adds that: 'Even allowing amply for imagination, fiction illusion and fraud, there is a large residue that appears to have been genuine.'

The effect of scepticism about such facts is that we have in the Western world 'two cultures' (though not in Snow's sense): an official one which denies the supernatural, and a popular one which admits it, or at any rate accepts the facts as they occur. There is no European country where belief in 'second sight' and the ability to foresee the future is not shared in some degree by large sections of the population; it is strongest, however, in regions where inbreeding seems to have accentuated the power and frequency of hereditary medium-istic gifts. According to Thorstein H. Wereide, 'second sight' occurs most often in mountainous, inaccessible and isolated areas such as parts of Scotland and Norway.[5] In Scandinavia it is known as *vardögr* (a word also signifying 'tutelary spirit'), and may take the form of hearing footsteps, whispering, a door opening, a whip cracking or a cart passing along; often many people hear these noises simultaneously, a certain time before they actually happen. There also appears at times to be a telekinetic factor: door-handles turning, objects moving inexplicably and so on, which is beyond the bounds of simple hallucination.

If we believe that 'magic' aspects of reality played a more important part in the infancy of the human race than they do today, we may suppose that such phenomena are survivals from an earlier time when social groups were more isolated and unexpected visits were things to be guarded against. In this case, the power to foresee them would be a faculty that has outlived its usefulness in modern society but is still an aid to survival in primitive communities. The Mixtec practices referr-ed to in Chapter 2 can be paralleled in Lapland, north-eastern Siberia, Tierra del Fuego and Polynesia. Lapland wizards, it is said, can foretell the approach of a Polar bear or the cracking of the ice. Among the negrillo tribes (Bushmen and Pygmies), medicine-men go into a trance in order to predict the result of a hunting expedition. Father Trilles in his monumental work[6] gives a graphic description of a Pygmy witch-doctor before an elephant hunt, consulting a heap of little bones —

the 'knucklebones of destiny' — and foretelling the whole course of the hunt and the fortunes of each individual taking part in it. 'He described the events as vividly as if he were actually witnessing them, . . . and the extraordinary thing is that he predicted correctly every detail of the hunt: how many beasts would be killed and where, how many would get away, how many tusks would be collected and how many men would be killed or injured.' The bones, it may be added, play a ritual or symbolic part like the 'magic mirrors' in use among other peoples, serving by means of a conditioned reflex to enable the seer to enter the requisite state of trance.

## Experiments with time

Although magic practices are commoner in primitive societies, it is wrong to suppose that they do not happen in the West. Eileen Garrett tells us that from her childhood onwards she practiced a psycho-physical technique to develop her powers of clairvoyance and precognition: she thus escaped from the 'illusion of time' and was able, as it appeared, to live simultaneously in the present and in the future.[7]

J.W. Dunne, who made an extensive study of precognitive dreams, also showed that the waking mind was capable of apprehending the future if it were given some sort of clue or starting point. The method he adopted was to impress on his mind the title of a book he had not yet read, or to open it at random and note the name of a character. He would then put the book aside and try to erase all impressions from his mind. creating a kind of vacuum — a feat of which not everyone is capable. Sooner or later an idea or image, or perhaps a name, would present itself, bearing no relation to his past or present experience. He would then open the book and, sure enough, the name or image would be found in it.[8]

Professor G. Zorab made a practice, every six months or so, of consulting amateur or professional clairvoyants and noting whether their predictions came true. In a paper read in June 1956 to the Bologna Centre for Parapsychological Studies he declared that many things he regarded as most improbable had taken place as predicted.

One September afternoon in 1962 the present writer, with his wife and son, were visiting Dr. Rol at Turin, who will be mentioned frequently in these pages. The international situat-

60

ion appeared calm, but our host began to speak of a crisis that would occur in exactly a month's time and would bring the world to the brink of war over Cuba. This of course did happen, and I would have been more surprised by its coming true if I had not know my friend to be a practised clairvoyant.

Ehrenwald suggests that the hypothesis of precognition should be rejected in all cases where it is not forced on us by the evidence; but this is to assume that nature shares our own prejudices. Precognition is certainly exceptional, but it does occur and is in many cases the most plausible explanation, especially when the subject is already known to possess the faculty of 'second sight'. Among subjects, past or present, are Pascal Forthuny,[9] Gérard Croiset (studied by the Dutch expert Tenhaeff), and the Roman ladies I.R. and Sandra Bajetto.

In 1962 Dr Eugène Osty made Pascal Forthuny sit on a chair chosen at random in an empty conference hall with 150 seats, and describe the person who would be sitting there when the hall filled in half an hour's time. Forthuny sat down and, after a moment's concentration, described the good and bad qualities, illnesses, hopes and disappointments of a middle-aged woman. In due course the hall filled up — the seats were not allocated in advance — and the woman who sat there, when the experiment was explained to her, confirmed that everything was as Forthuny had said. In this case the chair performed a similar function to the objects used in psychometry. The experiment was repeated with other subjects, nationals of various countries, with remarkable results in some cases, e.g. that of Croiset, who was able to predict events several days ahead.

Signora Bajetto relates the following incident. 'On 14 March 1953 I went to the Great Hall of the Institute of Human Physiology at Rome University with a small group including Professor Egidi, president of the Society for Psychical Research, and Sig. Vittorio Perrone of its Scientific Committee. They chose by lot the number of a seat in the hall and asked me to say something about the person who would be sitting there when the lecture began. I was afraid I would not be able to, as I had a headache, but as soon as I sat down I saw in my mind's eye a dark gentleman of middle height and florid complexion. He wore a brownish coat and grey flannel trousers, a white shirt and a red tie. He had musical ambitions and suffered from a rheumatic pain in the left leg; a friend was accompanying him, and would be sitting in the seat behind. All this was noted down and is in the Society's records. I was not at all sure if my predictions would be correct, but Sig. Perrone told me later that the experiment had been an outstanding success.'

## The mystery of time

We are still left with the problem of explaining how an event can be perceived before it happens; but if facts conflict with theories, it is the latter which must yield. Precognition indeed appears impossible if we believe in a three-dimensional universe in which the past no longer exists and the future does not exist yet, so that only the present is real. But what do we mean by the present? Since the theory of relativity was invented we know that it is not a absolute concept, but depends on the observer.

We may remember the classic illustration of a man at a roadside watching a procession. To him, the 'present' is identified with the individual who is passing at a given moment; but if he makes use of the third dimension, e.g. by climbing a clock-tower, he will see the whole procession simultaneously. In the same way we may think of retrocognition and precognition as taking place in a fourth dimension which transcends ordinary time-categories and the limitation of our sensory awareness to the present moment. To deny reality to the past and future is no more sensible than to claim that the instantaneous section of a film we are watching is the only part of it that has any reality. Far from the present being real and the past and future unreal, it is, if anything, the present itself which becomes illusory as soon as we attempt to fasten our minds upon it.[10]

According to Minkowski, space and time form a single four-dimensional complex; De Sitter and other relatives have adopted this conception, adding to it that of the curvature of space. A still more comprehensive scheme is that of Luigi Fantappiè, which we shall examine more closely in a later chapter. All these theories have been devised to explain the intricacy of a physical universe which seems to depart further and further from common-sense notions, so that many scientists — and notably Pascal Jordan, the Hamburg physicist — hold that three-dimensional space is only a cross section or 'limiting case' of total reality.

When scientists themselves invite us to abandon prerelativistic notions of the universe, students of parapsychology should be the first to welcome and take advantage of the new freedom. Precognition, far from being a logical or metaphysical impossibility, is merely a process by which we are able to catch a glimpse of something that exists in a higher dimension, whether we call it a-temporal or supra-temporal. Our concept of existence is thus enlarged beyond the limits of common-sense, or what Huizinga calls 'reason in its old form.'[11] The theory of 'total existence' or the 'eternal present', on the other hand, rules out such hypothesis as Laplace's determinism (according to which the future does not exist now, but is predetermined by a rigid sequence of causes) or William James's view that the future is semi-fluid, though determined in its broad lines.[12]

We see at this point that precognitive phenomena have a value of their own in causing us to revise our basic ideas of the universe, and to do so in a direction which normal science shows many signs of adopting. Man, in short, is a being who exists in more than three dimensions and can range mentally through time without being subject to the limitations of his bodily existence. His power to do so may as yet be exceptional only, but it opens the door to speculations and inferences of great importance.

One controversial question is whether the theory suggested above rules out the possibility of free will. Professor Zorab[13] considers that it does, but this is to limit ourselves to Euclidean or Cartesian logic. Others, such as Max Planck, take a different view. [14] Precognition does not imply that the will is bound: the future can be observed from the vantage point of a higher dimension, but that does not mean we are not free to shape it by our acts. Paradoxical as it may seem, our future acts exist at some distant point of the space-time continuum, although our conscious self has not yet performed them and is not yet aware of them.

# CHAPTER 5

## The dialogue with the secret self

*The dialogue with the secret self*

We have seen how problematical and uncertain is the dialogue between our secret self and our waking consciousness. Some of us do receive messages from the secret self, usually in dreams or in a state of meditation; others appear to receive no such messages, and others again receive them but do not heed or understand them.

One of the first modern students of the dialogue was Maeterlinck, who in an essay on 'Fate'[1] described the unconscious as a guide and counsellor with, among other functions, that of protecting the waking self from danger and disaster. He pointed out that 'It is a curious and constant fact that in great calamities there are generally fewer people killed and injured than might be statistically expected. . . . At the last moment, some chance circumstance nearly always occurs to dissuade half or even two-thirds of the prospective victims from going to their doom. A ship that sinks usually has fewer passengers on board than usual; two trains that collide, or an express that crashes into a ravine, are generally emptier than on days on which these disasters do not happen.'

Statistics have become more precise since Maeterlinck's day, and W.E. Cox in Britain has confirmed that the number of rail travellers tends to lessen during the period preceding a serious accident, as though many were dissuaded from travelling by a warning emanating from their unconscious.[2] This is only a working hypothesis as yet, but it is of more value than the lazy attitude which puts everything down to coincidence. Maeterlinck for his part did not believe in 'the clemency of blind chance', remarking that 'it is much more natural to suppose that there is something in man which enables him to scent disaster, and that an obscure instinct, very powerful in some cases, operates to save him from danger. . . . This may take the form of instinctive panic, a whim or a caprice, or some quite trivial incident which is nevertheless irresistible and providential.' In other words, we may call it an act of precognition which for some reason does not become fully conscious but stops, as it were, half-way.

Even though the promptings of the unconscious mind may not be fully articulate, they sometimes achieve their purpose equally well. On 7 October 1965 Queen Elizabeth II was on the quay at Charlottetown, Prince Edward Island, about to go on board the royal yacht *Britannia*. A crowd of several thousand were watching, but just as the Queen was about to step on to the gangway she drew back, saying it was not safe. A moment later it collapsed, to the confusion of the sailors who had hurried forward to make it fast. Some may think the incident proves the Queen to have had a sharper eye than the officers and men, but to others it will not seem improbable that she possesses, among her other gifts, that of heeding salutary presentiments. These, as Maeterlinck put it, are a whispered message from the life 'that knows everything but is aware of nothing' to that which 'is capable of understanding but knows nothing,'[3] To quote Giovanni Papini, 'Anyone who knows anything of introspection can testify to having heard interior voices that are not his own, faint suggestions and promptings that would have been unimaginable and incredible a moment earlier.' In Chapter 1 we related the mysterious warning received by Luigi D. at Asola; a similar case, reported in detail by Camille Flammarion, is that of a man who felt impelled to move his bed one night from one room to another, a few moments before the ceiling of the first room fell in. Other instances of the same kind are recorded at length by Louisa Rhine.

Professor Sir William Barrett, on behalf of the British Society for Psychical Research, investigated the case of a Captain MacGowan in January 1887, who planned to take his two sons to the theatre in Brooklyn, but at the last moment felt a strong impulse not to go. Despite the boys' disappointment he called off the party; that night the theatre burnt down, and three hundred people lost their lives.

The sculptor Giovanni Dupré (1817-82) was travelling in a carriage over mountain roads with his wife when they both heard a voice cry: 'Stop!' They did so and looked around, but saw nothing. They drove on, but the voice cried even louder, and Dupré got out of the carriage to find that a wheel was on the point of coming loose, on the side nearest the precipice.

The *Journal* of the American S.P.R. records that in 1928 a Mr Waldemar Brunke of Corona, California set out with his family on a trip to Newhall near Mojave, where they were to stay with friends. Suddenly, in obedience to a mysterious voice, he turned the car round and headed back for home. Next day the papers reported that a reservoir had burst at Newhall and hundreds of people, including the Brunkes' friends, had been drowned in their homes. These 'tutelary premonitions', as Richet calls them,[4] are reminiscent of the Socratic *daimon*.

A lady named Lucia Alberti has recorded that she received premonitions of this kind from her earliest years, and during the second world war, when she was in Vienna, they took the form of violent headaches and a sense of panic on the days preceding air-raids, so that her friends would ring her up to know whether a raid was to be expected or not. Stories of this kind appear less improbable now that psychosomatic medicine has drawn attention to the way in which our bodily organs can be affected by the processes of the unconscious mind.

Henry H. Price, a noted parapsychologist and professor of logic at Cambridge University, is so convinced that the unconscious continues to send us precognitive messages 'in code' that he has suggested half-seriously in the periodical *Light* that this phenomenon might be used to ensure a win at the races. The problem, he says, is to intercept the message from our unconscious mind, which is probably doing its utmost to circumvent our mental 'censorship.' To facilitate its task we should make our mind a blank and wait for a word or an image to appear. Nine times out of ten it will not itself be the clue, but will be associated with it in accordance with some psychological or associative law, as a kind of ruse to frustrate the vigilance of the conscious mind. If, for instance, the word that comes up is 'rainbow', we should look to see if any horse has a name like 'sun' or 'cloud', and so forth. This is a trivial example, but it is an instructive indication of the strange relationship between our two modes of consciousness, on which more depends than we are apt to think.

We have already noted that messages of a sad or dramatic character appear to be more highly charged because of their emotive content, so that precognitions of disaster are more frequent and better documented than others. It is as though waves of emotion could be projected through time in the same way as sound waves through space. Just as some people are quicker of hearing than others, so there are people more sensitive to emotional waves of the kind emitted by the Vaiont disaster or the assassination of President Kennedy.[5]

Ernesto Bozzano quotes numerous well documented instances of precognition relating to earthquakes that devastated great cities: Aleppo in 1882, San Francisco in 1906, Messina in 1908, Tokyo and Yokohama in 1923. In Britain there are similar precognitions on record concerning the Aberfan disaster of 1966, when a coal tip slid down and engulfed a school, killing 128 children and 16 adults.[6] J.W. Dunne and the Rev. Walter Franklin Prince listed several cases of dreams announcing rail crashes, etc., which often caused the dreamer great emotional stress.[7] On 11 June 1955 a member of Dr Marabini's staff told him how she had foreseen a motoring accident. 'I was somewhere else, not here in Bologna. There was a wide asphalt road like the Via Emilia. I saw a big lorry pass, and then a silvery car travelling like a meteor. Then, on the right-hand side of the road, I saw seven corpses stretched out over a distance of ten or eleven yards. Further along there were more bodies and a lot of bones and blood. I tried to shout: "Can't you see what damage the car is doing?", but I was unable to speak. The car had disappeared by now, as though it had gone round a curve. I woke up terribly upset.' That evening, when she went home, she learnt of the racing disaster at Le Mans. Commenting on the dream, this lady added: 'I knew nothing about the race at Le Mans, and I have never before had a dream about a car accident.' Dr Marabini described this case, and other instances of precognition by the same person, in a study which appeared in the supplement to *Minerva Medica* dealing with parapsychology. An accident similar to that at Le Mans occurred at Monza in Italy, and was foreseen, three weeks beforehand, by a lady at Florence named M.B., who dreamt vividly of an overturning racing car, red in colour and marked with the number 4.

Another celebrated disaster was that of the S.S. *Titanic,* which collided with an iceberg and sank on her maiden voyage on 14 April 1912. Four days earlier a Mrs Marshall, whose home was on the Solent, went to the top of the house with her husband and some relatives to watch the 'unsinkable' liner sail by. Suddenly she began to scream, declaring that the ship would sink before reaching its destination and that she could see hundreds of people jumping into the icy water. They tried to calm her, but she went on crying: 'Don't stand looking at me, do something! Are you going to let them all drown?' On the same day Vincent N. Turvey, the clairvoyant mentioned in Chapter 2, predicted that 'a big liner would be sunk', and on 13 April he wrote to a Mrs De Steiger confirming his prediction and saying it would come true within two days. The relevant documents, and others connected with the *Titanic,* were collected by Dr Jan Stevenson of Virginia State University.[8] Other predictions are cited in Walter Lord's book on the disaster, *A Night to Remember* (London, 1956). We may mention here some details of the fate of individual passengers, and others who were to have gone on the voyage but did not.

A business man named J. Connor Middleton, who had booked his passage on 23 March, had a dream on the 30th in which he saw the ship capsized and a crowd of people struggling in the water. He dreamt this again on two or three following nights, but did not cancel his journey until he received a telegram asking him to put it off, which he did with some relief. The journalist William T. Stead, on the other hand, went on the voyage although he had received four separate warnings from clairvoyants. One of these, named Harmon, had advised him in general to avoid sea travel and had written on 21 June 1911 to warn him especially against travelling in April 1912. A year earlier, a certain W. De Kerlor had 'seen' Stead embark for America on a ship which bore a funeral wreath at the stern in place of its name; and subsequently, De Kerlor told him he had dreamt of 'a catastrophe at sea, with over a thousand people struggling for their lives.' None the less, Stead sailed in the *Titanic* and was drowned.

We may wonder why it is that some people receive warnings from the unconscious while others do not, and why some who disregard the warnings are nevertheless saved by circumstances.

Maeterlinck, before the various predictions about the *Titanic* disaster were known, wrote: 'Let us take the example of a shipwreck . . . . Before the vessel sails, it is already marked by fate and its doom is certain. For months and perhaps years earlier, a mysterious process of selection has been taking place, and it may be that, out of fifty prospective passengers, only twenty will go on board.' In Maeterlinck's opinion much depended on the degree to which the unconscious is able to assert its claims *vis à vis* the waking self. This varies a great deal from one person to another; but there is another, more disquieting aspect, namely that some people appear destined to be saved in all circumstances and others to incur their own destruction[9] — as though our lives were governed by a puppet-master who takes a delight in bringing certain individuals to ruin.

There are in fact many cases of precognition, usually in dreams, in which the subject is allowed to know every detail of the approaching calamity except for some key fact which would enable him to avoid it.[10] Other warnings again seem designed to bring about the event they warn against. We are told, for instance, that Crœsus, having dreamt that his son would be murdered, entrusted the boy to the special care of the person who did eventually murder him. Could the crime have taken place if the warning had not been given? In the same way, Catherine Crowe in *The Night Side of Nature* (1848) tells of a clerk named Claude Soller who dreamt that he would be murdered on the road from Hamburg to Bergsdorf. His employer, to cure him of believing in dreams, sent him to walk along this road; by way of protection the lad took with him a workman whom he did not know, and this man murdered him for his money.

The 'puppet-master', or the secret self, seems at times to behave with cynical indifference or mocking cruelty, like the gods of some ancient pantheon. Elsa C. of Grosseto wrote some time ago to the author of this book: 'Three years ago I lost my only son. One evening, two years before he died, he told me that while standing on the terrace of our house, he had heard a voice say: "This is the last summer you will spend at Grosseto." He had just passed his accountancy exams, and we supposed that the words meant that he would be getting a job in a bank in another town. Some time later, also in the evening and on the same terrace, my husband heard the voice say: "Go and find your son and stay with him as long as you can, for soon you won't be able to." My husband took this as a premonition of his own death, but it turned out to be our son who died, of an illness that nobody could diagnose.'

In other cases the subject spontaneously manifests, usually in a symbolic way, his obscure awareness of impending doom, Jung believed that the unconscious mind is aware of approaching death and is not perturbed by it, but that the information is censored for the benefit of the conscious mind, which consequently fails as a rule to understand the warning presented to it.

Julius Caesar, it is said, had a long conversation with his friends on the eve of the Ides of March, debating which was the best form of death. The dictator indicated that he preferred a rapid and violent death, and next day his wish was granted, despite the warnings of Calpurnia and the soothsayer. On the morning of Kennedy's assassination, according to some press reports, the President remarked jokingly how easy it would be for a well-placed sharpshooter to pick him off as he drove through the streets of Dallas in an open car.

William Stead, it appears, was particularly interested in stories of the shipwreck of great liners, and had given talks on the subject from 1880 onwards. Facts like these may be dismissed as coincidence, but they are so numerous as to suggest a pattern. Giovanni Segantini (1859-99) was painting in the Engadine shortly before his untimely death; the picture, which he entitled *Death*, showed a peasant hut on the Schalberg, with some people standing round a coffin and a woman weeping. He never finished the canvas, but fell gravely ill of a mysterious disease and ended his days in the very hut which he had depicted. Thirteen days earlier he told his wife Bice, who left a detailed record, that the had had a sudden intuition that the painting was of his own funeral.

This recalls the belief of Dr. Eugène Osty that we all carry in our unconscious a sort of record of our own future. This would help to account for dream-premonitions of death, including those of Abraham Lincoln and Walter Reed, the conqueror of yellow fever. The painter Millais (as Robert Browning told Violet Tweedale) used to see the figures 13 and 1896 on canvases at which he was working, and sure enough he died on 13 July 1896. As P. Devaux says, 'It is probable that clairvoyance plays an almost continuous role in our daily life, but that it is repressed by the conscious mind, especially in civilized man, and takes on the attenuated form of presentiments.'

### Narrators of the future

Premonitions thus have their being in a world of dreams and images; this world is also the home of literary invention, and many writers have described the future without suspecting that they were doing so. We are not speaking here of rational projections of the present, but of events in the writers' own lives. According to Cornelia Brunner, Rider Haggard's characters, unknown to him, actually existed in real life, with the same names as in his books, and either had or were going to have the same adventures.[11] In one novel he gave a graphic description of a boy's death, and not long afterwards his only son, to whom the book was dedicated, died in similar circumstances.

Balzac used to meet men and women who bore a striking resemblance to characters he had just created; and Roger Gilbert-Lecomte, who died of a tetanic infection, had predicted for years that he would die of tetanus, and even composed a poem on the subject.[12] Jacques Buge, who records this, also quotes some lines from Rimbaud's *Une saison en enfer* in which the poet unconsciously predicted his death in a religious hospital after his return from Africa to Europe. Facts like these are unsettling for those who like to explain the world in cut-and-dried terms, but nature is not obliged to conform to our schemes of thought.

An American writer named Morgan Robertson wrote in 1898 a long story entitled *Futility* which contained an uncanny prediction of the sinking of the *Titanic* fourteen years later. The ship in the story was called the *Titan* and was described as an 'unsinkable' triple-screw liner (like the *Titanic*). It was 800 feet long (the *Titanic* was 882) and carried 3,000 passengers (actually 2,207). The *Titan* collides with an iceberg on its maiden voyage in April, while sailing at 25 knots (actually 23). Like the *Titanic*, it has watertight bulkheads. The large number of those drowned is due to the fact that the *Titan* has only 24 lifeboats: the *Titanic* had 20. In a diff-

71

erent order of fiction we may mention the 104 novels of Jules Verne, which describe in detail not only modern scientific developments but also political and social events that could not have been foreseen in the ordinary way.[13]

# CHAPTER 6

## Clairvoyance and telepathy

*A reader of closed books*

In March 1961 I met for the first time Dr Gustavo Adolfo Rol of Turin, a cultivated gentleman with an interest in painting and Napoleonic relics. I had telephoned from Milan on a Wednesday afternoon and arranged to go to his house on the Friday evening at 9.30. Having other business at Turin, I arrived there early on Thursday afternoon and had just checked in at a hotel, chosen at random among many others, when to my surprise the telephone rang: it was Dr Rol, to suggest that I should go and see him that evening instead of the following day.

'But how did you know I had arrived in Turin, and where I was staying?'

'I was doing a charcoal drawing, and my hand wrote your name of its own accord; then it wrote "P. Hotel, room 92." '

This was my first experience of Dr Rol's unusual powers, but I was soon to have others. I called on him as proposed, carrying an ordinary leather briefcase, and after offering me a chair he said: 'I see you have there two articles on telepathy, in final form but not published yet. It's an interesting subject.' Before I could express my astonishment he went on: 'But the story about Napoleon in the second article is not quite correct, as I will show you.' And so he did, after hunting for the relevant passage in one of his many books on the Napoleonic era.

I will revert to Dr Rol's amazing predictions, which included (at one of several later meetings) the prophecy of the Cuban crisis mentioned in Chapter 4. If he is less well known than his powers deserve, it is because he has long made it a rule not to gratify facile curiosity or to encourage theories that he does not believe in. I must confess that I would myself have hesitated to describe his exploits if they were not

73

vouched for by unquestionable authority.

That Friday morning, accompanied by a young photographer, I went back to Dr Rol, who teased the young man gently by mentioning some details of his private life. We then went into the library and chose some books at random, after which we moved to an adjoining room for an experiment. Dr Rol sat about eight yards away from us; the photographer had a number of books under his arm, and I would point to one, without mentioning its title, and invite Dr Rol to 'read' from it at page and line so-and-so. This he did each time without a mistake. To make sure that he was not 'suggesting' to us the choice of page and line, we based this on the face-values of playing cards drawn at random from a well-shuffled pack. We also repeated the experiment with myself holding books and the photographer pointing to them. We went on with the tests until we were both weary, and finally had to accept that the evidence was irrefutable.

### A remarkable predecessor: Alexis Didier

Simple-minded people who consider themselves hard-headed will, of course, be strongly tempted to explain this performance as some kind of conjuring trick. It so happens, however, that the writer of these lines has long taken an interest in conjuring, both in theory and in practice, and has published articles about it. A hundred odd years ago the French conjurer Robert Houdin, who specialized in exposing fraud, undertook to test the powers of Alexis Didier, a clairvoyant and former actor who had displayed his gift of second sight to the Countess of Modena, the Comte de Saint-Aulaire, the Comte de Broyes and the Marquis de Mireville.[1] After bandaging Didier's eyes with great care, Houdin, handed him a pack of cards that had just been unsealed, whereupon Didier read off their values without hesitation. Next, Houdin took a book, opened it and asked Didier to 'read', not from that page but from eight pages further on, at a distance from the top that he indicated with his finger. Here a slight slip occurred: Didier read from the correct line, but on the ninth page. However, after carrying out this and other remarkable experiments, Houdin in March 1847 signed a declaration to the effect that Didier's performance could not possibly be the effect of chance or trickery.

74

Another of Didier's feats was to enable Chopin to recover a parcel containing 25,000 francs that had been sent to him by a Mrs Erskine but had not arrived.[2] At Alexandre Dumas' house he played écarté with his eyes bandaged and was able to name the adversaries' cards; he read from a book, ten pages further on than the place at which it was open, and described exactly what was going on in a distant room, including some details that those with him did not know.

The incidents and experiments we have described illustrate two distinct faculties of the clairvoyant mind: that of apprehending thoughts and memories that are present in the minds of others (which is what we mean by telepathy, or the French by *diapsychie*), and that of apprehending facts without the aid of the senses or of any other mind, by some form of direct perception. For the second faculty, usually known as clairvoyance, various other names have been suggested:[3] but they are mostly inadequate and reflect the perplexity of the human mind confronted by a new form of reality that does not lend itself to categorization. It seems best to regard telepathy and clairvoyance, whether of the past or of the future, as part of a single cognitive process of phenomenon to which the English-speaking world, following Professor Rhine, has given the name of extra-sensory perception (ESP).[4]

Although few people possess these faculties in a marked degree, there are plenty of examples of their use. One evening in 1923 Professor William Mackenzie, who was at Warsaw for the second International Metapsychical Congress, made the acquaintance of a Polish engineer who, after half an hour's general conversation, looked intently into the Professor's eyes and for the next ten minutes gave a detailed description of the latter's house and its neighbourhood and of a member of the Professor's family. This was Stefan Ossowiecki, one of the great clairvoyants of history, who became a close friend of Mackenzie's. On another occasion he was able to perceive the contents of the Professor's pockets and also of a letter that Mackenzie had received but not yet read. When a student at the university of St Petersburg, Ossowiecki disconcerted his examiners by answering, 'sight unseen', questions that were handed to him in a sealed envelope. He met his death at the hands of the Nazis during the second world war, in circumstances that are not precisely known. Another engineer with similar gifts, to whom we shall revert later, was the Scandinavian Olle Jönsson.

*Clairvoyant children*

Mme Laplace, a well-known medium who figured in Osty's experiments for eight years, showed remarkable gifts even as a child. When she was six years old she suddenly exclaimed at dinner: 'Aunt Clotilde has died!' — which proved to be true. On another occasion a visitor brought her a chocolate fish; she refused to thank him and said: 'I don't like you because you beat your wife' — which was also later found to be the case. Francesco Waldner tells of a priest, an uncle of his, who discerned the sins of his penitents before they had time to confess them. Mme De Berly, another celebrated medium, lived almost permanently in a state of 'diffused consciousness' and appeared to those who conversed with her to share many of their memories, as though her mind interpenetrated theirs or was merged with it.

In general, clairvoyance cannot take place when the subject is fully aware of himself and his surroundings, but only when he is in the requisite condition of trance. This state, however, may not be perceptible to others, who may have the impression that he is merely absent-minded or plunged in thought: this was the case e.g. with Ossowiecki.[5] Some like the medium I.R., already mentioned, assume a fixed stare as though mesmerized or under a spell, while others, such as Sandra Bajetto or the engineer C.M., look as if they were intently following a line of reason or trying to remember something. From the point of view of cerebral physiology we do not know much about the symptoms or phenomena which accompany a state of trance, although neurologists have carried out observations by means of electro-encephalography and other techniques.[6] What we do know is that the condition is associated with a decrease in the 'level of vigilance' of everyday consciousness, due to some mechanism in the mind which may be touched off by a relevant object, as in the particular from of clairvoyance known as psychometry.[7]

On one occasion I performed the following experiment. I took three letters which I was about to post, put them into three identical yellow envelopes so that I no longer knew which was which, and asked Signora Bajetto to pick out one and describe the person it was addressed to. She agreed to

try, while objecting that according to the rules of psychometry a letter should give information about the writer and not
the recipient. However, she took up one of the letters and told
me it was addressed to an old lady with a pain in the left leg
and a tendency to bemoan her loneliness. This was perfectly
true. Signora Bajetto even adopted a pose characteristic of the
lady in question, and repeated one of her customary com-
plaints.

She then took up another letter and said, rightly again,
that it was addressed to a man of robust constitution who
would rather be doing a different job than his present one.

Some authors, like Whately Carington, do not believe that
clairvoyance, as opposed to telepathy with or without precognition, is possible. But these are subtle distinctions, and
most parapsychologists are of the opinion that clairvoyance
exists in its own right. Tenhaeff speaks in this connection of
a 'unitive' consciousness, and Lévy-Bruhl used the term 'mystic
participation', i.e. something transcending the normal bounds
of individuality.[8] We may recall Schopenhauer's notion of the
'thing in itself' and the more recent views of Gabriel Marcel
and others. Bergson defined supra-rational consciousness as a
'kind of intellectual sympathy which enables the mind to get
inside an object and thus apprehend its unique, inexpressible
quality'. He also refers to this faculty as 'intuition', and contrasts it with the reflective, ratioconative process which 'walks
round about' the object but does not penetrate to its essence.[9]
Alexis Carrel, the well-known biologist, expressed a very
similar view: he regarded intuition as a form of ESP, and
suggested that the difference between it and clairvoyance was
one of degree and not of quality.

On these lines we may regard clairvoyance and other forms
of supra-rational consciousness as a superior kind of intuition
which, though exceptional today, may in future be a normal
attribute of mankind, in accordance with Teilhard de Chardin's
view concerning the progress of the human race towards
'absolute consciousness'. This is certainly a more modern
conception than that of Lévy-Bruhl, who in his rationalistic
way regarded the intellect as paramount, and 'participation'
as an archaic and pre-logical faculty of the mind.

Despite the basic unity of clairvoyant experience, there is a
considerable variation in respect of procedure or 'ritual', according to the way in which each clairvoyant finds it possible

to penetrate what Quéant calls the 'dizzy unknown' beyond the confines of reason.[10] Today, in place of the fumes which once inspired the priestess of Apollo, we have various hallucinogenic substances that are known to primitive peoples and, in some cases, were known to the ancients also.[11] Some clairvoyants read hands, playing-cards or coffee-grounds; some use a diviner's rod, others handle an object, and others write at the dictation of their unconscious mind. In others, the sense of sight plays a part. The 'Seeress of Prevorst' had a vision of open coffins, each with a doomed individual inside; Ossowiecki used to discern dark circles around the eyes of people who had not long to live. Tenhaeff reports that some subjects perceived the organs of sick persons in symbolic form: a heart like that on a playing-card, veins like tubes and nerves like telephone-wires. A female 'sensitive' named Wiese had a system of special signs to express her perceptions, and Mary Tomeo of Bolanzo produces 'precognitive drawings' of a symbolic character.

### Dialogue at a distance

We should mention here the technique of spiritualistic mediums, which does not always involve the evocation of disembodied spirits. In some cases the medium's hand or arm moves of its own accord to produce 'automatic writing'; in others a *planchette* (a small board on wheels), or an inverted tumbler, moves about to indicate different letters of the alphabet, spelling out words and sentences at the dictation of the unconscious which roams independantly of time and space. The journalist William Stead, whom we have already mentioned, used the faculty of automatic writing to converse at a distance with living beings and obtain statements and information that they would never have given in the ordinary way.

Myers reports an experiment performed by a clergyman named Newnham and his wife: the two sat with their backs to each other, some yards apart, and Mr Newnham would write questions to which the wife wrote the answers. She would often begin writing before he had finished the question, and this on subjects of which she had no knowledge.

Still in the field of automatic writing, the Journal of the Italian Metapsychical Institute published some years ago an account by its former president, the lawyer Luigi Occhipinti,

78

of experiments he had conducted over a long period by the inverted-tumbler method, with remarkable results. On one occasion, two students obtained instantaneously the answers to complex mathematical problems; on another, two girls were favoured with 'literary inspiration'. Medical specialists put abstruse questions to which they received replies in technical language. Sig. Occhipinti also reports experiments by himself and his mother who, in a light trance, was able to write down poems, stories and various messages, including precognitive ones.

A related phenomenon is that of 'cross-correspondence' between two mediums in different places, often strangers to each other, who write down separate fragments of a single message, each contribution being unintelligible without the other. This again serves to bear out the idea of Mind as a single, indivisible ocean.

### Clairvoyance in the public service

A Turin policeman named Lanfranco Davito, a noted clairvoyant, was once asked by his superiors to find a suspected criminal. After a moment's pause he replied: 'it is not a man, as you think, but a woman in disguise; and she is not alone, but has two accomplices. She left Turin a few days ago.' He then named a certain town and said: 'Near by, at a bend in the river, there is a wooden building with overlapping planks; that is where the three are hiding.' Sure enough, the criminals were found and arrested.

The hypnotist, medium and clairvoyant Aldo Gabrielli was regularly consulted by the Italian police in difficult cases; and some years ago at Trent, a medium in a trance revealed the name of the murderer of Luigi Marsellier, a tailor. In 1956 Mr Nelson Palmer of Cape Town 'saw' the body of Myrna J. Aken, a girl of eighteen who had disappeared, in the place where her murderers had hidden it. From 1933 onwards the Budapest police made regular use of the clairvoyant János Kele (whose feats were studied by Hans Driesch) in order to trace missing persons.[12] The Dutch police similarly use clairvoyants, generally under the supervision of Professor Tenhaeff, who is qualified to interpret their cryptic or symbolic utterances in case of need. In Greece, on the initiative of the parapsychologist Dr Tanagras, lecture-courses were held to instruct the police force concerning paranormal phenomena.

Dr Maximilian Langsner, an indefatigable traveller who died in Alaska, rendered aid of this description to the police of various countries, but only when he felt a certain specific impulse: on one occasion he detected a murderer at Edmonton (Canada), who had left no clues. The Canadian police also received valuable help from the clairvoyant Cayce (cf. Chapter 2). Another sensitive, Peter Hurkos, aided the Virginia police to detect a fourfold murderer. However, clairvoyance cannot be relied upon as a regular adjunct to criminal investigation. In Italy, Gérard Croiset was called upon not long ago to trace a child that had disappeared: he declared correctly that the child was dead, but added various details that proved to be erroneous. It must not be forgotten that all clairvoyance is of an oneiroid (dream-like) character; its messages are often fragmentary, capricious and enigmatic, and one cannot rely on receiving accurate communications to order. If the clairvoyant is a genuine one there is nearly always some truth in his or her utterances, but there is also an element of distortion due to the labyrinthine workings of the hidden self. None the less, Professor Rhine suggested as long ago as 1957 that military use should be made of paranormal faculties, to prevent an aggressor enjoying the benefit of secrecy and surprise. From 1960 onwards this idea was taken up in both US and Soviet military circles. Psychological experts are on the staff of the Air Force research laboratory at Bedford, Massachusetts, and in 1960 the Soviet authorities made a grant to enable Professor Leonid L. Vasiliev to continue his researches into telepathy, which had previously been the object of official hostility or indifference. His followers at Leningrad are carrying on the work, as are other academies at Moscow and Kiev.

Both in the West and in the Soviet bloc, interest is shown in the possibility of mental communication with astronauts in orbit and men in submarines: attention was drawn to this aspect of telephatic science by Professor Lazar Sukharevsky in his introductory address to the first congress of Soviet parapsychologists in February 1968, under the auspices of the Association concerned with the science and technique of communications and electronics.

Thus, while in some quarters 'psi' or paranormal phenomena are written off as trickery, in others they are seen as having a contribution to make to scientific progress. The paradox reaches its height when, as in certain parts of the USA, professional clairvoyance is forbidden by law while astrology is allowed because it is 'based on calculation'. Certainly the public has a right to be defended against charlatanry; but the 'calculations' of astrology are more than dubious and our society will neglect at its peril the well-attested results of parapsychology.

## Statistical verification

Professor Rhine of Duke University (Durham, North Carolina) — who, as we noted, is responsible for the term 'extra-sensory perception' — also originated experimental techniques for the purpose of a statistical appraisal of the new science of telepathy. Such techniques had already been devised by Myers, Richet and others, but Rhine deserves the credit of adopting simple, uniform criteria which make it possible to repeat tests *ad infinitum* and evaluate the results on the basis of the accepted laws of chance and probability.

One of the devices first used by Rhine was the well-known pack of 'Zener cards', twenty-five in number, bearing five different symbols: a star, a circle, a cross, a square and a wavy line. The cards are shuffled by hand or by a machine and are then extracted at random by the person conducting the test. If the number of correct 'guesses' by the percipient is substantially greater than would be expected on the basis of pure chance, this is taken as an experimental proof of the operation of a 'psi' or ESP factor.

It is now over thirty years since Rhine's first experiments, which led to striking results, and during that period his method has spread considerably and has brought his subject to the notice of many investigators who might otherwise have paid no attention to it. He appears to have shown, among other things, that ESP is a universal phenomenon, although much more pronounced in some individuals than in others.[13] At the present time, some regard his methods as the only valid ones for the investigation of paranormal phenomena, while in other quarters a reaction has set in, for example on the part of G. Spencer Brown and Professor Marabini.[14] In 1953, at the international conference on parapsychology at Utrecht, Gabriel Marcel remarked that the results so far achieved were meagre in comparison with the effort that had been expended. Warcollier, again, expressed doubt as to whether statistical methods are best suited to the subject-matter of telepathy. Tenhaeff has experienced failure in applying Rhine's method to Gérard Croiset, and Rhine himself had difficulty in the case of Eileen Garrett. As Professor Tocquet puts it, 'the statistical method restricts and mutilates the phenomenon by depriving it of its affective character and of the human warmth which imparts an element of drama.'[15] Professor Ducasse, vice-president of the American Society for Psychical Research, has warned scholars against being 'enslaved to quantitative methods' and advised them to re-evaluate spontaneous instances of ESP occuring outside the laboratory, which are neither prepared nor expected, yet may be of great value to researchers.

Parapsychology, in fact, suffers from the same difficulty as psychology itself when it comes to reducing the subject-matter to strictly objective terms. European psychologists such as Mounier and Le Senne have for some time deprecated the tendency of American investigators to succumb to what they call the 'superstition' of the laboratory, or of numbers. Professor G.A. von Hayek of Chicago has, on the one hand, attacked the natural sciences for laying a false claim to epistemological certainty, while on the other he maintains that the human 'sciences' have done themselves an injustice by deferring to the methodology of physics and to a spirit of dogmatic rationalism which, in his opinion, can only result in sterility. Figures and statistics undoubtedly have their use within a limited field; but, as the psychologist Leonardo Ancona recently pointed out, 'human beings are not in all respects amenable to precise measurement; and it is above all in their most human aspects that they require to be studied in a manner free from preconception.'

Telediagnosis. Pasqualina Pezzola has the extraordinary power of diagnosing the illnesses of patients whose addresses are handed to her, and also that of mentally 'visiting' them. The accuracy of her results has been confirmed by doctors.

Foreknowledge in dreams and trances. Some time before the disaster at Vaiont the Bolognese medium Maria Lambertini 'saw' a huge tub, full of water, spilling its contents from a height and devasting the plain beneath. This is her own drawing of the vision. She also saw rows of coffins and a crowd of people in tears.

Time-travelling. María Reyes de Z. was handed a piece of marble from the Roman Forum and executed this drawing of the ruins: the site as it appears today is shown in the photograph above.

When this scrap of a letter, found in a bottle floating in the Atlantic, was handed to María Reyes de Z. during a trance, she described the despair of the passengers on a liner torpedoed by the Germans in 1917 and particularly the writer of the letter, who was drowned.

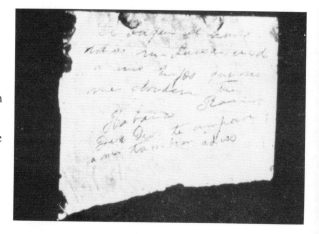

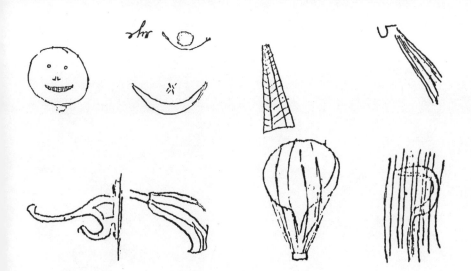

Mental television. The novelist Upton Sinclair discovered, in
experiments with his wife and others, that a telepathic subject can
reproduce with fair accuracy an image on which another distant
subject has concentrated for a moment or two. Each pair of drawings
above shows, on the left, the figure as transmitted, and on the
right as received.

In a programme organized by the
Italian Society for Parapsychology and
the Italian Radio, certain images,
including the plant on the left and the
model of a chameleon on the right,
were mentally projected by a group of
'sensitives'. They were picked up by
listeners with reasonable accuracy;
some took the plant for a starfish,
however, and others saw the chameleon
as a dazzling white light.

The Indian girl Kumari Shakuntala Devi gave a demonstration of her powers as a lightning calculator to an audience of journalists and students at Rome University. She is here seen with Professor Toddi (Pietro S. Rivetta), the Orientalist: The demonstration was preceded by a few moments of meditation in accordance with the rules of yoga.

Sandra Bajetto of Rome was handed a leather case (left) without any indication of its contents. She adopted a prayerful attitude and then described an Abyssinian scene, with a kneeling penitent advancing towards a round church. The case in in fact contained a Coptic gospel (right) which had belonged to an Ethiopian hermit,who copied and painted it and wore it round his neck for several years.

Artistic prodigies. This drawing was executed spontaneously at the age of five by Gianni Cavalcoli of Ravenna, who made thousands of similar pictures of unknown yet realistic animals.

Another 'metaphysical' artist, Iris Canti of Milan, was commanded by unknown forces to paint this picture, entitled 'Coming in to land', and dedicate it to Federico Fellini, to whom it was given.

Another of Iris Canti's involuntary works of art. The title, revealed to her after completion, is 'The salvation of humanity'. The eyes, below, represent the roots of human knowledge; in the centre is the flame of celestial love, and above are the protective hands of Providence; doves of peace hover around.

'Atalanta di Campofiore' is the pseudonym of a noblewoman of Sienna, a gifted medium who is inspired to paint human faces reflecting various strong emotions. Some, it is said, are portraits of dead people who have been recognized by their relations.

Lidoreau, a French industrialist, was the subject of a television programme introduced by Professor Tocquet. He had an extraordinary power over birds and used, by way of relaxation, to solve abstruse mathematical problems before going to sleep.

Fire-walking. On the feast-days of St. Helen and St. Constantine, members of the sect of Anastenarides at Langadhas in Macedonia walk over burning coals, barefoot and unscathed. This exploit has been filmed by Professor Cassoli of Bologna and others.

Colin Evans, a well-known British medium, demonstrating levitation at a mass seance at the Rochester Square Temple, North London in 1938. An infra-red photograph taken by Leon Isaacs.

Restless stones. Some years ago two sisters named Alida and Santina De Matteo experienced a wave of paranormal phenomena such as rains of stones and moving domestic objects. The photograph shows Alida with a 'vibrating stone'.

The Polish medium Stanislawa Tomcyzk could make scissors stand on end, as shown here, and stop or re-start a clock enclosed in a case. She could also make a roulette ball stop on a predetermined number and cause objects to appear and disappear mysteriously.

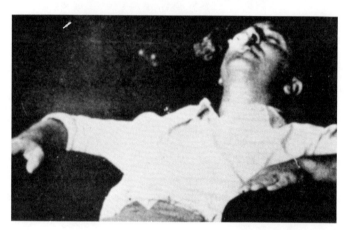

Domenico Musso in a trance, emitting ectoplasm — a substance produced by certain mediums in the past thought to provide the 'raw material' of ghosts appearing at seances. *Photograph by courtesy of Professor Giorgio Tron.*

Photograph of a 'double'. The ectoplasmic form is probably taking shape through the agency of the hypnotized medium (standing); it is that of Giovanni Andalini, now a celebrated faith-healer. The figure on the couch is in a cataleptic state.

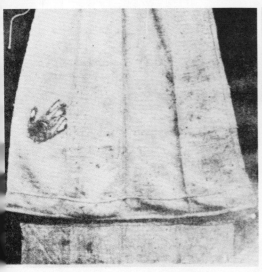

Physical traces of ghosts. Left: an imprint of the hand of the nun Klara Scholers, who died in 1637, on the apron of Sister Maria Herendorps at the Benedictine convent of Vinnenberg. Right: a similar mark imprinted on the nightshirt of Joseph Leleu of Wodecq-Mos, Belgium, by the ghost of his mother, which appeared to him on the night of 21 June, 1789. — Vestments with traces of fire due to ghosts that appeared centuries ago are preserved at the church of Sacro Cuore, Rome.

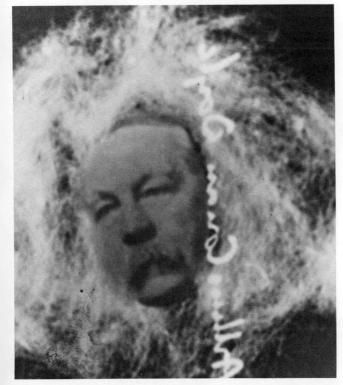

The spirit extra of Sir Arthur Conan Doyle, who was himself a very interested spiritualist.
*Reproduced by kind permission of Psychic Press Limited.*

A fairy dance: the first photographs of fairies seen in Yorkshire by two children, Elsie Wright and Frances Griffith. Sir Arthur Conan Doyle believed in the reality of the fairies and wrote books and articles about them. They were probably the effect of a mediumistic dream, which in exceptional cases can impart a degree of material consistency to products of the mind.

This is a psychic photograph which Houdini, seated in front, never tried to explain away. The picture was taken by his friend Alex Martin, a psychic photographer of Denver, US. The extras are clear. Houdini did not try to duplicate this kind of psychic evidence. Nor did he ever try to "expose" Martin.

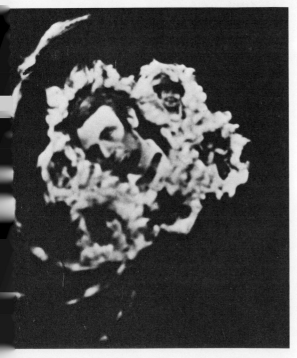

The striking spirit extra of Lincoln received at a seance to commemorate his birthday.

Mischievous and malignant spirits. Many cases are on record of domestic objects defying the laws of gravity, especially in the presence of a child or young person with mediumistic gifts; the phenomena generally cease after a few weeks. This happened in the case of Georges Bellone, a French-Italian boy aged fourteen (left) and of Sig. Locatelli (right), a dealer whose bicycles used to ride about of their own accord.

Haunted houses. Here the manifestations may go on for decades or even centuries, as in a house near the Sienna Botanical Gardens.

The Ring 'O Bells, Middleton, near Manchester, is haunted by the ghost of a Sad Cavalier, reputed to be the son of Lord Stannycliffe of Stannycliffe Hall. His ghost has appeared in and around the vicinity of the pub over many years, in particular when the tune 'Greensleeves' is played on the pub piano.

*Reproduced by kind permission of Mr. John M. Dale*

The 'calculating horses' of Elberfield. This shows Muhamed,
one of the four famous stallions, beating out the answer to
an arithmetical problem.

An enchanted fountain. One of the persons shown is a telekinetic
medium at Treviso, whose presence causes stones and other
small objects to perform strange antics. On one occasion he and
his friends threw some pebbles into the fountain; as they were
driving away, the pebbles, still wet, hit the bodywork of the car
as if thrown back by a human agency.

Sig. Alfredo Beltrame, a
friend of the Treviso medium,
had his spectacles whisked off
his nose by a mysterious agency
and transferred to the inside of
his car, which was locked
and protected by an anti-
theft device.

Two assiduous investigators of paranormal events: Bruno
Lava (left), a geometrician, and Dr. Cino Boccazzi (right).
Dr. Boccazzi is a well-known urologist and also finds time for
archaeology and mountaineering, at whcich he is an expert.

A derelict cemetery, near Treviso, where a gravestone once glided through the air and came to rest at Dr. Boccazzi's feet. Other striking and well-attested instances of telekinesis have taken place here.

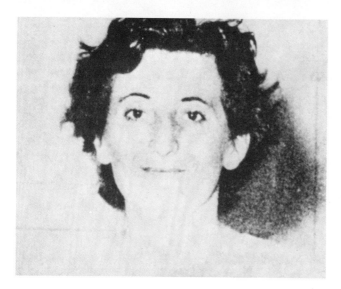

Maria Lambertini of Bologna (above), a seamstress by trade, was out walking by the riverside when she heard a voice telling her to take home a lump of chalk and carve it into a head of her son (below, left). At the bidding of the same mysterious power she has executed other carvings of strange masks (below, right), vampires, friendly demons etc. Despite her lack of artistic training the works have been much praised by critics.

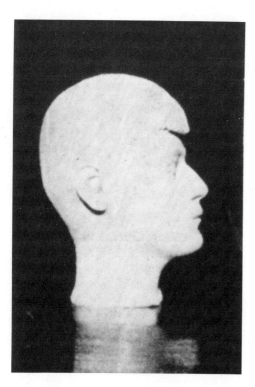

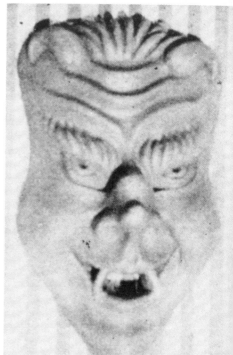

# PART II

The unknown sources of knowledge

# CHAPTER 7

## Knowledge that is not ours

*Knowledge that is not ours*

Therese Neumann of Konnersreuth in Bavaria (1898-1962), who was famous for her visions of Christ's passion, was visited several times by the Indian swami Paramahansa Yogananda.[1] The two established a close *rapport* despite the difference of their cultures, and on one occasion the swami was present when Therese relived, as she did every Friday, the stages of the Via Dolorosa and crucifixion. With trembling lips she addressed an invisible presence in an unknown language, as her white garment and kerchief slowly became imbrued with blood. At a certain moment the yogi found himself sharing her vision:[2] he has described how he saw Christ struggling through the mocking crowd, and how Therese lifted her head with a horrified expression as the Saviour stumbled beneath the weight of the cross.

Many other instances of 'shared consciousness' can be quoted. The French explorer Alexandra David-Neel[3] reports that the Tibetans who engage in psychic practices attribute the phenomenon to a state of intense mental concentration bordering on trance. Giuseppe Ticcu, describing the process of initiation whereby lamas instruct their pupils, says that in some cases there is no communication by word of mouth: the master and pupil sit side by side, absorbed in meditation, and their attunement is such that ideas and doctrines gradually pass from one mind into the other.

In cases like this, where a whole body of experience can be shared without being reduced to words, it seems inadequate to speak of telepathy in the usual sense. If the secret of such communication has been lost among Western peoples, it is no doubt because with us the conscious self lays claim to absolute independence, with the result that we are cut off from the depths at which mysterious links are forged between one mind and another.[4] Some draw a comparison here with the process of biological evolution. In a bird such as the ostrich, the wings have become atrophied but the strength of the pectoral muscles has transferred itself to the legs, so that the creature can run at great speed. Modern civilized man has opted for 'legs' and has great powers of physical motion, but it is not a hundred per cent certain that he has made the right choice: as W. Tudor Pole suggests,[5] we ought perhaps to give more attention to communion and less to communication. The present trend is all towards speed and intensified individualism, ignoring the glimpses of a deeper unity that religion and philosophy open up to us. Some, nevertheless, have the courage to go against this trend: for instance Liselle Reymond, a Swiss intellectual, some twenty years ago turned her back on the West and went to live among the Brahmans.[6] One of the first lessons her *guru* taught her was: 'There is no lesson to learn, no task to perform. When I speak to you, you are my thought, and when you speak to me, I am your thought, just as there is only one roof above both our heads. An eagle does not make up its mind to fly: it plunges into the void and finds itself flying.' Lizelle Reymond followed this counsel and found herself attuned, as Yogananda put it, by virtue of gifts that were not so much mental as spiritual: we may recall Warcollier's ideas on the unity of the human race, and Gabriel Marcel's view that there are no barriers at the unconscious level.

Alexis Carrel, the biologist and Nobel prizewinner, wrote that it is an illusion to suppose that each of us is independent of his fellows and of the universe, and that what we call telepathy may consist in an encounter, 'outside four-dimensional reality', between the immaterial portions of two minds. A curious example of such an encounter is related by Tudor Pole, later a major in the British army, who in 1910 was a well-to-do young man touring the world in search of unusual experiences. At Alexandria he met Abdul Baha, the Persian Bahai leader, who was proscribed as a heretic by official Islam but venerated by his followers throughout the Arab world as a religious reformer, seer and healer. They conversed haltingly through an interpreter whose English and Persian were both inadequate; but, when the interpreter withdrew, Pole found himself not only understanding what Abdul Baha said in Persian but able to reply in the same language, though he had never heard or spoken it in his life.

## The mediumistic gift of tongues

It is difficult, not to say impossible, to explain phenomena such as these in terms of ordinary psychology or cerebral physiology, but it may help if we adopt Bergson's hypothesis that the brain acts as a filter, admitting some perceptions and excluding others; or we may think of it as a net with meshes that are capable of enlargement.

Richet tells the story of Laura Edmonds, whose father was a US Senator and member of the Supreme Court of New York State. She knew no language except English and a little French, yet she was able at times to converse in Modern Greek, Polish, Hungarian and one of the Indian dialects. The term 'xenoglossy' has been used for this mysterious gift, which usually manifests itself under séance conditions when the medium is in a state of trance. The clairvoyant Cayce, to whose diagnostic powers we referred in Chapter 2, used to reply to consultants in this way in their own language. Mirabelli, a Brazilian subject studied by Ringger, knew only Portuguese in the ordinary way, but when in trance spoke fluent English and Italian. Other mediums with this gift were Alfred Peters and Valiantine.

To what minds are we to suppose that these mediums were attuned? The simplest view is perhaps to imagine that they were closely linked psychically with the persons they were talking to, or the others present at the séance; but we may also recall William James's theory of a cosmic reservoir of consciousness, or the 'super-minds' to which Whately Carington refers in his work on telepathy, or again the 'group minds' and 'psychic fields' postulated by some biopsychologists. These and other hypothesis alike involve the existence of a psychic world upon which the individual can draw, but which is greater than he. We may imagine a profound and secret self whose contours are indefinite and which is in contact with wider psychic entities, on the ocean-wave analogy already mentioned. This theory would not be accepted by the school of thought which limits the scope of the subconscious to memories and impressions that have been in the conscious mind but which it has, so to speak, mislaid. In the last century this school coined the term 'creative automatism

87

of the subconscious' which, according to them, suffices to explain every instance of new knowledge supposedly acquired by paranormal means; and indeed there are cases which can be understood simply as the revival of forgotten knowledge. For example, in 1946 the violinist Kreisler suffered a brain injury which caused him to forget the six modern languages he knew but to regain a complete knowledge of Latin and Greek, which he had learnt as a boy but forgotten: until the injury was cured, he could only express himself in these two languages. Quéant records the case of a French soldier in the first world war, who after receiving a head wound, found himself able to speak English, but lost the ability when the wound was cured.

*Unknown sources of knowledge*

It is of course generally known that the subconscious works on impressions and memories and recombines them in ways that escape the observation of the conscious mind, but are a valuable aid to the creative intellect. Sometimes this process leads to odd results, as in the case of Hélène Smith, studied by the Swiss expert Théodore Flournoy. This medium, whose real name was Elisa Müller, used to drop into unknown languages which she claimed were extraterrestrial, but which Flournoy recognized to be subconscious inventions based on French. Such feats as those related to Laura Edmonds and Tudor Pole, involving the fluent speaking of languages previously unknown, of course go far beyond anything the subconscious could achieve in this way, and presuppose access to a wider mental universe. This was recognized e.g. by Eileen Garrett, who declared that some of her own performances in the way of automatic writing did not spring from the subconscious with its reflections of day-to-day life, but from a larger and less personal sphere: she felt as though she had attained a higher mental level and had penetrated to the primal springs of knowledge that, as she put it, 'unite every aspect of life'. At such times she perceived 'amazing colours and vivid pictures of unknown persons and places', scraps of strange music and unknown tongues.

The case of an English medium who spoke and wrote the Egyptian language of about 1300 B.C. is described in detail in a book by Frederic Wood and Howard Hulme. Another well-known case is that of an American lady, Mrs Pearl Leonore Curran, studied by Walter Franklin Prince, who in 1913 produced by automatic writing a novel set in early Christian times and a story of medieval life, *Telka*, in authentic period English. Mrs Curran, who had no special education or knowledge of history, believed that these works were dictated to her by the disembodied spirit of a seventeenth-century girl named Patience Worth.[7] Examples like this seem to show that the past is indestructible and continues to influence the present through the minds of living persons who, as it were, bring experiences back to life, in a transfer or merging of consciousness which may turn into an actual merging of personality. This is analogous to retrocognition in dreams, but in the present case the dreams are wide-awake ones and produce tangible and immediate effects.

## Artists by compulsion

Mrs Curran is not the only medium to have produced literary work at the behest of a mind outside her own. In 1948 a writer named Frances Dale returned to her publisher the sum of money he had sent her for a novel, on the ground that it was not written by her but by a priest of Atlantis. The Turin policeman Lanfranco Davito, already mentioned, wrote and published stories about Tibet although he had no previous knowledge of that country's history and customs, as a prefatory note explained.

Margaret Bevan, an old lady living in London, painted portraits of people who had died and whom she had never known, and in 90 per cent of cases their accuracy was confirmed by photographs. She felt as though an unknown person were guiding her hand and forcing her to paint whether she wanted to or not. Signora Iris Canti of Milan similarly finds that, although she has no wish to paint, she is compelled to from time to time, and has no peace of mind if she tries to struggle against the *daimon,* or whatever modern name we prefer to give it. Her pictures are of decided interest, although they fall into no ordinary classification: they are symbolic, fantastic, allegorical and dream-like, and appear to express themes drawn from esoteric Indian philosophy, a subject of which Signora Canti has no knowledge. Even when a picture is completed she does not understand it until an 'occult force', to use her own expression, enlightens her by dictating explanatory verses, which rhyme but have no poetic merit. Nor is she allowed to sell a picture until these forces give her leave, which apparently they very seldom do.

Maria Lambertini, the Bologna medium, who earned a modest living with her needle, one day brought home a large lump of chalk from the banks of the Reno and, using only her fingertips and thumbs, modelled it into a brilliant likeness of her son. Later, under the same impulse, she produced a faun and a series of demoniac figures, grinning vampires etc. Since then she has made a regular practice of sculpting in this way, and feels lost on the fairly frequent occasions when her 'spirit-guide' withdraws his inspiration for the time being.

This phenomenon of 'metapsychic art' is not a new one. It generally happens that the impulse to paint or sculpt occurs suddenly in adults who have never shown any disposition to do so and have no technical knowledge. Examples are Augustin Lesage, an almost illiterate miner, and the playwright Victorien Sardou, both of whom suddenly began painting pictures in a style unrelated to contemporary trends.

The work is generally executed at great speed, and the involuntary artist is often incapable of explaining its meaning. Victor Spencer used to paint his pictures upside-down, so that until they were finished it was not clear what they represented. Marian Gruzewski, in Poland, made his first drawing in five minutes, in the dark, and on another occasion produced in a quarter of an hour a highly expressive composition with a large number of figures. In childhood he had been classed as 'unteachable' because his hand insisted on writing independently instead of at the master's dictation. Professor Egidi[8] relates that a tanner named Machner was discharged from a drawing school because his spontaneous style proved impossible to reconcile with that of the teachers; yet his strange pictures of flowers and Martian scenes were certainly not devoid of artistic interest. Another case is that of F. Lowley, who, before the mysterious gift asserted itself, was a skilled draughtsman but in a quite different style. His former drawings, as described by Egidi, were delicate and meticulous, but from 1931 onwards he produced works of chaotic appearance at frantic speed and with a convulsive trembling not only of his drawing-arm, but of the left as well.

From time to time there appeared in these drawings historical characters of every period and country, the detail of which was always accurate. He would throw off dozens of such drawings in a day, some taking as little as twenty seconds and others a minute or so. Even if blindfolded or in the dark he would proceed with the composition unerringly. Some of these works expressed future events in symbolic fashion, e.g. the Abyssinian war or the bombing of Rome.

The salient characteristics of metapsychic art are its rapidity and independence of the artist and, on occasion, its precognitive aspect. Even if this is lacking, it displays the luxuriant, fantastic quality of a dream: this is true of the works by Hélène Smith and Machner, and of Sardou's bizarre yet harmonious scenes of 'family life on the planet Jupiter'. The artists in question are in fact endowed with the ability to present their dreams on canvas: so do other artists, it is true, but metapsychic art is distinguished by the dominant role of the subconscious.

### The roots of artistic creation

We may begin to discern here a point of contact between artistic creation on the one hand and mediumistic powers on the other. As Jung says,[9] an uncreated work of art tends to impose itself on the conscious will in a tyrannic or insidious fashion, taking no account of the subject's well-being or personal interests: the 'autonomous creative complex' is bent on emerging into the light of day, as though it were a separate part of the soul and were independent of the authority of consciousness. The yogi Ramacharaka[10] similarly writes of an 'extraneous presence' forcing itself into the mind and assuming a conscious role of its own. Neither of these authors are referring here to a 'presence' in the spiritualistic sense, but merely to something which is foreign to that part of the mind which knows itself. Jung refuses to believe that a genuine work of art can have its roots in the subconscious, considered as a mere repository of day-to-day experience: the source of authentic inspiration, in his view, is to be sought 'in that sphere of unconscious mythology whose primordial images are the common patrimony of mankind.' Although Jung's terminology and philosophic background are different from those of William James and Whately Carington, he agrees with them in postulating a source of inspiration that transcends the individual mind.

In general the creative role of the unconscious has been neglected in the past, but there are exceptions. Alfred de Musset said in effect that 'We do not work with our brains'. but listen to a stranger speaking in our ear.' Henry Maudsley, the English alienist, observed that 'A writer's best ideas are those by which he himself is surprised. A poet engaged in composition is practically under dictation as far as his conscious mind is concerned.' Rilke spoke of receiving his verses as a gift, and the Danish poet Grundtvig declared that he had sung of 'things unknown" The critic Jacques Buge remarks that 'It is as though an archetype of the work to be created already existed in some mysterious way, so that the poet's task consists of drawing it hither by an effort analogous to that of memory: he is, as it were, summoning up a future that exists in the past.' Oliver Quéant, another adventurous thinker, considers that 'All that we know, foresee or guess is not simply our property but is the reflection of something extra-human that exists in an imponderable and unknowable form at the very centre of consciousness, that ether of the supreme, universal intelligence.' This recalls Carrel's image of something located 'outside the four dimensions of our universe'. We may use such metaphors as these provided we realize that, presupposing as they do our earthly notions of space and time, they are bound to be inadequate to the thing described. We are certain to make mistakes in exploring the mystery of knowledge and artistic creation, but we cannot go wholly wrong if we base ourselves on indisputable facts.

# CHAPTER 8

Glimmers of another consciousness

*Rationality and genius*

Louis Pasteur, on the occasion of his admission to the *Académie des Sciences,* made a speech which must have seemed audacious to his more rationalistic colleagues. Among other things he said: 'The most valuable notions that the human mind possesses are all in darkness, in the background. If we were cut off from this background, the exact sciences themselves would be stripped of the greatness which derives from the secret affinity between them and other truths of infinite scope that we are beginning dimly to apprehend, and which constitute a link with the mystery of creation.' It is unusual for a scientist of Pasteur's calibre to pay such a bold and honest tribute to the rich though obscure possibilities that lie outside the range of our conscious or subconscious minds.

Henri Poincaré, in *La Valeur de la Science,* expressed a similar point of view when he wrote: 'Guesswork before proof — need we recall that all important discoveries have been made in this way?' And Louis de Broglie, the noted physicist, remarks that 'Intuition enables us to perceive all at once, by a kind of inner light that has nothing to do with laborious syllogisms, some profound aspect of reality.' Bergson affirmed the priority of intuition over intelligence, and Maudsley observes that reasoning only brings to the level of full consciousness what was already known by intuition. Despite authorities such as these, many lack the humility to admit that our most rational sciences have their roots in unfathomable mystery. We can well believe that the original sin was one of pride, when we find *homo sapiens* attributing his own progress exclusively to a tiny part of the psyche, adapted to the comprehension of a limited section of the universe, and refusing to believe that what lies outside it can be of any importance or that evolution can have any other purpose than to enhance the powers of the reasoning faculty. Certainly we should be proud of this faculty, but not to the point of embracing a superficial, one-sided rationalism that denies value to a whole area of experience.

Not only are some perceptions, as we have seen, independent of the conscious intellect, but it is precisely the higher forms of mental activity that have this non-rational quality. Genius itself can only be described in terms that presuppose a form of consciousness superior to ours, obeying rules of which we know nothing. As Myers says, when we contemplate a supreme work such as the *Agamemnon* of Aeschylus we cannot help feeling that it is in part the product of an intelligence distinct either from subliminal reasoning or from conscious planning. It is more like the imperfect presentation of a schema based on perceptions unknown to us, than the kind of perfection attained by the rational manipulation of known data. Walstein comments similarly on the work of other great artists. Although genius is a force that wells up from the unconscious, we cannot agree with Adler or Freud that it is adequately explained in terms of sex or the inferiority complex, of compensation or sublimation. It should be noted, on the other hand, that inspiration is often bestowed most fully on individuals of less maturity and fewer resources than their fellows. Traditional psychology, ignoring as it does the contribution of the secret self, is powerless to explain the existence of infant prodigies — young children who suddenly display mental abilities beyond the adult range, and also technical knowledge in such fields as music, art and literature, not to mention mathematics and chess.

### Over-gifted children

'Genius is a secret of infancy', according to Aimé Michel,[1] who is inclined to explain it by the predilection for a certain subject which exists in some families, so that an increasing measure of aptitude is passed on to each succeeding generation. This may account e.g. for the Bach dynasty in music, but Michel himself admits that it does not fit every case: for instance, the poet Ovid lisped in hexameters, though it appears that his parents found this rather irksome than otherwise. (When his father told him angrily to desist, little Publius, still

94

in hexameters, begged forgiveness). A child named Christian Heinechen, the fifth son of a painter, who was born at Lübeck in 1721 and died there about five years later, is said to have conjugated Latin verbs before he could walk; in the course of his short life he learnt Hebrew and studied geography, art, history and the Greek classics. Even if this is a legend, it is not wholly out of keeping with known instances. Pico della Mirandola, at the age of five, was able to repeat backwards, from the last word to the first, a poem that had just been read to him; at ten he was a protonotary apostolic, and at fourteen he was studying canon law at Bologna university.

In music, Mozart is the best-known of a long line of infant prodigies, and every now and then we hear of children conducting orchestras. As in the case of the painters mentioned in the last chapter, these artists are characterized by a devouring passion for the activity thrust upon them. Some, we are told, 'cannot live without music,'[2] and others cannot stop teaching themselves dead or living languages.[3] At Vienna in 1917 a Polish boy named Rzeszewski displayed his ability to play six games of chess simultaneously. He usually won them, and this without making any conscious plan, but by a kind of intuition. At that time he was passionately keen on chess, but later — as is true of many musical prodigies — he lost his extraordinary skill and also his overmastering interest in the game.

In 1953 I myself observed the performance of a boy from Ravenna named Gianni Cavalcoli, who was six years old and had an astonishing power of throwing off highly expressive drawings at great speed. He made twenty thousand of these in three years, after which his creative frenzy slackened by degrees. They were mostly drawings of unlikely-looking prehistoric animals, in elaborate and harmonious compositions.

As with metapsychic artists, these juvenile productions are the work of the unconscious breaking through the barriers set by the conscious mind. This luminous, cognitive aspect of the unconscious has in general been ignored or undervalued; but even in academic circles there are some who hold that we possess a third faculty, the 'super-conscious', which is the domain of mental and artistic creativity and corresponds, as it were, to the ultra-violet rays of the spectrum as distinct from the luminous band which we can see and the infra-red area. This idea was first put forward by Myers and has been taken up by such scholars as Assagioli and Disertori, Martiny in France, Bucke in Canada, Kenneth Walker in Britain and Urban in Austria, all of whom are experts in the field of psychology and neuro-psychiatry.

### Calculating prodigies

The feats of child mathematical geniuses are, if anything, even more remarkable, though their gifts seldom last into adult life. André-Marie Ampére, the founder of electro-dynamics, showed a passion for calculation even before he went to school. He used beans for the purpose, until a time came when he was ill with fever and was not allowed any. After three days of strict dieting he was given a biscuit, but instead of eating it he divided it into fragments so as to continue his calculations, which evidently meant more to him than food. This story is told by François Arago, who was himself a child mathematical prodigy. It is interesting that as Ampère developed into an eminent mathematician on the conscious level, his aptitude for mental calculations declined. This is usually the case with infant prodigies, though not always.

Giacomo Inaudi, a shepherd-boy of Piedmont who had never been to school, performed elaborate calculations by means of stones. Later he became one of the most celebrated calculators of all time, while still following the Indian custom of performing additions and subtractions from left to right. Other famous child arithmeticians are the seventeenth-century Mattia il Gallo; a Sicilian peasant boy, Vito Mangiamele, who was presented to the French Academy of Sciences in 1887 at the age of ten; Henry Mondeux, and Ludwig Kahn, who when he grew up turned from mathematics to clairvoyance.[4] An Indian girl, Kumari Shakuntala Devi, taught herself arithmetic before going to school and was soon able to correct her elders' mistakes. In 1951, when she was just twenty, I saw her give a demonstration at Rome University under the supervision of Pietro Silvio Rivetta (also known as Toddi), the Orientalist. I was struck by the bird-like grace of her fragile form, her jet-black eyes and hair and her serious, even sad expression, as well as the amazing speed with which she answered questions. After overcoming her initial shyness she proceeded to extract the square, cubic and even higher roots of twelve-digit numbers, to multiply huge sums together and give the day of the week corresponding to dates chosen at random. Other, even more abstruse questions were put to her, and she solved them without difficulty. When asked what her system was she replied that she had none, except for the unimportant exercise with dates; she added almost anxiously that she would be grateful to anyone who could explain how her feats were possible.

Sig. Rivetta declared that in his view it was a question of yoga techniques and the 'secret self', and he pointed out that Shakuntala had gone into a brief state of meditation before answering the questions: this was a type of concentration called *dharana*,[5] which enables the subject to mobilize the resources of the innermost depths of the psyche. After this she had no need of ordinary calculation, but discerned the answers by pure intuition. Professor William Mackenzie emphasizes that calculators of this type are a kind of medium with paranormal powers, their knowledge proceeding from a non-rational source.[6]

Another calculator named Bidder was able to analyse huge numbers into their primary factors by what he called an 'innate instinct' — a term which biologists and psychologists may find difficult to accept in the present state of their respective sciences. Ferreol, whose feats were studied by Paul Möbius, declared that the answers to problems were dictated to him by an 'interior voice', and that he afterwards did his best to check them in the ordinary way. Calculators indeed appear to have the advantage over clairvoyants that the latter can and do make mistakes, whereas the former's results are always accurate.

Another curious fact is that calculators are often undistinguished as far as ordinary mental gifts are concerned. Inaudi, according to Binet, was of less than normal intelligence; the Belgian Oscar Verhaege, according to Myers and Tocquet, was thought in youth to be mentally retarded; Thomas Fuller, a slave in Virginia, died at the age of eighty without having learnt to read or write; another American, Zerah Colburn, was always at the bottom of the class, and in Britain, Jedidiah Buxton was incapable of writing his own name.

We may note, too, that in this field the powers of the secret self appear to be placed systematically at the disposal of the conscious mind, and not merely in a fitful and enigmatic fashion: as though nature had at last found an efficient way to co-ordinate the two planes of the psyche, and this in a highly specialized sphere with, to all appearances, no bearing on biological evolution.

Different calculators have had different ways of performing their feats and of explaining them. Inaudi used to chat with the audience while doing simple sums in the ordinary way, and simultaneously performing abstruse calculations in his subconscious mind. Dagbert, a friend of his, states that he himself once solved seven problems at once at a public session while playing a tune from *Trovatore* on the flute, which he claims was of great assistance.[7] Lidoreau, who died not long ago, declared that if he was not fatigued by solving problems it was because his subconscious did most of the work. He used in fact to devise and solve still more complicated mathematical problems as a form of relaxation, to help him get to sleep at night. Like Shakuntala and others he had 'mathematical visions' or perceptions of the relationships between numbers, but was never able to explain them in more detail to others.[8] This goes to confirm the hypothesis that there is a system of thought transcending the ordinary possibilities of language and logic — a system which the British school of cybernetics calls 'heuristic', in contradistinction to the algorithmic mode of calculation which is that of the normal human mind and also of computers.[9] As is well known, these machines are infinitely superior to us in their own domain, but it is hard to believe that they can ever emulate the method which is confined to human beings and appears to spring from unfathomable depths.

## The mysterious course of evolution

Unfortunately human beings have an inveterate tendency to mistrust whatever is 'different' from everyday psychology, and to regard it as abnormal or pathological. 'Great wits are sure to madness near allied'; the idea was taken up bu Lombroso in his psychological writings, and it is a comforting one to the mediocre, but a dangerous myth for all that. In one of its modern forms, it serves to bolster the suspicion that those who experiment with paranormal mental powers are engaged in an anti-social flight from reality. This prejudice is widespread in the scientific literature on clairvoyants and others, who tend to be stigmatized as *'idiots savants'*: yet by no means all of them are mentally subnormal or ill-equipped for everyday life. Lidoreau, for instance, was a cultivated, intelligent man and a successful industrialist; at the same time he had a childlike passion for numbers and birds, and used to compare one to the other when trying to explain the exercise of his extraordinary mathematical powers.[10]

The ways of evolution, we must remember, are impenetrable to the human mind. According to Myers, who in this anticipates Teilhard de Chardin, we cannot interpret it except on the assumption that its general tendency is to develop intelligence and, sometimes, pleasure; but we must not imagine it as a single-track or inexorable process. Certainly the conscious mind can never completely dissociate itself from the latent consciousness of a different kind that exists in all of us; and we may assume that every faculty which cannot be suppressed is intended to develop into a higher state of perfection. As Jean Charon points out in the context of mathematical prodigies, it may well be that these intuitive or supra-rational powers are the germ of a higher form of intelligence which will, one day, be grafted harmoniously on to the intellect as we know it.

Nature indulges in experiments and what may appear to us false starts, but sooner or later its ends are realized. The *coelacanthidae* with their long fins were a clumsy kind of fish and were not yet reptiles, and the eohippus was a long way short of being a horse. In Teilhard de Chardin's view the universal mind or psyche evolves from the pre-living state of inert matter to that of instinct and intelligence; but there is a still higher or 'ultra-living' state which man may attain, and perhaps has already begun to attain, in which these powers will be linked with that of intuition, the cognitive faculty *par excellence*. Meanwhile nature's experiments continue, and every now and then they throw up extraordinary results. Bernard Vives relates that Wolfgang Pauli, the Austrian physicist and Nobel prizewinner, was visited one day at Zurich by a young Hungarian refugee who had had no higher education but claimed to have discovered an important principle of mathematical physics. Pauli, supposing the young man to be crazy, passed his manuscript to the psychoanalyst Jung; but the latter persuaded him to read it, and it turned out to contain elaborate equations similar to those of a study on which Pauli was then engaged with Heisenberg. Questioning the youth, Pauli found that his conscious knowledge of mathematics was at a much lower level than the paper, but any idea of plagiarism was ruled out by the discovery of detailed notes on which it was based.[11]

### The spirit bloweth where it listeth

It is hard to know how to define powers of this kind, which are akin to genius but are distinguished from it by the sporadic and irregular way in which they manifest themselves, like the dream-knowledge discussed in earlier chapters. Myers defines genius as the ability to perceive, in a waking state, the profound associations of ideas that come to us in dreams; and he cites the case of John Stuart Mill, who composed whole chapters of his *System of Logic* while threading his way through the crowds of Leadenhall Street. In mental absorption of this type the conscious self is reduced, as it were, to its lowest terms and is subordinated to a wider, more potent form of awareness, if not actually merged in it. This, as we have seen, can be facilitated by entering into a state of trance, or by yoga practices designed to 'unify the states of consciousness'. But such preliminaries are not always necessary; and here we may cite the extraordinary case of José Pedro de Freitas, also known as Arigò ('simpleton' or 'bumpkin'), an untaught Brazilian clerk who performed surgical operations.

Arigò, on whom a documentary film was made by the journalist Rizzini, died in his early forties in 1971, having cured as many patients by surgical means as Pasqualina Pezzola with her clairvoyant diagnoses. In the morning he earned a living in a government office at Congonhas do Campo, ten hours' drive from São Paulo, and in the afternoon he performed operations, free of charge, with an assistant named Altomir Gomes. His 'theatre' consisted of the kitchen at his home, divided in two by a curtain, and his instruments, kept in a biscuit-tin, were an old lancet, a pair of scissors and a forceps. With this equipment he not only lanced abscesses

100

and small subcutaneous cysts but removed stones from the liver and kidneys, excised internal tumours and was particularly successful in eye operations. Nor were his patients only simple peasants: they included political and religious personalities and foreigners from distant countries. His activity was the subject of books and lively debate; attempts were made to forbid him to practise, but without success. His patients queued up in the kitchen, and when their turn came they underwent the operation with no visible sign of pain; the incisions stopped bleeding at a word from the surgeon. Unlike Pasqualina's matter-of-fact performances, Arigò's were carried out in the setting of a syncretic form of religion, common in rural Brazil and involving elements of spiritualism and Christianity. An obituary notice appeared in the Italian *Tempo Medico* for April 1971.

A similar case of 'psycho-surgery' is that of a Philippine youth named Antonio Agpaoa, whose operations were studied by Dr Motoyama of Kyoto. But his performances have been called in question, although it appears that the patients were satisfied. Instances of remarkable cures by shamans and witch-doctors have been reported by explorers and missionaries. Very often these extraordinary powers seem to be conferred on simple and childlike people, in whom the voice of the conscious ego is less clamorous. We may be reminded of St Paul's words: 'God hath chosen the foolish things of the world to confound the wise; and God hath chosen the weak things of the world to confound the things which are mighty.' (I Cor. 1:27).

# PART III

Beyond the frontier

# CHAPTER 9

Encounters with oneself

*Escape from the body*

In 1917 a British infantryman at Waille in Alsace, who had been on guard for hours and was overcome with cold, hunger and fatigue, fell in a faint and had the curious experience of being 'outside himself': that is to say, his ego was detached from the body and appeared to hover outside it, contemplating with a touch of contempt the wretched figure that lay there in its military uniform. The sensation was similar to that which an escaped prisoner might feel, looking back at the place where he had grown accustomed to suffering. It was only a few moments, however, before his conscious mind returned to the body and its privations.

This case was reported by Sir Oliver Lodge in the *Journal* of the S.P.R. for 1929. Similar occurrences were discussed at the beginning of the century by Dr Sollier, who called them 'autoscopic hallucinations'. In terms of cerebral physiology they are thought to be due to toxic or mechanical stimulation of encephalic centres in which the 'corporal schema' (to use Professor Bonnier's expression) resides.[1] For practical purposes it is as though the subject merely dreamt that he saw himself, and we may concede as much to sceptical psychiatrists; but there is room for doubt as to the nature of this kind of dream. As is known, there are hallucinations or apparitions which possess a true content, i.e. they reflect some part of reality that exists objectively although it is not, then and there, perceptible by ordinary means. In Eugène Osty's opinion, autoscopic phenomena may well belong to this category, as evidenced by the following incident reported in 1930 in the journal of the *Institut métapsychique,* of which he was then director.[2]

A woman named Natalie Annenkof, whose small daughter had lately died, went on a warm spring day to the cemetery to visit her grave. Looking at the flowers she had planted, and watching the bees buzzing to and fro, she suddenly felt a curious weakness and weightlessness: she lost the sensation of being in the body, and appeared to herself to be hovering in the air. 'I gazed at my body down there and was struck by how sad it looked; I also noticed small details, like some marks on my coat. "This must be death," I thought; but at that very moment I felt immense joy, as though I were living several lives at once. . . The keeper came along, touched my hand and face, shook me and then ran off in terror. "What will my husband do without me?" I thought at that point, and resolved to get back into the body if I could.' When she did so, she was struck by the sensation of physical weight; she also felt once again her mental anguish, as well as minor discomforts of the kind that are usually too familiar to be noticed, and the effect of all this brought her close to tears.

How far can an incident like this be ascribed to involuntary self-deception? The subject's perceptions were accurate in detail, as was confirmed by witnesses, so that it cannot have been a case of pathological hallucination. In cases of this sort a natural pattern of genuine experience seems to manifest itself between the extremes of credulity and scepticism. Autoscopic vision is in fact a particular case of dissociation (*dédoublement*) or extra-corporeal experience, such as that of the mind-travellers referred to in Chapter 2. Many similar cases have been recorded by Muldoon and Carrington, Hornell Hart, Whiteman and others.[3]

In a study which appeared in 1960 in the *Proceedings of the S.P.R.*, Miss Celia Green and Sir George Joy described 300 incidents of this general kind, selected from over 1500. Among the six which related to autoscopic vision, one was experienced by a lady who tells her story as follows. 'I was awakened by a light shining under the bedroom door, and got up to see if I had left it on by mistake. . . I felt a sudden sense of peace and harmony and great well-being. . . I returned to the bedroom and sat on a chair. After a while I got up and went to the bed, but was amazed to see my own body lying in it. I recognized it quite distinctly. At the same moment I felt an irresistible force compelling me to identify myself with the body. It was a painful feeling; my heart throbbed; I could neither breathe nor move. . . At breakfast I told my friends, who thought it must have been a dream; but I am sure it was a real experience, though a most extraordinary one.'

Psychiatrists may insist on treating such occurrences as dreams pure and simple, but we may wonder, with Chauvin, whether psychiatry as understood today is any more than a study of the physiology of the nervous system.[4] In the future, perhaps, it will take account of the possibility of objective hallucinations of an extra-sensory kind. Meanwhile, autoscopic phenomena appear to be commonest among mediums and poets. Goethe and Alfred de Musset are eminent examples, and Byron relates a remarkable experience of Shelley's. Late one night the poet was in bed reading a play by Calderón, when a muffled and hooded man appeared and beckoned Shelley to follow him. When they were outside the room he revealed his face, which was Shelley's own; the household was awakened by the poet's scream of horror.

We may also recall De Musset's lines in *La Nuit de décembre*:

*Du temps que j'étais écolier,*
*Je restais un soir à veiller*
*Dans notre salle solitaire.*
*Devant ma table vint s'asseoir*
*Un pauvre enfant vêtu de noir,*
*Qui me ressemblait comme un frère.*

Musset told Louise Colet that he regarded this *Doppelgänger* as a 'persistent image' of himself. His experience was less disturbing, however, than that of Guy de Maupassant, who, as related by Paul Bourget, used to return home from walks and find his 'double' seated in his own armchair; shortly after this, he became incurably insane. In such a case we may agree with the psychiatrists that autoscopy may be a symptom of a disintegrating personality; but it would be as arbitrary to predicate this of all instances as to identify genius with neurological disorder. Paranormal subjects are in fact the 'fifth column' of man's invasion of the psychic universe, and without them a whole dimension of reality would remain unknown.

Eileen Garrett has related that, when in a state of meditation, she once found herself 'some yards away from her body', which appeared to be 'wrapped in a cloud or cocoon of delicate hues', varying as she breathed. Frederica Hauffe of Prevorst 'saw' herself on 28 May 1827 in the presence of Dr Kerner, who was attending her for a nervous disease: remaining in her own body, which was lying in bed, she had a momentary vision of herself, or her double, seated on a stool close by. Violet Tweedale relates a somewhat similar occurrence: she had just awoken in her sunny bedroom when she saw her own double approaching rapidly to resume its proper place in her body. She was distressed to find it less handsome and dignified than she believed herself to be, and concluded from this that we all, perhaps, wear a mask expressing what we would like to be rather than what we are.

Elizabeth d'Espérance records that one day she got up from a sofa where she had been reading and suddenly felt full of life and health, whereas a moment before she had been in a state of discomfort. 'I felt as if I knew for the first time what life was.' Then she saw, on the sofa, a person reading — this was her own self, or rather its corporeal base. Her sense of well-being was indescribable. Time and space had disappeared; she felt like the tiniest of atoms, but as if merged with the universe that had given it birth.

### Infinite bliss

It is inevitable that a medium should interpret experiences in the light of his or her personal convictions about the nature of reality; but similar sensations have been recorded by such different subjects as the serene, objective René Warcollier, the poet Tennyson, the novelist Rosamond Lehmann and the simple, illiterate Pasqualina Pezzola. All these describe a sense of liberation and ineffable bliss, a vision which in human and symbolic terms can only be defined as one of brilliant light. In addition there is a final stage reserved, as we shall see, for those who achieve such detachment from their everyday ego that they are able to meet themselves in a cosmic dimension.

Warcollier, a well-known parapsychologist who died not long ago,[5] records an occasion in his youth when, under the influence of a mental shock (the accidental sight of a festering sore), he felt as if he were about to faint, but instead found himself removed into a new dimension of being, a state of deep and perfect awareness. 'I had no sense-perceptions of any kind, but felt absolutely aware of myself, or rather of the universe. Instead of the visual sensation of light, I felt as if light and I were one. . . I could only describe my experience in the inadequate terms used by mystics to depict their states of ecstasy. . . All this seemed to last for an eternity, but it was in fact only a few minutes. I forgot nothing of my marvellous experience: I was again myself, but enriched by a memory that I have never been able to describe to anyone. I do not know what the "beatific vision" may be, but I know that in that state I enjoyed a matchless felicity and awareness that completely fulfilled my own idea of beatitude.'

In Tennyson's case we read that, while still a boy, the poet heard himself being called insistently by his Christian name 'Alfred', and that each time the call seemed to reach a deeper level of his being; at the same time his own self appeared to melt or expand into an indescribable state of unlimited freedom. The loss or merging of his personality did not feel like a state of extinction but of true life, a condition in which death had no meaning.

Rosamond Lehmann[6] relates that during a time of sadness in her life she had an experience of superabundant joy accompanied by the intensification of all her perceptions. States of this kind may be dismissed by sceptics with words like 'autosuggestion', but we know now that they may lead to unsuspected realms of knowledge.

Pasqualine Pezzola, a simple, level-headed woman and not a myatic, was once asked, while under observation by Dr Giuseppina Mancini, to 'rise as high into the air as she could'. She went into a trance and, as Dr Mancini relates, her expression became more and more gentle and finally ecstatic, almost superhuman. On returning to herself she spoke of celestial visions and planes of light. This sense of metaphorical 'height' may be interpreted in terms of what Jung calls the collective unconscious, the seat of recurrent and fundamental human experiences that are expressed symbolically by 'archetypes'. The terms 'light' and 'illumination' are of course frequent in descriptions of religious and mystical states, and that of an 'upward' journey is met with in shamanistic ritual, which uses the technique of ecstasy and is practised by different peoples in many parts of the globe. Mircea Eliade, who has made a close study of shamanism, sees it as an attempt to renew that contact with the higher powers which was destroyed by original sin, and believes that it can give rise to genuine mystical experience. Ecstasy, he maintains, is a universal human faculty, though different cultures may interpret

107

and value it differently.[7]

Other authorities prefer to speak of 'super-consciousness', and B. Disertori of Padua University writes of a 'higher unconscious', an unknown, luminous facet of the ego that is manifested in ecstatic states and moments of supreme mental illumination — which, he emphasizes, have nothing to do with pathology but reflect an aspect of the soul that has not lost contact with Deity.

## The unknown continent

This realm of experience has long been deliberately ignored and is, as it were, an unknown continent that humanity must now explore. The instances we have related are no more than a foretaste of immensely wide possibilities, but they show that the heights of consciousness can be scaled without doing violence to nature. The ecstatic experience may well be part of an evolutionary design characterized by the awakening of a form of awareness more direct, penetrating and universal than the intellect is capable of, even at the height of its powers. This awareness appears to partake of the nature of a dream, but it is a vivid and waking dream which enables the 'self that thinks and wills' to escape from its normal bounds and become merged without loss of identity, in a greater self which may be that of the universe. Such is the end that may potentially be attained by all, though few as yet have reached it — great mystics and ascetics for the most part, who have left us in obscure yet fascinating language such descriptions of the mystery as we possess.

The Blessed Henry Suso (c. 1295–1366), a Dominican mystic who was accused of heresy in his time, wrote: 'When the morning star rises in my soul I am penetrated by charity, truth and sweetness so that I forget all sorrow. . . I feel as if I had passed beyond time and space into the abode of eternal bliss. Is this Thou, O Lord, or is it I, or what is it?' Another Dominican mystic, Meister Eckhart, goes some way to answering this poignant question when he says: 'The soul is no longer a creature, but is blessedness itself, unity of essence and substance with the Godhead: it is its own blessedness and that of all creatures.' Eckhart in the fourteenth century was condemned for heresy and for speaking a language unpalatable to the Schoolmen, and four hundred years earlier a similar fate befell the Persian mystic al-Husain ibn Mansur for holding that the Divine Spirit descends and makes its abode in the soul of the pure-hearted ascetic. This man, generally known as al-Hallaj (the carder), was put to death at Baghdad in 922 after cruel tortures which, he declared, he did not feel in the least, as he was rapt in contemplation of the One God and felt as though alone with Him.[8]

It is interesting to note how the mystics of different creeds and civilizations speak a similar language. The third-century philosopher Plotinus describes in his *Enneads* the stages of ascent towards contemplation of the One and unity with Absolute Being. The One, he declares, is also the Good, but is more than the Good; it is beyond thought, transcending all, yet living and comprehending all. 'When the One is present, the soul will be all in Him — it will be He, forgetful wholly of itself.' Expressions like these recur in the work of mediaeval Jewish mystics who proclaimed the ideal of *devekut*, i.e. 'cleaving' or loving adhesion to God. Comprehension is here replaced by communion or self-identification, at a level transcending human logic and intelligence — where, as the Jewish mystics put it, 'all knowledge becomes useless.'[9]

In Hindu mysticism the same thought is expressed by *samadhi* (concentration or devotion), which J.C. Chatterji describes as 'a state of ineffable happiness in which union and separation are perceived at one and the same time, so that we are ourselves and are also everything that is.'[10] Raja Yoga Ramacharaka writes that 'the self experiences the truth of real existence, of being rooted in the supreme reality of the universe and forming part of it. It does not know what this reality is, but feels it to be true and different from everything else in the world. . . something transcendental, beyond all human experience.'[11] Paramahamsa Yogananda describes an ecstasy of his own as follows: 'An ocean of joy beat upon the calm, infinite shores of my soul, and I understood that the Divine Spirit is an inexhaustible benediction, clothed in a body woven of lights without number.' The same author tells us that when a yogi attains the state of perfection his mind is no longer linked to a single body but to the whole universe. The Orientalist Tucci speaks of 'a harmonious process directed towards the recovery of self-awareness: consciousness not of a mere individual but of the cosmic Self from which all things derive and to which

109

they return: pure consciousness, which is not clouded by any concrete thought but is the precondition of such thoughts, constituting as they do the reality of the individual psyche.'

Such is the result of the 'unification of states of consciousness' that is the supreme goal of yoga asceticism, seeking through *samadhi* to achieve contact with something greater and richer than ourselves — a new mode of existence in which the centre of gravity of the self is displaced towards the heart of that ocean whereof the self is a wave. Psychologists are right to endeavour to integrate the unconscious with the conscious mind, but they should not ignore or reject the higher form of integration attainable on the level of the 'transcendent self.' as Novalis called it. We are like exiles hankering after our lost homeland, but hampered by the pride of the conscious intellect that seeks to conceal its riches from us.

### A light that cannot be put out

For the last two hundred years and more, the flame of mysticism has been declining in the Western world despite isolated and shamefaced exceptions. This is a natural consequence of the individualism and hedonism of our era, which have developed to the point of downright alienation. Elemire Zolla in his anthology describes mysticism as the revival, in an atomized civilization, of the experience of tribal initiation — a return to tradition in the true sense, an unconscious memory of buried things; and Mircea Eliade calls it 'an archaic mode of spirituality'. This recalls Lévy-Bruhl's conception of primitive thinking as communal ('participationist') and pre-logical, expressing man's emotional fellowship not only with other men but also with nature and whatever lies beyond nature. It behoves modern man not to reject this mode of thinking out of hand but to ask himself if it does not embody something of lasting value.

As Remo Cantoni observes, it is not a question of extolling primitive ways in general or abandoning the path of rationality that humanity has chosen, but of realizing that our choice has involved sacrifices and spiritual losses that have affected our happiness and the balance of our existence. The debit side of the account is emphasized by several writers, such as Huizinga who contends that 'knowledge is more than reasoning' and that intuition and contemplation can attain to knowledge that is forever barred to the intellect. The Greek word *gnosis* and the sanskrit *jnana,* he points out, both signify 'knowledge' (they derive in fact from the same root) and, used as they are in relation to mysticism, serve to indicate that it is a true form of perception and understanding. Maurice Blondel observes that pre-logical thought and mysticism, intertwined as they are in primitive superstition, represent in a distorted yet perfectible form the highest intellectual, social and religious truths. Gilson goes further and asks whether, once we have discarded the illusory notion of a 'primitive and limited' way of life, we may not discern in mysticism a function no less vital and natural to mankind than that of logical thought. But these are isolated voices, and our universities continue to relegate mysticism to the realm of historical and ethnographical studies. However, the Princeton philosopher W.T. Stace is an exception to this rule: from a pragmatist point of view he draws heuristic and practical inferences from the general similarity of mystical experience, which he believes should be respected if only as a 'source of truer morality'.[12]

Among the opponents of mysticism are those who deny the supernatural altogether and also some psychiatrists who dismiss it with such disparaging terms as 'immaturity' and 'regression'. But against this fashionable contempt we may invoke the authority of Jung, who contends that nothing in the human soul is outdated or destined to disappear completely, though it should be our business to see that the past and present are in proper balance. 'The Orient is not a Tibetan monastery, but a reality within us.'[13] For the present to think itself independent of the past is about as sensible as for a wave, or the crest of a wave, to think itself independent of the ocean. It is especially absurd for the *nouvelle vague* of rationalism to attempt to refute the claims of mysticism — the *cognitio Dei experimentalis* — by means of biochemistry and neurophysiology, or with drugs and laboratory instruments. Such neo-positivists as Julian Huxley and J.B. Haldane have encouraged this line of enquiry, and of course it cannot be denied that every psychic manifestation has its physical counterpart. Hallucinogenic drugs can excite the brain beyond its normal limits, and in Central America and the USA there is a sect numbering tens of thousands who claim that they can achieve a direct experience of divinity by consuming peyotl, the plant from which mescalin is extracted. But there is a difference between the intoxication produced by drugs and the mystical state, which, while it may be stimulated in various ways, presupposes a natural or acquired capacity to explore the higher levels of consciousness. Aldous Huxley, Julian's cousin, knew and described the effects of mescalin at first hand, but he also knew true mysticism and did not confuse one with the other; nor did Rosamond Lehmann, who expressly distinguished the effects of the drugs she had tried from the preternatural experience related earlier in this chapter.

The phenomenon of ecstasy has been studied from a neurophysiological point of view by Drs Das of Calcutta and Gastaut of Marseilles and by Maryse Choisy, by means of electro-encephalographs of yogi subjects in a state of *samadhi*.[14] These tests, as far as they go, suggest that the psychological state in question is accompanied by an equally special neurophysiological one which, however, is normal and not pathological. A similar result has been obtained by Professor Kasamatsu in observations of a subject in a state of *zazen*. Experiments of this kind may finally convince psychiatrists that a state of ecstasy is not synonymous with delirium, as many have contended: it is a dream, but of the same kind as those dreams which reveal portions of reality that we would otherwise never know. But prejudices die hard, and, as Bernanos's country priest observed, the testimony of all the saints weighs little in the balance against the opinion of a few psychologists.[15]

# CHAPTER 10

## Extraordinary powers of the body

*Fire-walking*

'Constantine Liuros, a blond, handsome youth with a cheer-ful smile on his face, suddenly stepped into the fire. His feet, gleaming white, moved forward through the burning coals like a ploughshare tracing a furrow. The others followed him: once, twice, ten times, the spectators becoming less agitated as the men's feet gradually beat the coals into ashes. Theodore advanced with a lingering step; he held an icon in his right hand, resting it on his shoulder so that the edge touched his cheek. It was as though he and the saint were conversing with each other, all alone in a world of fire.'

This strange account is not the record of a morbid display of masochism, but of a religious rite which has taken place annually for the last four hundred years at Langadhas in Greek Macedonia, on the feast-days of St Helen and St Constantine. The above description dates from 1963, when the ceremony (which also takes place at the neighbouring village of Ayia Elena) was made the subject of a documentary film.[1] It should be made clear that the fire consists of a stretch of burning coals generating a heat of two or three hundred degrees centigrade. The ceremony is not popular with the higher clergy, but is tolerated on account of its deep roots in history and local folklore. Those who take part are not fanatics but belong to a small clan which has performed the feat for centuries, to commemorate events now lost in the mists of legend. Besides being an act of faith, it is a testimony to the existence of mental powers that can temporarily suspend the operation of natural forces — a fact which is anathema to the complacent and closed minds of official science.

Of all such facts, the phenomenon of pyrobatics is one of the best documented. Thick layers of burning coals have been photographed and filmed time and again, as have the unharmed soles of the fire-walkers' feet, be they men or women, peasants, artisans or students. In May 1957 a film was made at Langadhas and Ayia Elena by an Italian team including Dr P. Cassoli, Professor B. Beonio-Brocchieri and the anthropologist L. Cipriani. In earlier years the performance was observed by General Tanagras, a doctor and parapsychologist, L. Cipriani and Professor R. Salvadori. Other accounts have been furnished by Marianthi Diamantoglou, M.C.A. Romaios and Georges Roux.[2] Similar testimony comes from the most distant countries: India, Japan, Hawaii, the Sunda Archipelago, Fiji and Mauritius. In England in 1935 an Oriental named Kuda Bux walked along a track created by burning seven tons of wood: this was at Carshalton, under the supervision of Harry Price.[3] The scientists present included Professor Pannet, who measured the temperature of the soles of Bux's feet after his walk and found it to be normal. Two onlookers tried the walk themselves, but had to give up after a step or two and suffered severe burns. Before embarking on the walk, Bux had carefully washed his feet under Price's supervision.

Naturally all this evidence does not suffice to convince those who are wedded to scepticism for reasons emotional rather than scientific, or who demand the application of controls that make the experiment virtually impossible. It is all very well, for instance, to insist on measuring the temperature of the fire-walkers' feet before and after, but it has to be borne in mind that they too have a ritual to observe if they are to perform successfully. At Langadha and Ayia Elena the villagers concerned spend the previous night preparing for their feat by means of a special dance, accompanied by drum-beating and curious whistling and puffing noises, for which they are nicknamed *anastenarides* or 'sighers'. These may be compared with the breathing techniques that enable yogis to control their bodily functions. According to the account already quoted, 'They enter into an ecstasy of concentration. The music draws them into an ever-closer spiral, an endless motion that strains the nerves to breaking-point and perhaps beyond it, into a spiritual realm to which we have no access.' That realm, however, exists inside every human being, and can be discovered by entering into the appropriate state of consciousness, which will bring to light — as we shall see —

unsuspected mental and physical powers.

The eminent chemist and physicist Sir William Crookes relates that he saw the medium Daniel Dunglas Home (1833-86) take a brand out of a large wood fire, hold it in both hands and blow on it so that the flames played about his fingers, which showed no sign of being burnt, then or afterwards. Home repeated this performance several times, always in a state of trance. Olivier Leroy, in a study published in 1931, spoke of a Parisian lady, Marie Sonnet, known as 'the salamander', who could remain for half an hour suspended immediately above a blazing fire without showing any signs of injury, not were her clothes singed.[4] The Jesuit Father Herbert Thurston records many such cases in his book on the physical phenomena of mysticism. A curious fact is that the power of incombustibility can be transferred to others, at least for a time and to a certain extent. Devaux reports that Annie Hunter of Bournemouth, who used to chew burning coals as if they were sweets, once (in 1923) placed a coal on the head of a *Daily Express* reporter who was interviewing her: he was not harmed by this, but burnt his fingers badly when he tried to remove it.[5]

### 'Sheet-dryers'

Alexander David-Neel, whom we have already mentioned, spent fourteen years in Tibet and the neighbouring countries; she learnt the language, became a Buddhist and joined a religious order which permitted her to travel about and study the occult aspects of Tibetan spirituality. Aided by her adoptive son, who was himself a lama, she learnt to dissociate fact from legend and to develop in herself unusual psycho-physical powers. In 1929 she published in Paris *Mystiques et Magiciens du Tibet* (English translation 1931), with a preface by Dr A. d'Arsonval, a member of the *Academie des Sciences* and the *Académie de Médecine,* who had previously invited her to give a series of lectures at the *Collége de France*. In the preface he wrote: 'This Easterner, this complete Tibetan, has nevertheless remained a Westerner, a disciple of Descartes and of Claude Bernard, practising the philosophic scepticism of the former which, according to the latter, should be the constant ally of the scientific observer. Unencumbered by any preconceived theory and unbiassed by any doctrine or dogma,

Madame David-Neel has observed everything in Tibet in a free and impartial spirit.'

The book tells, among other things, of hermits who spent the winter unscathed, in unheated caves at an altitude of between 13,000 and 16,500 feet, clothed only in a simple cotton garment or *respa* (which term was used as a nickname for the men themselves). They were able to do this thanks to a mysterious inner heat called *tumo*, which they generated by a particular method of concentration and holding the breath, reminiscent of yogi practices and the *anastenarides*. The authoress was able to acquire this art in some degree, and once spent the night in a deserted spot, unclothed and motionless in meditation, after bathing in an icy mountain stream. She remarks that 'Winter had not yet begun, but the level of the place, about 10,000 feet high, made the night rather chilly, and I felt very proud of not catching cold.' Other travellers in distant lands have reported similar phenomena, and there are instances in the history of Western mysticism.[6] In Tibet public ceremonies are held to celebrate the prowess of the respas and fire-walkers. Alexandra David-Neel relates that: 'Sometimes a kind of examination concludes the training of the *tumo* students . . . The neophytes sit on the ground, cross-legged and naked. Sheets are dipped in the icy water, and each man wraps himself in one of them and must dry it on his body. As soon as the sheet has become dry, it is again dipped in the water and placed on the novice's body to be dried as before. The operation goes on in that way until daybreak. Then he who has dried the largest number of sheets is acknowledged the winner of the competition. It is said that some dry as many as forty sheets in one night. One should perhaps make large allowances for exaggeration . . . yet I have myself seen some *respas* dry a number of pieces of cloth the size of a large shawl.'

Madame David-Neel's testimony is all the more precious as it may well be the last from that particular area. Even at the time she wrote, the ancient lore and customs of Tibet were being supplanted by modern ways, and later political upheavals may have completed the process. In fifty years' time, perhaps, the Macedonian fire-walkers will also be a thing of the past, to the gratification of those who ascribe such practices to a 'magic' and anachronistic phase of human development. Once contemporary evidence has ceased to be available, it is easy to dismiss the whole phenomenon as legendary. Meanwhile official science adopts a kind of compromise, not seeking to investigate occult manifestations but treating them as *terra incognita,* in the hope that if resolutely ignored they will disappear.

## An untirable athlete

Alexandra David-Neel also relates that during a journey in northern Tibet she encountered a lama running, or rather bounding along, at preternatural speed, with a trance-like expression and with his gaze fixed on a point high above his head. 'He seemed to lift himself from the ground, proceeding by leaps. It looked as if he had been endowed with the elasticity of a ball and rebounded each time his feet touched the ground. His steps had the regularity of a pendulum. He wore the usual monastic robe and toga, both rather ragged.' This was a *lung-gom-pa*, a kind of ascetic with the special power of covering hundreds of miles in this way at great speed She would have stopped the man to speak to him, but the servants warned her that if she broke into his meditation, the 'god' would depart from within him with so abrupt a shock that he would die. Whether or not this was an exaggeration, she obeyed the warning and the mysterious athlete passed by, ignoring their presence. He was going in the same direction as they, and she ascertained later that he must have continued at the same pace for a day and night without stopping, in addition to the time he had been travelling before passing the group of riders in the heart of the tableland.

## Weightlessness

Phenomena such as these show that what we regard as the absolute laws of physics or physiology are often only applicable to 'normal' conditions, using this term in a statistical sense and not in opposition to any kind of pathology. Further evidence is supplied by the well-known phenomenon of levitation. This has most often been observed in the case of mystics,[7] but it also occurs with mediums (e.g. Home, Paladino, Eglinton, Maria Vollhart and Willy Schneider), and sporadically in individuals such as a son of Lord Torphichen who, on occasion, had to be held by the legs

117

to prevent him rising into the air. This took place at the age of puberty, which is often associated with unusual manifestations in people with mediumistic gifts. Sometimes they begin earlier: a Berlin girl aged five, later a famous medium. possessed the power of 'floating' down a marble staircase in her parents' home, and felt inexpressible joy as she did so, but after a few years this faculty left her.[8]

Home, according to Crookes, went into levitation hundreds of times before witnesses while in a state of trance. Once, in the presence of Lord Adair and others, he floated out through an open window while still in a horizontal position, and came back into the room through the window adjoining. When Lord Adair asked how it was done he replied, still in trance, 'I'll show you,' and repeated the feat.

Hereward Carrington suggests that it may be possible, by means of respiratory techniques, to liberate oneself from gravity for a moment or two; but this can hardly suffice to account for levitation in physical terms, though it does recall the Oriental practices which accompany concentration and can be described as paraphysiological. Levitation is of course familiar to yoga practitioners, whether Hinduist or Buddhist: according to the mystical treatise known as the *Visuddhi Magga* it belongs to the fourth and penultimate stage of meditative technique. The second-century writer Philostratus, in his life of Appollonius of Tyana, relates that the latter saw a Hindu sage suspended in mid-air. The *Illustrated London News* in June 1936 published a three-page account, with photographs, of a display of levitation that took place in India under strict experimental conditions.[9] Instances can be multiplied: in all of them the performer is in a state of trance, ecstasy or mystic concentration.

### Mastery over the body

It should be noted here that yoga practices have a double aspect: as Mircea Eliade puts it, they can produce either saints or sorcerers. True ascetics are concerned above all with attaining the supreme degree of illumination and liberating their secret self from the trammels of the body: in the course of this endeavour they acquire unusual psycho-physical powers, but these are not an end in themselves and may even be regarded as a temptation. False ascetics, on the other

118

hand, use these powers as a means of dominion over others: the eighty-four *siddhis* or 'perfections' taught by the *Hatayoga,* the 'six secret doctrines' of lamaistic Tibet or the 'five exalted sciences' of primitive Buddhism.

The technique in all these cases is much the same, the Buddhist practices being derived from those of Hinduism. Long discipline, complete stability of mind, concentration of the intellect and will on a single object — such is the basic formula, though it may be embellished by Oriental metaphors and hyperbole. *Hatayoga* and Tantric practices emphasize physiological and gymnic aspects and the cultivation of little-known organs in which resides the mysterious energy called *kundalini.* Whatever we may think of the physiological theory, it is hard to blink facts that have been scientifically established. Some thirty years ago Doctors Charles Laubry and Thérèse Brosse carried out rigorous experiments in India to verify the power of certain yogis to control their own breathing, heartbeats, blood-pressure and intestinal motions.[10] Dr Brosse returned to India in 1950 under the auspices of Harvard University and, with Dr Milovanovich, carried out electrocardiographic tests showing that the subject was able to reduce the contraction of his heart muscle almost to zero — a state of affairs that, in a normal person, would have aroused grave fears for his life, but which the yoga was able to reverse at will. Some were able to hold their breath for fifteen minutes, and others to exist for three hours while breathing so shallowly as to leave no trace on the recording device. Others again could enter into a state of suspended animation (anabiosis) similar to that found in creatures on the point of death or in some species of lower animals.[11] Similar demonstrations of *hatayoga* were given in November 1950 by the Indian doctors Pramanick and Goswami to an audience at the *Faculté de Médecine* in Paris.

*A priori* scepticism in this field has been criticized by such eminent writers as Jung and Disertori. Among its causes is the physical monism of the Western world, which tends to subordinate the mind to the body, whereas the Oriental outlook is the opposite of this: as the *Dhammapada* puts it, 'Mind predominates in all, and all things are subject to it'. If Western thought admits the independence of the psyche at all, it is usually in terms of a harmful dualism between mind and body, an attitude which goes back to Greek philosophy. Only

119

in the last few decades have we seen the beginnings of psychosomatic medicine, which studies the influence of the subconscious mind on bodily functions but usually does so from a pathological point of view. Yet in the field with which we are concerned the mysteries of the body are one with those of the soul, and cannot be dissociated without grave consequences. We have already seen several ways in which the mind can influence the body and suspend the operation of physical laws; to these may be added the fact that the body can be made to emit light or a special scent, to change its shape, voice or appearance, to live without food for long periods or go into a death-like state of catalepsy.[12] All these phenomena are well attested, as is that of extra-retinal vision.[13] None of them can be explained by physiology, yet they are not miraculous or contrary to nature, merely the effect of a state of consciousness in which the *daimon* is sometimes able to manifest its powers, drawing on the resources of a wider world than that or ordinary science. States of meditation, trance or ecstasy may be likened to dreams; at all events they are specific modes of being and are probably fundamental, since they can subject reality to their own laws. In them the unconscious rises to the level of ordinary consciousness, merges with it and transports it into a wider dimension. Some attain this state by natural aptitude, others by long practice or mystical fervour. Such methods are alien to the spirit of modern man, who prefers to transform his body by means of drugs and the material world by means of physical force. All this is legitimate, no doubt, but it involves what Mounier has called the polarization of culture in a utilitarian sense. 'Dazzled by our own specialization and its marvellous results,' he observes, 'we run the risk of ignoring infinitely wider fields.' Or, as Alexis Carrel wrote in the 1930s: 'It is one of the most tragic facts of human history that we have made so much more progress in the science of matter than in that of mind.'

# CHAPTER 11

## The dream-self

*Goethe's encounter with a ghost*

Nathalie von Echstruth relates that Goethe's friend Johann Friedrich Rochlitz once travelled from Frankfurt-on-Oder to visit the poet at Weimar. He was caught in a shower on the way there and, finding that Goethe was not at home, changed into the latter's dressing-gown and slippers and went to sleep in an armchair. There he dreamt that he met Goethe on the road to the Belvedere and that the poet said to him: 'What are you doing here at Weimar, wearing my things?' At that moment, unknown to Rochlitz, Goethe was actually on the Belvedere road and had a waking vision of Rochlitz which impelled him to address the latter in the very words his friend had dreamt. Klemm, another friend of Goethe's, was with him and witnessed the occurrence, which seemed to him of evil omen. When Goethe reached home and found Rochlitz asleep in the chair, he took him for a ghost and ordered him to disappear! We shall see in due course other instances of Goethe's extra-sensory powers.

Some authorities, such as Tyrrell, would describe this as a case of telepathic hallucination or clairvoyance. A large number of 'phantasms of the living' were reported in the book with this title by Gurney, Myers and Podmore (1886), and Professor Hornell Hart speaks of 'apparitions of living persons in places that they were at that moment dreaming of, or thinking of intensively.'[1]

In November 1954 the journal *Light* published an account of a red-headed bank clerk who, while ill in bed at home, was 'seen' by several customers at his usual counter, but disappeared when spoken to. Other customers who were there at the same time, however, did not see him. One may suppose that the apparition was caused by his concentrating mentally on his place of work, perhaps while in a state of delirium, i.e.

a particularly vivid kind of dream. We have already seen in Chapter 2 cases of 'travelling clairvoyance', but the unusual feature in this one is that observers actually saw, or thought they saw, the individual concerned. Was it in fact he they saw, or a kind of phantom?

As Tyrrell observes, anyone whose unconscious mind is so disposed may believe that he sees an object that does not in fact exist. This may come about if the unconscious receives a telepathic message from some non-sensory source: it goes to work on this datum in the same way as a film director goes to work on a given subject, and produces a kind of private 'film' for the percipient's benefit. Hence, according to Tyrrell, inter-mental contact may produce the appearance of a ghost: 'The percipient's personality is fully capable of presenting a figure to his conscious mind without any external or physical help. . . The apparatus involved is largely psychological and appears to have extraordinary creative powers.' This is an attractive theory and fits many instances, but is hard to apply to others such as the following.

Signor Paolo F. of Nimis in the province of Udine writes: 'During the last war I was in the civil service in East Africa until captured by the British, who moved me to Tripolitania. There I spent a year or two in isolation. . . One day I saw a vision of a relative of mine who lived in Friuli: he showed me his right arm with the hand cut off and bleeding, and said "Look what has happened to me." Long after, I found out that he had indeed lost his right hand in a bombing attack.'

Isolation and silence are certainly conducive to experiences of this kind in sensitive subjects, and so is a state of alarm or emotional intensity. The following incident is one which I was able to verify by questioning those concerned. At dawn on 7 September 1943 — the eve of the announcement of the Allied-Italian armistice and the German occupation of Italy — Signora Maria Luongo Cortese, then living at Naples, awoke with a start and saw beside the bed her eight-year-old son Tancredi, who was supposed to be at Frasso Telesino near Benevento: he looked desperately thin and pale and cried to her for help, then disappeared. She made her way with difficulty to Frazzo Telesino, found him in the pitiful state in which she had 'seen' him and was able to take him back to Naples. Such experiences only happen to people with mediumistic gifts, and this was true in Signora Cortesi's case.

There is a long history of cases of 'telepathic hallucination', and those recorded by the British and American Societies for Psychical Research run into hundreds, in addition to more recent studies.[2]

One of the American examples is that of Miss Jane Griffling, who was kept awake one night by a high wind and, looking out, saw her servant Lena walking towards some clothes that were hanging on a line. Next day it turned out that Lena had lain awake in bed thinking of the clothes and how they might be blown away by the wind, but was too tired or too lazy to get up and rescue them. This is a variant of the more usual phenomenon in which people dream of things they would have liked to do during the day, or, if they are somnambulists, get up and do them. Unlike the 'travellers' referred to in Chapter 2, in a case like Lena's it is the unconscious and not the conscious self that seems to perform a 'psychic journey', and, as already mentioned, a further distinguishing feature is that the travelller is visible to others.

The self may travel to a distant spot in this way, not merely for purposes of exploration but in order to affect the mind or visual sense of another person. Thus Eileen Garrett relates that two women friends of hers, one living three hundred miles away and the other thirty, wrote during a period of a few days to say they had 'seen' her in their respective homes and to ask if anything was the matter. She came to the conclusion, some years later, that she must have been thinking of her friends while in a state of trance or semi-trance and this must have caused her psyche to project itself in their direction. This is also compatible with Tyrrell's theory; but he is too categorical when he states that 'the explanation of all this must be sought in our perceptive apparatus and not in the external world', and that 'there are no centres of physical emanation in space.' This would mean that no ghost is actually there, i.e. perceptible to ordinary sight and not only to the mind's eye. This purely 'subjective' theory of ghosts is rejected by René Sudre and other experts. Tyrrell, however, maintains it even in the case of apparitions that are seen by several people at once, since hallucinations and mental states in general can quite well be shared (cf. Chapter 1). But Tyrrell's theory breaks down in the case of ghosts that not only appear but also perform some action and leave physical traces of what they have done. There are in fact apparitions that are merely visual, others accompanied by a sound-track and others again that have telekinetic properties, as we shall see.

## A ghost in church

Two or three years ago a cavalry officer, Major F.P. of Naples, told me that during the first world war, when he was a lieutenant in the infantry, he was in action at Castagna-vizza on 23 March 1917 and was wounded in both hands. That same afternoon, in his home at Salerno, a noise like a thunderclap was heard, the balcony windows shattered and the books in his study fell off the shelves. At that moment his sister Anne ran into their parents' room crying that she had seen him sitting on a chair with blood on his arms. This, he believed, was when the Germans captured him and a fellow-officer and took them off to Mulhouse. Tyrrell's theory may explain the hallucination, and perhaps even the noise, but what about the broken glass and the falling books? We know that the *daimon* or secret self can affect objects at a distance, and we shall see further examples of this, but we may note here once again that it can manifest itself in various physical and mechanical ways to people with mediumistic faculties who are in the appropriate state of consciousness.

A remarkable case of second sight accompanied by tele-kinesis was reported in 1896 by a clergyman named Stead in the English journal *Borderland*. One of his parishioners, the elderly Miss A., was an assiduous churchgoer but was from time to time confined to bed by a serious illness. One October afternoon, after a severe attack, the doctor gave her an in-jection and left her in the care of her maid and a friend, who subsequently declared on oath that she had not got out of bed. Nevertheless, that evening Mr. Stead saw her appear at church, looking extremely pale and wearing an unmistakable black hat. Knowing her condition, he looked at her reproving-ly, and those next her in the pew also showed anxiety. One of them offered her a prayer-book, which she laid on the seat beside her; she took no part in the hymns, and left the church just before the end of the service. Several of the congregation afterwards confirmed that they had seen her; some children

124

walked with her, when she came in, from the door as far as the choir. Here again, it is clear that someone or something went to church in Miss A's place: we must think of it as a disembodied phantom or simulacrum, created and impelled by her longing to carry out an action of which her body was incapable.

## Ghosts at sea

Some may find it hard to believe that a ghost can open doors, express its thanks or be seen by several people for over an hour; but, as Chauvin-Duval says, it is not a question of what we can believe but what in fact happens. It is curious that although mankind accepts the supreme mysteries of life, mind and the universe because they are indisputably there, many people reject other mysteries that happen occasionally and at unexpected times. Even scientists are apt to demand that paranormal events should be reproducible in laboratories, though in many cases they do not depend on the will of the performer. Others reject the evidence for such events because in the past they have been quoted in support of certain non-scientific beliefs; but the facts and the interpretation are two different things, and the evidence continues to multiply.

The following story is related in *Gnomologie,* by 'Enel' (Paris, 1959): the author's real name is Mikhail V. Skaryatin, a Russian prince who emigrated at the time of the Revolution and became an Egyptologist. As a young man he was an officer in the Tsarist navy, serving in the corvette *Yastreb* ('Hawk'). The ship's company were in a depressed state, as their much-loved commanding officer had had to quit his post owing to a nervous breakdown. At the end of a stormy day, when visibility was still bad and the ship (*en route* for Shanghai) was navigating among shoals and strong currents, Skaryatin took over the midnight watch with strict instructions not to change course. Suddenly, in the dark, he heard what appeared to be the ex-commander's voice telling him to alter course half a point to westward. As Skaryatin did nothing the voice repeated its order in urgent tones, and an arm appeared from behind his back and pointed to the chart. He recognized the commander's hand, with the swollen bluish veins and signet ring. This time Skaryatin obeyed, and the ship sailed on without incident. He told his fellow-officers what he had done, and next day, when the weather cleared and a bearing was taken, it was found that if the ship had not altered course she would have struck a rock.

A similar incident happened in 1828 to a Scotsman named Robert Bruce, who related it to his friend Captain J.S. Clarke: the latter's account is quoted in *Footfalls on the Boundary of another World,* by Robert Dale Owen (1861). Bruce, aged thirty, was first mate on a vessel bound for New Brunswick. The ship was due to reach port in about thirty hours, but it was foggy and there was a risk of drift-ice. Bruce was in his cabin studying charts when he saw an unknown man in the captain's cabin opposite, writing something on a slate: he was dripping wet and looked ill and exhausted. Bruce jumped up, but had only time to notice the man's harrowed expression before the figure disappeared. On the slate, however, was what looked like an urgent message: 'Steer to the nor'west!' The captain did so — it was some 45 degrees off course — and a few hours later they sighted a group of men on an ice-floe near the wreckage of a cargo-ship. One of the men, who had been adrift for three weeks, was to all appearances the one who had appeared in the captain's cabin, and when asked to write the words of the message he did so in an identical hand. It turned out that some hours before the rescue he had fallen into a deep sleep, and on awaking told his fellows that he had seen a ship on its way to save them; moreover he described its appearance in detail. Curiously, he had no recollection of the message, which was the one objective proof of the incident. It appears that in cases of this sort the completeness of the subject's trance is in proportion to the importance of the action, and a deep trance is analogous to a deep sleep, from which we emerge with no awareness of what we have dreamt.[3]

Pierre Devaux relates numerous well-documented cases of a dream-reality imposing itself on the physical world. One is that of a clergyman named Hamilton, who dozed off late one night at his club, but slept uneasily as he knew his family would be anxious. When he got home, they told him with amazement that they had already seen him enter the house and go up to his room; his father had heard the noise of the front door closing and his footsteps on the stairs. This recalls the case of the servant Lena, who was seen performing an act that she knew she ought to be doing at the time in

126

question.

It is related of St. Antony of Padua that, while preaching an impassioned sermon in a Spanish town, he fell into a trance and appeared — or his *alter ego* did — at Padua for a short time in order to give evidence on behalf of his father, who was falsely accused of a serious crime: having indicated the true culprit, the Saint returned to his sermon.

In 1811, when George III of Great Britain suffered his final attack of mental illness, several witnesses 'saw' Lord Byron sign the visitors' book at the Palace, whereas he was in fact in Patras in Greece, confined to his bed by malaria. His heart was evidently in London, for he was seen there several times and his publisher, convinced that he had returned, stopped forwarding his mail. When told of the matter Byron merely said: 'I hope my double behaves like a gentleman.'

# CHAPTER 12

===

## Self-projection

*Self-projection*

During the second world war a French lieutenant in charge of Italian prisoners at Guelma in Algeria was returning to his quarters late one night and met a medical officer named Lefébure under a row of trees outside the camp. To the question 'Hullo! What are you doing here?', Lefébure replied: 'It's not me, it's my double' — and disappeared. The other officer ran to Lefébure's lodging and found him sound asleep. The sentries guarding the camp had not seen him, as they would have been bound to do if he had really gone outside. It turned out, however, that Lefébure had been trained by an Oriental sage in the art of passing outside the body and entering a mysterious dimension of the universe in which the mind is able to exist without its normal physical integument.[1]

The difference between a case of this kind and most of those dealt with in the last chapter is that it involves a deliberate intention to project the self as a physical phenomenon, informed by the conscious mind of the subject. P.E. Cornillier records similar experiments by an American lady, Mrs. Mary C. Wlasek, who in 1922 represented California at a spiritualist congress at Los Angeles. While still *en route* for the congress she manifested herself at séances there on 27 and 29 September, to the astonishment and delight of a large audience.[2]

Such feats differ from those of Pasqualina Pezzola (Chapter 2) inasmuch as Pasqualina transported her mind but not her body or simulacrum to the distant place, and was not seen by the people there. Probably, however, it is a question not of two different faculties but of the same one at different degrees of intensity; and if so, this tends to confirm the view that there is no strict division between mental and physical phenomena.

Some subjects, like Stefan Ossowiecki, have been able to project themselves in either of the two ways, and apparently this is true at the present day of a Danish engineer named Olle Jönsson. Such people are exceptionally endowed by nature, but there are others who cultivate powers of this type according to the methods of different schools of yoga. Dr Francis Lefébure, already mentioned, wrote a large book on his experiences in which he attempts to blend the esoteric wisdom of Asia with some aspects of Western neurophysiology, but with a clear bias towards the former.[3]

Among serious students of self-projection are Hereward Carrington, Nandor Fodor, H.H. Price, Nornell Hart, Raynor C. Johnson, C.I. Ducasse and J.H.M. Whiteman. The last-named drew up a report on the subject after the parapsychological congress at Utrecht in August 1953: in this he discussed 550 cases of 'detachment from the physical body', some of which he had observed himself. He distinguished between 'complete detachment,' when the subject loses consciousness, and the state in which the subject remains conscious while projecting his mind elsewhere. In the latter case Whiteman refers to 'mystic liberation' and 'simplication of the personality, with the dissociation and total or partial elimination of disharmonic elements.'[4]

## Dreams that conquer distance

Primitive societies, which have fewer inhibitions about acknowledging myeterious facts, supply many examples of what we have been describing. In such communities self-projection usually serves some practical purpose such as tracing a thief, summoning a distant friend or finding out where game is hiding. Shamans and witch-doctors possess powers of this kind which make up for the technical backwardness of their societies. A Dyak medicine-man, according to Mauss, goes into a trance while his 'double' is off elsewhere, gathering herbs and other remedies which he then applies to his patient. Mauss also tells us that among the Kurnal tribe in Australia there is a kind of wizard who can 'send forth his soul' to spy out the advancing enemy. The Tungus shamans of eastern Siberia are supposed to have the same powers, as are their opposite numbers in Lapland, Tierra del Fuego and parts of central Mexico. The natives of Gabon (central Africa) use the term

129

'*ngwel*' for an area of reality 'where time and space do not count', and Zulu witchdoctors claim to be able to 'open the gates of distance'.

Alexandra David-Neel speaks of a village woman of Tsawa-rong in Tibet who remained in a state of inanition for a whole week, during which she was able to travel great distances with a sense of extreme lightness, walking across rivers, through doors, etc., but still attached to her body by an almost impalpable cord which she could not break. According to Dr J. Shepley, similar powers are believed to exist in Ghana.[5]

Sir James Frazer dismissed phenomena such as these by stating that primitive man confuses the operations of his own mind with natural laws. As E. de Martino has observed, there is a gulf between ethnologists in the field who record 'magical' occurrences, and ethnologists back in Europe or North America who devise psychological theories to account for them. We shall revert to this when discussing the existence of psychokinetic powers. Meanwhile we may observe that self-projection, or bilocation as it is sometimes called, exemplifies the power of the mind, whether conscious or unconscious, to transcend limitations of space and time even in the physcial sphere.

Olivier Leroy, in a book published in 1927, relates an incident which was told him by Father Trilles, to whom it happened twenty or more years earlier.[6] Ugema Uzago, a witch-doctor and head of the Yabiku tribe, told Fr. Trilles one day that he was going to a place on the Yemvi plateau which was normally four days' journey away, but which he would reach by magic instantaneously. To prove his powers he undertook to tell a friend of the missionary's named Esaba, who lived at Ushong three days' journey away to bring him a packet of cartridges for his sporting rifle.

That evening Fr. Trilles went to Uzago's hut; the witch-doctor undressed, rubbed himself with a special oil and danced round a flame on to which he threw aromatic herbs, reciting lengthy incantations the while. Finally, at nine o'clock, he stretched out on a pallet and fell into a kind of catalepsy. Fr. Trilles watched over him until morning, when he awoke and said he had been to the Yemvi plateau for a witch-doctors' council and had also given the promised message to Esaba. Sure enough, the latter turned up three days later with the cartridges, saying that on the night in question, at nine o'clock, a 'wandering spirit' had told him to bring them.

Some occultists and others, following ancient Egyptian or Hinduistic doctrine, hold that every individual is possessed of a 'double' or 'astral body',[7] a semi-material entity which is capable of leaving the body for a time but remains attached to it by a kind of ethereal cord. But this underrates the power of the unconscious to create not merely one but several simultaneous images of its owner's body, and even to give transient life to other shapes which bear no resemblance to the latter, as we shall see in later chapters.[8]

# PART IV

## The past invades the present

# CHAPTER 13

___

## Visual messages from the past

*An appointment with the unknown*

Some years ago Dr Naegeli Osjord, a distinguished neuro-psychiatrist and specialist in paranormal phenomena, had the courage to spend the night alone in a haunted German castle which, in the Middle Ages, had combined the functions of a prison, feudal court of justice and torture-chamber.[1]

Dr Osjord, a man of strong nerves, slept peacefully for a time, but awoke to find with astonishment that his body was occupied not only by his own personality but also by that of an unjust mediaeval judge who was racked with remorse for his misdeeds. The intruder emitted groans through Osjord's mouth and trembled with his limbs; the bed shook violently, and an infernal din was heard in the neighbouring rooms and passages. Osjord continued to observe events calmly, noting however that he felt a degree of muscular tension and was unable to move. After the judge's spirit had left his body he went to sleep again, but was awakened by the sound of blows and cries of pain from the next room. He listened to these for as long as they lasted, and then went to sleep for the rest of the night.

It is of course possible that Dr Osjord was the victim of dreams or hallucinations 'suggested' by the castle's unpleasant history; but there is also no reason why he should not have had a retrospective dream involving a true perception of the past, such as we read of in Chapter 1. As for this identification of the dreamer with the person dreamt of, this is analogous to some of the cases discussed in Chapters 3 and 4. We may revert here to Pasqualina Pezzola, who was once set a task that involved the transcending of time as well as distance. Drs Cassoli and Marabini told her to 'visit' an old lady at Bologna, whose name and address they gave her on a slip of paper, but omitted to tell her that the lady had died some time ago. Pasqualina duly went in spirit to the address and, not finding the lady there, was 'taken' to her present abode, i.e. the cemetery. Her account continues: 'I was led to a place where there was no need to knock, and found the woman shut in by walls. It was very uncomfortable, as all sorts of "fluids" were trying to drive me away. She came forward as if to speak to me, but then disappeared. This happened more than once. It was very dark. I realized that she was in great distress, and I felt the same in her presence.' Pasqualina was so upset by this episode that she went straight to bed and remained there till next day.

Clairvoyants, as we know, are apt to identify with the person towards whom their 'second sight' is directed: in the psychic universe, 'to understand' and 'to share' mean very much the same thing. Darkness is a symbol of distress, and the 'fluids' may correspond to traces or recollections which past events leave of themselves — or we may conceive of these as having some more tangible reality, in line with modern ideas about the nature of existence. We have referred (in Chapter 3) to Toddi's 'hyperphysical' conception of the past, and the physico-chemical one of Fantappiè, who sees it as the cross-section of a higher dimension embracing all time. Theories of this kind are linked with that of a cosmic reservoir of individual memories, a 'psychic dimension' as we may call it, to which the unconscious affords access. As Jung writes in his posthumous work, 'When the soul enters into contact with the unconscious it is, in a sense, in touch with the community of the dead, for the unconscious corresponds to the legendary country of the dead and of our forefathers.' Legendary it may be, but it is a source of true information for mediums who have the power to enter it and receive its messages. These may be purely subjective or they may be in a form which the medium can transmit to his fellow-men, while unconsciously colouring it with his own interpretation.

In April 1938 Natuzza Evolo of Mileto, a servant-girl of fourteen in a lawyer's household, began to 'see dead people' — that is to say, they appeared to her as real persons but were invisible to anyone else. Some thought her mad, others possessed by a devil. Bishop Albera carried out a rite of exorcism, but the visions continued while it was going on: Natuzza saw people arriving in groups and crowding around her, some of whom had been dead for a long time while others were unknown. There is of course no absolute proof that the visions were genuine; but the story is similar to that of Frederica Hauffe of Prevorst, who, it appears, had more converse with the dead than with the living, and also that of a Berlin bookseller named Nicolai, who suffered an apoplectic stroke in 1791 and for some time afterwards reportedly had clear visions of people who had died and others who were living far off. He saw these engaged in ordinary pursuits and, by degrees, was able to hold conversations with them, including the dead.[2] Such visions may be called hallucinations, but they differ from those of madmen in that they convey information which, in many cases, has been checked and found to be true.[3] Nicolai's conversations may, like Pasqualina's, be termed symbolic in so far as they represent attempts by the secret self to impart information to the conscious mind, and it is generally found that these conform to patterns which are partly determined by the medium's own constitution or mental state.

Jacopo Alighieri, as we saw in Chapter 1, had a dream-conversation with a dead person; others, like Pasqualina, have encountered the dead in trances, while Natuzza, Nicolai and others have conversed with them while in a waking state. Finally, as we saw in the case of Dr Osjord, it is possible for communication with the dead to take the form of identification and physical possession. Sometimes there are two stages, so that the medium first 'sees' the person in question as a separate individual and then identifies with him or her. This was the case with a Belgian clairvoyant, denoted as 'Delta' by Professor Tenhaeff, who on several occasions helped the Dutch police to find missing persons, usually those who had died by violence or accident or done away with themselves. He would be taken to the place where they had lived and, after a short time, would be aware of a kind of nebulous ghost that appeared first in space but was then 'absorbed' into himself. At this point 'Delta' would tremble and sweat and show every sign of undergoing the same sufferings as the missing person had done; he would describe the latter's feelings and intentions and often their last acts, e.g. if they had been drowned or committed suicide.

The question arises whether to regard this, as many would do, as a form of spiritualism, or rather of psychometry as defined in Chapter 3, i.e. direct cognition of the past, which, in the psychic dimension, coexists with the present and future. As Schopenhauer observed, 'A living person who was able to cast his view backwards might bring forth reminiscences that appeared to be communications from the dead.'[4] Many of the phenomena we have described could well be regarded as stormy contacts between the human mind and past events, involving clairvoyance of a psychometric kind — i.e. induced by 'atmosphere' — and also a unitive form of cognition or participation. It would seem in the light of this that ghosts have no power to manifest themselves independently of human beings, but require the assistance of the living.[5] We may add that the medium's retrospective vision may be so intense that he can project it in a visible and tangible form, and that a phantom thus objectified may appear to produce physical effects by making a noise or moving other objects. However, it is not the ghost which produces these effects but the medium himself, who unconsciously brings his paranormal powers into action so as to project his vision to the full.

### The Millvale ghost

One of the few really well attested cases of recurrent apparitions took place in 1937 in a Catholic church at Millvale near Pittsburgh. A young painter of Yugoslav origin, Maxo Vanka, was in the church one evening putting the final touches to an allegorical fresco depicting 'Religion in the New World', when the organ started to play loudly. No one could be seen; the parish priest, Fr. Zagar, was in the presbytery and probably asleep. Nothing could be heard outside except two watchdogs, barking furiously. Vanka went on painting — he was in a hurry to finish the fresco by the due date, which was why he was working at night. But his attention was next distracted by heavy blows on the church walls and by the apparition of an old priest, with a wrinkled, unhappy face. who walked up to the high altar, blew out the lamp and disappeared instantaneously.

Vanka, besides being an unconscious medium, was a man and the people of Millvale, but had paid no attention. However, the sound of the organ once more filled the church and he began to feel a profound sense of distress, which seemed to come from outside himself and presumably therefore from the ghost. He told the tale to Fr. Zagar, who said it was nothing new: the mysterious priest had been appearing for the past twenty-five years and had been seen by Fr. Zagar, his curate Fr. Nezitch, and the housekeeper, Mrs Dolinar, The first living creatures to notice his approach were always the dogs, which barked loudly and then howled as though in terror.

Vanka, besides being an unconscious medium, was a man of fortitude and went on working in the church at night from 9 April to 10 June. The phantom continued to appear and once, it is said, lit a row of candles on the high altar — but possibly Vanka himself did this, in a somnambulistic trance which caused him to identify with the ghost. At all events, whenever it appeared he was seized by a sense of anguish; this had also been the case with Fr. Zoritch, the previous parish priest, who had been driven to apply for a transfer.[6]

It is natural to speculate on the motives of ghosts' actions in terms of ordinary human ones. Some students assume, explicitly or otherwise, that there is a direct equivalence between the ghost and the dead individual's personality, but this should not be taken for granted. Hereward Carrington writes that 'Many ghost stories indicate clearly that there is something dynamically operative — something that occupies space and has a mind of its own.[7] Myers held that 'something ethereal and semi-material' might, as it were, be captured by the mental act of a living person and obliged to remain in space for a limited period; we shall see in a later chapter that this is quite a plausible view. On the other hand, as Myers also observed, the actions of ghosts are often pointless or trivial, like events in a troubled dream.[8] It is conceivable that the dead, in some eternal dimension of reality, are capable of having dreams or nightmares and that these may assume bodily shape, as do the dreams of the living in certain cases. This explanation, of course, would rule out the one suggested earlier in this chapter, that the mind which does the dreaming is that of a living medium whose unconscious mind is able to explore the universal archives of the past.

Basically our view as to the nature of ghosts will depend on whether we regard them as 'dreams' in the mind of the dead or of the living. In the former case their existence is sometimes invoked as a confirmation of life after death; in the latter, they may represent no more than fragments of the past perceived by living mortals with mediumistic gifts — of which they may or may not be aware — and sometimes projected by them. Those who identify the visible phantom with the personality of a dead individual would do better, in any case, not to argue from this to views of human survival which would be more soundly based on metaphysical or religious grounds. As Whately Carington says, the problem of survival may be one of those to which Nature prefers to give an ambiguous answer. Human personality is so complex and involves so many levels of consciousness that there may well be room for speculation as to what truly survives and what does not.[9]

### The strange psychology of ghosts

It appears rash, therefore, to seek explanations for the behaviour of ghosts in terms of ordinary human life, or to infer from it the nature of life beyond the grave. None the less, such attempts are often made and we should examine them. According to Gabriel Delanne and many others, ghost-behaviour is generally obsessive and consists of returning again and again to the same point, like a gramophone needle stuck in a groove. In the Germanic countries, ghosts are often thought of as souls that have somehow lost their way between the material and the spirit-world: thus Hans Holzer writes that 'a ghost is a diseased spirit in need of help, just as a mentally sick man needs psychiatry.[10] Oscar Goldberg saw the Millvale ghost as the soul of a priest torn by conflicting impulses, one of devotion and the other of rebellion. Some go further and suggest that explanations of this sort can be tested in particular cases by inducing the wandering spirit to take up its abode in a medium who can then be questioned.

Violet Tweedale tells the story of two ghosts that successively manifested themselves through the same medium in 1917 at 'Castel a Mare', a villa in Torquay: one was the spirit of a murderer who had killed two people in the house fifty years before, while the other ghost was that of one of his victims, a young woman who used to haunt the place and emit bloodcurdling screams. It is hard to explain on anthropomorphic grounds why both the murderer and the victim should feel a compulsion to return to the spot and re-enact their violent history; and, in the light of this and many similar cases, we do not believe that the psychology of ghosts, if there is such a thing, resembles that of ordinary humans, except perhaps in a distorted way. One can, of course, understand ghosts appearing in a dream or waking vision to reveal the identity of their murderers and to demand vengeance — as in the case of Lieutenant James B. Sutton, reported by Hyslop,[11] and another instance related by Myers.[12] But why, for instance, should an old lady, buried a few hours ago, appear to a total stranger and ask the latter to search for a wine-coloured dress that had been left behind in a cupboard;[13] or why should two brothers who were smugglers return, night after night, to the cellar of an old house in Cornwall and re-enact a fight to the death which took place between them?[14]

In the face of such examples we may be inclined to agree with Maeterlinck that ghosts are often no more than 'incoherent, precarious manifestations of a transitory state, a reflection of ourselves — disconnected scraps of memory that float in the void for a time after our death, and then vanish for ever.' One might suppose from this that Maeterlinck disbelieved in survival, if we did not know that he posited the existence of an indestructible psyche, quite distinct from normal consciousness. René Guénon used the term 'psychic residue' to denote the enigmatic spectral forces which, in his view, were completely distinct from the soul, whose destiny lay elsewhere.[15] Taking into account all these theories, and with due regard to the obscurity of the subject and the inadequacy of human thought, we ourselves incline to the second of the alternative views suggested above, viz. that ghosts are not independent apparitions but are the content or product of retrospective dreams by living persons.

### Children and the 'forbidden dimension'

Animals, as we saw in the Millvale case, are particularly sensitive to psychic phenomena, perhaps because they are closer to nature than we; and the same is true of children, though indifference or hostility often causes them to lose the sensitive faculty as they grow older.

When Violet Tweedale was a small girl, the ghost of a

woman used to walk past the bedroom where she and her brother slept; it was not visible, but the two children could hear the unmistakable rustling of a dress, and they listened for it — at the same hour every evening — with curiosity unmixed with fear. The mysterious visitor would climb the stairs up to their landing, walk down the passage and disappear. She was never heard to go downstairs, and the children's only perplexity was how she got back to the starting-point. Eileen Garrett, again tells of a little old lady who used to appear when she, as a child, opened the drawers of a particular chest, and Elizabeth d'Esperance had a childhood visitor of a similar kind.

Frederica Hauffe of Prevorst was twelve years old when she first saw a ghost — a tall, dark-faced old man who walked past her in a dark passage, sighing deeply, and then turned round and looked piercingly at her. She ran to tell her grandfather, Johann Schmidgall; the latter was a medium himself and already knew the ghost but to set the child's mind at rest he told her she must have imagined it.

Franek Kluski and Florence Cook, when children, used to see ghosts which they mistook for living people, as did Natuzza Evolo and a certain clairvoyante of Bologna, who was treated for 'hallucinations' without success and was later pronounced perfectly sane by an eminent Austrian psychiatrist. One may choose to believe that all the clairvoyants in the world at all times are in league to tell false stories of this kind, but it seems less improbable to suppose that supernatural powers of perception really do exist.

## Ghostly playmates

Eileen Garrett was orphaned in infancy and was brought up by an aunt who did not understand the child and treated her unkindly. She lived an unhappy life until the appearance of 'the children' — a boy and two girls — whom she saw one day standing in the house doorway. Torn between fear of her aunt and a desire to play with them, she waited until next day, when she found them still looking at her with mingled shyness and curiosity. A friendship then began which lasted until she reached puberty: the four children played together, told one another secrets and so forth, exactly as though the 'visitors' belonged to the ordinary world, with two im-

140

portant differences: first, they were 'made of light'; and secondly they conveyed their thoughts to Eileen without speaking.[16]

Ghosts, it is clear, are not always sinister, dramatic or tragic. Contact with the past is a complex phenomenon depending on at least two variables: the medium's aptitude for what Tyrrell calls 'retrocognitive telepathy', and the creative activity of the medium's unconscious mind, which interprets the past and re-works it into a more or less dramatic pattern. using symbols of its own choice. The result is something intermediate between reality and imagination, as in the case of Eileen Garrett's visionary playmates. From her experience of the phantom children Eileen learnt, no doubt, that adults either do not know or do not tell the whole truth about things, and that it is sometimes salutary to disobey their orders. Like most children in a similar position she was subjected to close questioning and a good deal of pressure, but did not budge from her belief in the reality of her playmates.

Fifty years earlier another lonely, introvert child, Elizabeth d'Espérance, used to spend hours every day in certain empty rooms of her parents' house, where she encountered a succession of amiable strangers who never failed to smile or greet her while going about their business. Her mother and the doctor questioned her at length about these mysterious beings, who sometimes disappeared for months on end, especially when her father (who spent much time travelling by sea) was at home. It appears that even a natural medium may be unable to evoke spirits at a time when his or her mind is focussed on concrete reality. A difficult question, in cases like these, is to determine what is pathological and what is not. Eileen Garrett was suspected of neurosis, but this is too summary a way of dismissing what is merely 'different' from the ordinary mind. It is true, however, that frequent excursions into the 'forbidden dimension' are not conducive to the stability of those who would prefer to remain anchored in the normal universe. As Eileen Garrett asks somewhat sadly, after discussing the flimsy evidence on which psychiatrists pass judgement on the retrospective or fantastic visions of those with second sight: 'How much fancy is allowed to a human being before he is classified as a neuropath?'

# CHAPTER 14

## Ghosts and mediums

On December 15 1929 the journalist Harry Price,[1] an assiduous investigator of the supernatural, took part in a séance at the home of the modest London family with whom he was staying. The medium was one of those who possess the extraordinary power of giving visible and tangible form to the objects of their dreams, whether these are based on their own memories or other peoples' or on clairvoyant contact with the past. On this occasion the medium called up the image of her small daughter Rosalie, who had died six years before. Price describes the scene: in a room lit only by the illuminated dial of a wireless set, half a dozen persons sat round the medium, who repeated her daughter's name several times until the child materialized. 'I cautiously stretched out my left arm and, to my amazement, felt what seemed to be the naked body of a small girl aged under seven. I drew my hand slowly across her chest and then touched her chin and cheeks. The flesh was warm, though less so than in a living person. I laid the back of my left hand against her right cheek . . . then touched her chest again and could clearly feel her breathing.' Price says that the girl was 4′ 3″ in height and that he felt her long, soft hair, reaching to the shoulders. 'I took her right arm and felt the pulse, which was beating fast, at about ninety to the minute. I placed my ear in the region of the heart and was clearly aware of its beating. I took both her hands in mine,' etc. With the aid of a fluorescent mirror, Price was even able to glimpse the girl's features. 'Her face seemed pale; she had bright, blue, intelligent eyes. Her lips were pressed together, giving her a curiously firm expression.' To such questions as 'Where are you now?' and 'What do you generally do? play with other children?' she made no reply; but when Price asked 'Do you love your mother?' her face lit up and she said softly 'Yes, yes.'

The medium thereupon clasped the child in her arms and

142

burst into tears, as did the other women present. Price was also moved, but when he came to write his long account two hours later he was already beginning to wonder if the séance was genuine. 'Despite all the precautions that a long experience has taught me,' he writes, 'I could not be quite certain that I had not been deceived; but by what means, and what motive would those highly respectable people have had for doing so?' Price, it should be explained, was also interested in the theory and practice of conjuring; he had conducted a crusade against bogus mediums and had actually unmasked one or two. This may account for his ambivalent attitude towards the apparition of Rosalie; moreover it appears that his editor had put pressure on him to express some doubt of its genuineness. He had in fact taken a whole series of precautions before the séance: he had inspected the room sealed the doors and windows, looked inside cupboards, knocked on the walls and floor to see if they sounded hollow, removed pictures and strips of wallpaper and even a wall clock, and had strewn starch all over the place to pick up any fingerprints or footmarks. He also searched the men who were present: not the women, it is true, but a child of Rosalie's size could not have hidden under a 1929 skirt. After the séance was over he confirmed that everything in the room was as it had been, and the starch showed no traces. After all this, his scepticism can only be construed as 'professional deformation'. The art of deception, after all, has its limits. The attitude of such as Price — the 'ghost-hunter', as he styled himself — was summed up by Jan Ehrenwald when he wrote: 'Modern man has constructed a picture of the world on the ruins of magic and animistic beliefs, mistrusting the secret attraction of the primitive forces of his own psyche. Consequently he is now at pains to ensure that nothing of what has been banished should return to form part of his everyday life. Hence the contempt and ridicule that he visits on all those who engage in out-of-the-way research.' This attitude whereby important subjects of study are ignored as 'poor relations' of science is all the more insidious because it is often unconscious.

## The magic of 'Don Luisito'

Some years ago the international journal *Parapsicologia*, edited by Professor William Mackenzie, published a well-documented account by Professor Gutierre Tibón of Mexico describing instances of materialization that had been produced over the years by the medium Luis Martinez ('Don Luisito'). These took place under the supervision of Sr. Alvarez Alvarez, a wealthy and cultivated industrialist, and were seen by hundreds of witnesses including Alberto Barajas, a mathematician and co-ordinator of scientific research in Mexico; a Jesuit who had written books against spiritualism; a Director-General of UNESCO; two former Presidents of Mexico, and two ex-Ministers of Foreign Affairs.

Professor Tibón, a distinguished psychologist and sociologist, attended numerous séances between 1951 and 1953 in which he saw the figures of Don Luisito's dreams materialize and walk about, talking to those present and performing various actions. As soon as the medium fell into a trance, small phosphorescent globes — white, yellow or green in colour — were seen for a time dancing above people's heads; then they disappeared and the true materialization began, with human faces and hands striking the walls or patting members of the audience on the shoulder. At other times they would play with drumsticks on a drum that moved about in mid-air, or pull flowers out of a vase and scatter the petals over those present. Professor Tibón relates that 'Once two little lights came close, and in a few seconds tied my arm, neck and feet to my chair with amazingly clever knots.' After the stage of lights and hands, small quivering forms appeared in the centre of the circle and gradually took on human shape, after which characters came on the scene who had been created or evoked by Don Luisito's unconscious mind with the help, in all probability, of that of members of the audience.

The first of these wore a turban and presented himself as an Oriental doctor named Amahur. Then came 'Sister Belen' [Bethlehem], a little wrinkled old woman, and a talkative figure named Dr del Castillo, who always wore a black ribbon tie. Less frequent apparitions, who never spoke, were a Crusader with a shining sword, a priest wearing a gold-embroidered stole, and a personage adorned with a twelve-pointed diadem, some of the points being brighter than others. Then followed a lively throng of 'children' — little luminous beings who seized hold of a quantity of toys and made a din with cymbals, tambourines, castanets and all manner of devices, including the kind of doll that squeaks when you press it. Among this group was a single soloist named 'Botitas', who could play tarantellas and sentimental tunes on the accordion.

All this brings to mind the views of Claparède and Baudouin on the analogy between dreams and games,[2] or what Flournoy calls the 'sportive' aspect of mediumistic phenomena.[3] In Don Luisito's case the sequence lasted for two hours, after which he showed signs of discomfort and exhaustion. Sr. Alvarez would then awaken him from his trance and turn on the lights, whereupon the floor would be found strewn with flowers, petals and toys of all kinds.

Professor Tibón, like Harry Price, took every imaginable precaution against fraud, but never found any. He too was initially sceptical but, being a man of scientific mind, finally surrendered to the evidence, as Price did not. It is of course possible to suppose that Don Luisito, whom Tibón describes as a slow, clumsy individual, was a brilliant illusionist who had missed his vocation, or that Sr. Alvarez was a rogue, or that Tibón and the other hundreds of witnesses were emotional, credulous and simple-minded. But, while this attitude may perhaps be expected from official science, it is strange to meet it among professional parapsychologists, some of whom appear to accept the reality of paranormal phenomena only when they can be produced at will in laboratory conditions. Yet the most remarkable of such phenomena are surely the 'wild' as opposed to the 'tame' or predictable ones — for instance projection of the self (*dédoublement*), the spontaneous appearance of ghosts endowed with material consistency, or the evocation of such ghosts at a séance.

Summing up the Rosalie episode, Price concluded: 'Only if I had been able to observe the materialization in my own laboratory would I assert confidently that the great question of human survival has been experimentally resolved in the affirmative.' This, however, involves two basic fallacies. In the first place, mediumistic phenomena can only occur if the medium feels at ease and, so to speak, on the same wavelength as the audience. In some cases, as we have seen, there has to be an elaborate ritual, and in others, such as that of the dead child, a contributing factor is no doubt the emotion of all those present and the fact that the scene itself, unlike a laboratory, was full of memories and associations. The second fallacy in Price's observations is that one cannot argue from necromancy to individual survival after death. We can no more assume that the 'personality' of a ghost is identical with that of a dead person than, for instance, that an image on a cinema screen is identical with a particular actor. The medium's subconscious mind may indeed be likened to a film projector, with the difference that what it projects is in three dimensions and may possess a degree of physical consistency. The same psychic power that can give life to a *Dopplegänger* or cause a 'replay' of some past event (as by summoning up ghosts of the dead) is clearly able to call into being the material counterpart of a dream experienced by a medium sunk in a trance. The dream, as we saw, may embody the medium's own recollections or, by way of clairvoyance, those of others; or it may be inspired by one of the indelible traces that every human life leaves behind it in the ever present past; or again, we may hold with William James that the mediumistic mind has access to a 'cosmic reservoir of individual memories'. Whichever way we care to express it, the conclusion that follows is that certain minds are endowed with extraordinary powers; but nothing more.[4]

At spiritualist séances the minds of the audience are generally intent on evocation of the dead, and this no doubt influences the medium's subconscious mind, but there are many cases where the materialization takes the form of animals, grotesque drawings or inanimate objects. The medium's dream derives its content from all those present and mobilizes their psychic resources (the medium acting as a catalyst), so that all are generally exhausted at the end of the séance. The medium, however, expends more energy than any of the others, and apparently he or she is the source of the 'ectoplasm' of which ghosts are made, and which endows them in some cases with great physical strength.[5] The dream, in fact, represents a high degree of creative power, involving the dissolution, to some extent at least, of the protoplasm of which the medium's body is made, and its transformation into creatures possessed of a certain autonomy. Some scholars have tried to interpret this in neuro-physiological terms: thus Dr Nicola Brunori suggests that the seat of this 'magic'

146

creative power is the middle brain or diencephalon, released temporarily from the control of the cerebral cortex — the latter being the normal seat of consciousness, while the 'palæo-psyche' or primeval self is associated with the deepest layers of the brain. The fact that there is a correlation between mediumistic phenomena and certain types of cerebral activity does not, however, mean that the latter is necessarily the cause of the former, any more than the printed characters which make up a book are the cause of the ideas it contains.

## The creative force of the collective psyche

The Polish expert Julian Ochorowicz coined the term 'ideoplastic' to describe the unconscious power of a medium to create tangible and apparently autonomous physical forms. The notion was adopted by Geley as the basis of a unitary conception of metapsychic phenomena,[6] and also by Richet, Osty and many others.

Professor Richet was once present at the materialization of a female ghost: he clasped one of its hands and, without speaking, wished that it should be wearing a ring; immediately the ring was there. He then wished a bracelet on to the arm in the same manner. This seems to bear out the view that all those present have a share in the medium's creative power: the dream is everybody's dream, and the events that take place are as volatile and unpredictable as those in dreams of the ordinary kind. During a séance directed by Eugene Osty a squirrel materialized beside the medium and jumped from shoulder to shoulder round the room. This medium — a Pole named Jan Guzik — was evidently fond of animals and especially wild ones: on one occasion he summoned up a bear, and on another a small dog which bit Professor Le-clainche in the finger, leaving a mark to prove it.[7]

Another Polish medium, Franek Kluski, who died in 1944 and also wrote poetry, materialized on different occasions at least two hundred and fifty figures, many of them animals and birds, including a golden eagle which perched on his shoulder. At a séance under Professor Geley's supervision on 20 November 1921 he even conjured up an extinct type of creature, a shaggy ape-man which rubbed against the Professor and emitted the acrid smell of a wild beast; it was well-disposed, however, and licked the hands of the others present. On another occasion, on 10 August 1923, a hairy creature of the same kind overturned a sofa and lifted up several chairs on which ladies were sitting, so that the organizers hastened to stop the proceedings by awakening the medium from his trance.

The exact nature of these materialized beings is a matter of much uncertainty. According to Flournoy they result from a dissociation of the medium's personality, i.e. they are, so to speak, latent or secondary personalities repressed by his normal consciousness;[8] but this seems to do insufficient justice to the audience's co-operation in producing the phenomena, or to the latter's autonomy and physical reality, temporary though it be. We must, in other words, transfer our attention from the individual to the collective psyche, and from the purely psychic to the psycho-physical plane. According to Mackenzie's 'polypsychic' theory, what happens at a séance is the formation of a new mediumistic personality resulting from the fusion of psychic elements and potentially physical ones — all these being contributed unconsciously by the participants through a process of psychophysical dissociation occurring in each of them with the medium as catalyst. The creation of the new personality may be compared to childbirth, an effect enhanced by the medium's travail and suffering during the time that elapses before the apparitions begin. The new entity, as Mackenzie maintains, is of a higher order of strength than any of the participants, in accordance with the biological law whereby collective organisms display supranormal powers compared with individual ones.[9]

Apart from Don Luisito and Guzik (who is mentioned by Professor Mackenzie in the introduction to this book), the most celebrated 'teleplastic' mediums of recent times are Rudi Schneider (whose séances were attended by Jung and Thomas Mann)[10] and Einer Nielsen, who was studied by Gaston de Boni. Powers of this type excited much interest in the nineteenth century, but now appear to be under a cloud in parapsychological circles, owing in part to the discovering of fraud in certain cases. Undoubtedly Trevor Hall was right to bring to light the senile loves of Sir William Crookes and the medium Florence Cook, who blackmailed the old gentleman into covering up her deceit over the séances at which the ghost of Katy King was alleged to have appeared. But the real question is whether she did not in some cases produce genuine materialization, and the same applies to Eusapia Paladino, Guzik and other mediums who have been known to commit fraud but have true achievements to their credit as well. Such an eminent scholar as Charles Richet was taken in by a medium, but others, such as Osty and Geley, have detected fraudulent mediums yet have not given up their faith in mediumistic phenomena. Infrequent though these phenomena may be, they open up vast perspectives, and it is highly probable that in future ages the sceptics' names will be forgotten while honour will be paid to those who pioneered the new science — Myers, Geley, Osty, Richet, Crookes and Crawford, to name only a few.

# CHAPTER 15

---

## Living creatures of the mind

### Living creations of the mind

'Think what you like', said the monk smiling: 'I exist in your imagination, and your imagination is part of nature, so I am part of nature too.' — Chekhov.

### The importance of believing in fairies

In 1920 an article appeared in the Christmas number of the *Strand Magazine* signed by two authors, one of whom was Sir Arthur Conan Doyle, and entitled: 'Photographs of fairies — an event which opens a new era.' This reported that two small girls at Cottingly in Yorkshire claimed to have seen fairies frequently and photographed them on five occasions. The pictures were reproduced, and their authenticity was said to have been confirmed by a photographic expert. The fairies appeared beside the girls as tiny winged beings of the conventional kind, and in one picture there was also a gnome.

One of the girls, Elsie Wright, declared that she had played since early childhood with gnomes and fairies in the meadows and woods around Cottingley, but had soon realized that no one could see them except herself. However, when Frances Griffith arrived from Australia she could see them too, and the girls decided to photograph them. Sir Arthur Conan Doyle and his colleague believed that the fairies really existed, that the girls possessed the faculty of clairvoyance or second sight and that Frances, in addition, had mediumistic powers that enabled her to 'materialize' the fairies so that they could be photographed.[1]

The article aroused lively controversy, and opinions were divided as to whether the girls' testimony could be believed. Books on fairies began to appear, including some by Conan Doyle himself; other writers were Edward L. Gardner, Dr

Geoffrey Hodson and C.W. Leadbeater, a theosophist who developed a theory of *'devas'* or luminous beings with subtle, ethereal bodies, living 'in an atmosphere in which thoughts and feelings are true forces.' Gardner shared this view, as did occultists in other countries, e.g. Rudolf Schwarz in Germany and Anne Osmont in France.[2] Schwarz believed in an extra-sensorial world inhabited by fairies, gnomes, dragons and other legendary creatures, while Anne Osmont was content to postulate 'forces, probably endowed with consciousness, which preside over different manifestations of natural elements'; she warned the reader to be on his guard, since either he would dominate these forces from the outset or they would dominate him.

### A child in the 'Mole Kingdom'

George Foot Moore, the American Orientalist and historian of religion (1851-1931), took the view that phenomena of this kind are mental projections or personifications which characterize man's first steps towards the knowledge of nature; but it is not clear how far this explanation applies to 'collective projections' — the myths, legends and tales which are the dreams of mankind, to borrow Mackenzie's expression. It appears natural that such dreams should occur from time to time in individual minds, participating as they do in the universal 'psychic ocean'. It may be that Eileen Garrett's dream-children belonged to the psychic universe in the same way as the Yorkshire fairies or the 'Mole Kingdom' of Franek Kluski, the Polish medium mentioned in the last chapter. Kluski describes how, as a child, he used to spend hours quietly in a corner, generally lying on his back; then, when evening fell, he would arrange two chairs with a rug over them, under which he would hide. When asked where he was he would inevitably reply 'in the Mole Kingdom'. His parents left it at that, but one evening he invited several children to join him there, including an older girl who looked after his little sister. Crouching together under the rug, they heard mysterious sounds: a vase breaking, the striking of a clock that had been out of order for some time, and the soft footsteps of the Mole, which made its approach wrapped in a bluish cloud. At the same time they were aware of two more children in their midst, a boy and girl whom they all knew

151

and who had died some time ago. They were not frightened, as Franek had told them that dead children often came to life in the 'Mole Kingdom'.[3]

Such was the way in which Franek and his comrades discovered the 'dream dimension', to which thinkers of different types give different names. Jean Cocteau once remarked that 'there is an unknown, invisible world — the real world, no doubt — to which our own in a mere accidental fringe.'[4] Charles Richet, as a scientist, spoke of the 'cryptocosm', and occultists refer to an 'astral world . . . that reflects all the beings, objects, actions and thoughts of our own,' as Hutin puts it, adding that some have the power to make these reflections visible and tangible, for a short period, in everyday life.[5] Others, such as J. Evola, use the Sanskrit word *akasha* to denote a 'mysterious omnipresent substance or energy, immaterial and psychic rather than material and physical, which may be thought of as a light pervading all regions and endowing them with virtues and mysterious properties'. In more ordinary language we may recall William James's 'cosmic continuum' or what others have called the psychic universe or *psi* plane. It may be doubted, however, whether these attempts at scientific phraseology tell us anything more than a simple imaginative term such as the 'Mole Kingdom'.

*Where dreams come alive*

The English parapsychologist G.W. Lambert observes that all 'sensitives' possess two distinct fields of vision, the ordinary one and the hallucinatory or spectral field, in which subjects obey the laws of dreams.[6] He recalls that Swedenborg was able to walk about for hours without getting lost, while concentrating on his own interior vision. In the cases we are speaking of, the 'spectral field' includes psychic phenomena which are the creation of one or several unconscious minds, such as the Yorkshire fairies, the 'Mole' of Kluski's childhood or the ape-man which he called into existence when grown up. This account of the matter may disappoint those who, like Air Marshal Dowding, believe in the real existence of fairies,[7] but they may console themselves with the thought that psychic creations have a reality of their own.

As we saw in Chapter 3, material objects may serve as a clue or stimulus with which to evoke the past, and it is noteworthy that they can also enable a clairvoyant to enter into someone else's dream-world. This is illustrated by the case of a small girl who suffered from typhoid fever and, in that state, dreamt of a highly elaborate doll's house with a marble staircase, cars in front of the door, a massive gold birdcage on the first floor and so on. As was the custom in those days, the girl's hair was entirely cut off as a health measure, but a lock of it was kept and came into the hands of Dr Pagenstecher, who handed it one day to a medium we have already mentioned, María Reyes de Z. The medium, who was already in a state of trance, 'saw' the little girl's head and proceeded to give an exact description of the doll's house. After the experiment she realized that it was her own daughter Leonora, who had been promised a doll's house during her illness.

María Reyes, among her other powers, was able to perceive images in the mind of Dr Pagenstecher, who was also her medical adviser. 'I can see in his mind the luminous figures of people he is thinking about at that moment or has been thinking about intensively, as though he had a sort of portrait gallery in his head.' This recalls, with some difference, the inter-mental contacts of Chapter 6. Another example is that of a novelist who, in a foreign country, handed his watch to a clairvoyant who thereupon described, not the watch's owner, but a character in one of his books, with whom — so Professor Tenhaeff informs us — the author had 'identified' to a great extent.[8] Mental images of this kind, or *clichés mentaux* as Osty calls them, are frequently responsible for errors on the part of clairvoyants. It may be said that we all carry our own dreams about with us, and sometimes the dream may outlive the dreamer. Professor Tenhaeff relates another story: a clairvoyante, Mrs. M., informed a certain Mrs. S. that she 'saw' her in the company of a senior naval officer in an old-fashioned uniform. In actual fact, the Professor explains, Mrs. S. believed herself to be the descendant of a Dutch naval hero of former times, and was very proud of this, but her belief was without foundation.

## Unwanted company

It is clear from instances such as these that dreams and other constructions of the mind are not purely subjective, but have a reality of their own which can impress itself on out-siders. This may also be true of deep-seated mental feelings and dispositions, which manifest themselves to clairvoyants in sensorial form. Violet Tweedale relates that at a fancy dress ball she was dancing with a rich and handsome debauchee named Prince Valori, when she saw beside him a curious lean figure with pointed ears that looked like a satyr: it was not, however, a guest in fancy dress. When she mentioned it to her partner he turned pale and replied: 'If you see it too you must be clairvoyant: luckily very few people can. I have tried to get rid of it, but I can't.' Violet Tweedale also mentions a general who had a ghostly companion of the same kind, but was more nonchalant than the prince and even made jokes about it.

One of the archetypes of human dreams and imagination throughout the ages is that of the devil, corresponding to the dark side of our nature. Modern thought accepts this in terms of psychiatry and psychoanalysis but is apt to rebel at the idea that demons, *qua* projections of the mind, can assume a material shape in the same way as Kluski's Mole and ape-man. We can conceive that mental events may be the effect of physical ones, but not the other way round. In the Orient things are different: for instance, in Tibet it is believed that by concentrated thought one can call into existence a kind of spirit known as a *tulpa*, with a life of its own. This is attested by Amaury de Riencourt and Alexandra David-Neel, who relates that one day she was visited by a Tibetan artist who specialized in depicting wrathful deities, and to her sur-prise saw behind him a nebulous shape resembling one of these beings. Stretching out her arm towards it, she felt the touch of a soft object; then it vanished. The painter himself had not been aware of it, but said that he had indeed been concentrating on that deity during the past few weeks for a purpose of his own, and had been working on a painting of it all morning.

Inspired by this and other examples, Alexandra David-Neel resolved to attempt to create a *tulpa* herself in the shape of a monk, not resembling the gaunt lamaistic pictures she saw about her, but short, fat and jovial. After months of concen-tration she succeeded: the phantom assumed a solid, lifelike form and lived as a guest, first in her apartment and then on a tour which she undertook, with servants and tents. The phantom behaved like an ordinary traveller, performing various day-to-day actions that she had not consciously commanded. After a time his independent existence began to get on her nerves and she resolved to get rid of him, but it was easier said than done: he had partly escaped from her control, and his face took on a 'vaguely mocking, sly, malignant look'. She adds that 'Once a herdsman who brought me a present of butter saw the *tulpa* in my tent and took it for a live lama.' Finally, after six months of hard struggle, she managed to deprive the phantom of existence.

On Tyrrell's view phenomena of this kind may be put down to collective hallucination; but all the evidence seems to show, if nothing else, that we cannot tell where to draw the line between mental and material things, between hallucinations and projections on the one hand and plastic, objective manifestations on the other. It may be, for instance, that the secret self possesses the power to confer life of a certain kind on the figures of a dream-world, and that any idea or image that is cultivated for long enough by an individual or still more a collective psyche tends to become autonomous and interfere with the physical world, as do the phantoms of mediumistic dreams.

Examples of this may be found in the realm of artistic creation, though not many authors are so unfortunate as to have their characters get completely out of hand, in life as well as on the printed page. However, the Finnish novelist Mika Waltari (born 1908), author of *Sinuhe the Egyptian,* was persecuted over a considerable period by his own female character, Neferne-Fernefer. There may be some objective truth behind Pirandello's *Six Characters in Search of an Author*. At all events, we read that Balzac used to talk and argue with his own characters, and similar stories are told of Dickens and Harriet Beecher-Stowe.

All activities which involve, to use Brunori's terminology, a partial depression of the cortical area of the brain and temporary hyperactivity of the diencephalon or 'middle brain' — e.g. self-hypnosis, profound meditation or a partial state of trance — are conducive to hallucinations with an element of objectivity, i.e. something that can be physically recorded, measured or verified. From this point of view magical and mediumistic phenomena are essentially alike,[9] and so is the collective psyche which comes into being when, for example, a number of people are gathered around the death-bed of a loved individual. There is a vast literature of death-bed apparitions, many of which probably reflected states of mind of the dying person. [10] A large number of cases have been investigated by Karlis Osis of the Research Department of the Parapsychology Foundation.[11]

## The photography of thoughts

A special type of phantom is that which can be created by a clairvoyant projecting visions of the future into a mirror or crystal ball. (Frederica Hauffe of Prevorst also used to perceive images in soap-bubbles). Father Trilles, when a missionary among the pigmies, once told the local witch-doctor that he had been robbed. The man took up a mirror and told him to look in it, and to his great surprise he saw the face of a man whom he had suspected of the theft. The question arises whether an image of this kind is purely hal-lucinatory or has some physical reality. Nandor Fodor, in his *Encyclopedia of Psychical Science,* opts for the second hypothesis. He points out that in some cases the image in the crystal appeared larger when seen through a magnifying glass;[12] in others it was reflected in a mirror, and in others again it was seen by several people at once; more-over, it could be photographed. This last point seems to us a decisive one: do we possess photographs of ghosts, or of thought-creations in general?

There has been fierce controversy over this, with extremes of credulity and scepticism. Sceptics refused to believe in the Yorkshire fairies, [13] and thirty years ago Professor T. Fukarai lost his chair at the University of Tokyo for defying an academic veto by publishing a book entitled *Clairvoyance and Photography* (London, 1931). In this he reported a long series of 'psycho-photographic' tests carried out by himself with the aid of teleplastic mediums who, by concentration, had transferred images from their own minds on to photographic plates. Some of these were merely letters of the alphabet, while others were complex entities belonging to the 'spectral field', as Lambert calls it. One of Fukarai's most remarkable experiments was carried out as a result of the appearance of a ghost at a place called Funagata. This was seen by a clairvoyant named Mita, who said it resembled a holy man in prayer. Enquiry showed that a sage named Kohboh Daishi had in fact stayed there in bygone times to carry out the 'hundred days' prayer'. Fukarai thereupon organized a large gathering at Funagata and commanded Mita to concentrate on the figure of Kohboh Daishi, while blank photographic plates were confided under seal to the chairman of the assembly (whose proceedings were inaugurated with prayer). When the plates were developed, they proved to bear the representation of Kohboh Daishi as Mita had 'seen' him and as he had been in life.

A somewhat similar incident was reported from the Lebanon in May 1950, when the superior-general of a Maronite order was shown a photograph taken some days earlier by a seminarist who had been with some companions to visit an ancient monastery. This showed, alongside the other figures, an aged monk kneeling in prayer, whom none of the young men remembered having seen but who was identified as Sharbel Makluf, who had died in the odour of sanctity in about 1900.[14]

Prayer is itself an important form of concentration, and it is not surprising that it should play a major part in the psychic universe. As Eileen Garrett observes, 'Thought is an active force produced by the human psyche and able to influence other minds, like a flash of light traversing space' — and, she might have added, passing through time, like the light of a star which conveys a never-ending message even though its original source has ceased to be.

Photographs can of course be faked, as was shown in the early days of spiritualism, but there is something obsessive in the attempt to explain away the whole body of evidence on this basis. This evidence includes results obtained by Lindsay Johnson, a medium and photographer, who, Devaux tells us, worked with 'the utmost experimental rigour', and by W. Hope, who convinced even Harry Price. (As already stated, photographs of the dead do not prove human survival: they only prove that a mediumistic faculty has been in operation). In the case of Sharbel Makluf, the negative was examined by experts who declared that it had not been tampered with. Other paranormal photographs were scrutinized at Paris by a committee of experts under M. Lemoine, two of whom — MM. Cressac and Chevalier — wrote that 'After eliminating cases where the alleged "ghost" results from some

157

accidental effect interpreted under the influence of emotion, it must still be recognized that mysterious phenomena exist and require to be explained.'

Psycho-photography is undoubtedly a rare phenomenon, as are photographic mediums, but we should be wary of denying their existence. An important series of experiments was recently carried out with the medium Ted Serios, by Mrs Pauline Oehler and then by the psychologist Dr Jule Eisenbud of Denver, Colorado, in the presence of academic researchers, photographic experts and illusionists, so as to exclude any possibility of fraud. Serios for his part is aware that the results are not produced by his conscious mind: often he is unable to recognize the human figures, landscapes, and buildings that appear in more or less distorted shape when the Polaroid negatives are developed. Most of them, no doubt, are latent memories that emerge into consciousness with the deformation usual in dreams. In some cases they represent places unknown to Serios but known to the experimenter, signifying that the former reproduces them by a process of clairvoyance. Dr. Eisenbud has assembled the results of his experiments in a remarkable book, *The World of Ted Serios* (New York, 1967), which speaks for itself despite the author's frequent warnings and reservations.

# PART V

Magical relations with the outside world

# CHAPTER 16

## Conscious objects

### Conscious objects

The novelist and critic Luigi Capuana (1839-1915), who was keenly interested in spiritualism, had a curious adventure in a Roman art museum (the *Galleria dell'Accademia di San Luca*). He was looking closely at a painting when he suddenly felt obliged to look in another direction, and met the gaze of two passionate eyes. They were not, however, those of a human being of flesh and blood, but belonged to an 'Unknown Lady' in a portrait by Van Dyck. He tried to ignore the lady's appeal, but felt as if she was following him wherever he went. Late that night he returned home, and had hardly closed the front door when he felt a warm breath on his face and realized that the ghostly presence was still with him. He ran upstairs and into his bedroom, where he found the mysterious lady awaiting him with all the ardour of someone who has had to be patient for two hundred and fifty years. This curious and frustrating state of affairs continued for several days.

Capuana's predicament may be ascribed in part to his spiritualistic beliefs and in part to retrospective clairvoyance. In any case, pictures and other objects do seem at times to possess a mysterious psychic quality enabling them to symbolize particular situations. They seem almost to deserve the name of 'living objects', but this is of course only a metaphor. Everyone has heard of pictures that fall off the wall in sympathy with some fatal event, and some stories of this kind are well founded. For instance, when General Sir Henry Havelock-Allan was killed in action on the North-West Frontier in 1897 his portrait, hanging thousands of miles away in the mess of the second battalion of the Northumberland Fusiliers, crashed to the ground for no apparent reason.[1] M. Flammarion tells a similar story of an officer whose portrait

161

fell to the floor before his wife's eyes; she believed him to be out of the firing line, but three weeks later a delayed message came to say that he had been transferred to the front and had been killed at that precise moment.

Professor Albert von Schrenck-Notzing (1862-1929), a specialist in parapsychology, died in hospital after an appendicitis operation, and at that time all the clocks stopped in his house. His wife, on her way to visit him, noticed that a large clock in the hall had stopped; she then saw that her watch had done likewise, and so had a clock in the study. She rushed to the hospital and found, as she had feared, that he was dead. It also turned out that a watch in his waistcoat pocket had stopped at the identical time.

Bells have been known to ring, and pianos to play of their own accord, as a signal of untoward events, and a symbolic part has also been played by flags. When the Earl of Ypres (Lord French, commander of British forces in the first world war) died in 1925 in his home at Deal Castle in Kent, the large banner of the castle was seen to flap wildly, then collapse and fall to the bottom of the staff; at the same moment an American flag in the great hall of the castle fell to the ground, breaking an iron ring which had held it in place.[2]

### "Nothing happens by chance"

Some people may write off such events as pure coincidence, but it is a lazy explanation and would not have appealed to Laplace, the mathematician and determinist who taught Napoleon. Charges of superstition, neurosis or Freudian 'regression' are sometimes levelled against those who bring forward evidence of apparently sentient objects; but these, as Professor Hagenbuckner has pointed out,[3] are often merely an excuse to save their authors the trouble of rational investigation. Official science takes the view that a physical cause must be assigned to every physical event, but there are scholars who call this in question: Jung and Pauli, with their theory of 'synchronicity', suggest that the principle of causality is of relative and not absolute value and is part of a more general law whereby all occurrences that coincide in time, be they objective or subjective, are linked together by something more than pure chance, a kind of interdependence.[4] This may seem a revolutionary idea, but it is rooted in ancient

162

Chinese thought, in the philosophy of the Stoics and the theory of magic and alchemy, codified in the document known as the Emerald Table.

Jung observes that if we throw down a handful of matches the resulting arrangement cannot be accidental, but is determined by the subjective and objective circumstances. For many centuries the Chinese used a similar method of divination in connection with the *I Ching* (Book of Changes).[5] The ancient Greeks attached a providential significance to any chance remark heard by a person in grave distress, and the Romans believed that the flight of birds must have some relation to the questions or hopes confided to the augurs. We may dismiss these ideas as superstitious if we will, but we cannot say the same of the intuition which declares that there is no such thing as chance and that beside the laws observed by science there are other laws of which we still know nothing. Examples of the operation of these mysterious laws may indeed by found in microphysics. Two gamma photons produced by the collision of an electron with a a positron ought, by the rules of physical science, to be completely independent entities, but we find that a physical event undergone by one has inexplicable effects on the other.

## Rebellious objects

The behaviour of 'sentient' objects such as those which announce a death may be conditioned by the psyche of the dying person or that of the receiver of the news, or by the two jointly as we have supposed in the case of ghosts. This applies also to unruly manifestations such as the following, reported in 1935 by Eugène Osty in the *Revue métapsychique*. Paul Monet, a retired officer of the French colonial army, found himself unable to sleep for the curious reason that his bed kept shaking about. He discovered later that a former subordinate of his, Jean Kutska, who had a violent grudge against him, had been in delirium at the time owing to an attack of fever and had been uttering curses against him — no doubt he did the same when he was well, but delirium is a kind of dream-state and may have superior magical powers. (By 'magical' we mean simply 'obedient to laws that science cannot yet explain, and that may be extraneous to the physical universe').

163

In November 1943 the gendarmerie of the French department of Deux-Sèvres recorded the case of a girl named A.G. who could not sit on a certain chair, because whenever she tried to do so it rose in the air and shook her off.[6] H. Durville relates that a boy of fourteen named Raymond Charrier had difficulty in putting on his shoes because they used to slip from his hand and disappear.[7] Durville kept him under observation for some days, and found he had various mediumistic properties.

Father Thurston records that a Mother Superior named Costante Maria da Fabriano had a prayer-book which used to escape from her grasp and float about in the air, to the consternation of the nuns assembled in choir.

In the case of young people such as A.G. and Raymond Charrier there may be an association between the mischievous behaviour of chairs and shoes and the rebellious attitude of early youth. At all events, a large number of such extraordinary occurrences do involve children or teenagers. In August 1956 a series of strange events were reported from Rigaud di Ramat, a mountain village near Chiomonte in the province of Turin. Georges Bellone, a thin, quiet boy of eleven, had come from Marseilles, where he lived with his father and mother, to stay with the latter's parents, Augusto and Cristina Sibille. On the night of the 18th he was heard thrashing about in bed as though he had a nightmare; at the same time his blankets started to float in the air, and the same thing then happened to the crockery and cutlery and the remains of the old people's dinner. Bits of straw came out of the mattresses and swirled around together with scraps of food. Most extraordinary of all, a certain lamp refused to remain alight: every time it was lit, it went out immediately as though blown out, and finally it rose into the air and shot out of doors.

Friends and neighbours were summoned in haste; one was attacked by a fork which planted itself in the seat of his trousers, but the tough mountaineers did not lose their heads or raise the cry of witchcraft. Instead, realizing with remarkable discernment that Georges's nightmare must have something to do with the disturbances, they hauled him out of bed and stuck his head into a water-trough. The nightmare left him, and the domestic objects returned to their obedience.

We are now in the realm of the poltergeist — named from

164

the German word for a noisy, mischievous spirit — and, following Fodor,[8] students generally ascribe such phenomena to latent conflicts in the personality of the mediumistic subject, who, as already remarked, is often close to the age of puberty. In other cases, as Dr Assailly[9] suggests, it seems that a polypsychic element may be involved.

An incident of this type happened in 1958 at Omignano (Salerno province) to two sisters aged twelve and ten, Alida and Santina De Matteo. According to the evidence of their parents, doctor and teacher, every now and then a rain of stones of various sizes and unknown origin took place in their presence. One fell on the head of the local chief of *carabinieri,* but in general they did no harm to anyone. The phenomenon was most noticeable when the girls were asleep in bed and became restless: the stones would then hurtle about in the air as though in sympathy with the children's inner life. The matter was fully investigated by a member of the Italian Association for Parapsychology, and the results published in its Bulletin.

In 1956, at Scerne in the Abruzzi, the authorities were alarmed by an epidemic of burning mattresses. A thin dark girl of twelve with piercing black eyes was present on each occasion, but — luckily for her — never alone: she explained that every time she went near a bed, she saw fire in front of her eyes. Another series of apparently spontaneous fires took place at Aspio (Ancona province) in 1959. In 1961, in the house of Guglielmo Locatelli at Brembate (Bergamo), brooms, mattresses and flower-vases started to move about of their own accord; drawers opened and shut, and stones occasionally came gliding in and landed gently on particular objects. All this occurred in broad daylight, and often before several witnesses. Attempts at exorcism were in vain, but the happenings ceased after a young girl who used to help with the housework gave up her job in terror at the strange events. She too was around the age of puberty; but there are also cases in which the mediumistic faculty comes to life in adults, especially as a result of illness or emotional strain, and is associated with phenomena of the poltergeist type.

In February 1955 Teresa Costa, a young woman of Calabria whose husband had migrated to France, moved with her two children to join him at Saint-Jean-de-Maurienne (Haute-Savoie). Perhaps because of the change of atmosphere, she began to feel ill and to have fainting-fits, and on these occasions strange events happened: towels and napkins flew through the air, and there was a noise as though people were knocking on the walls. The village folk took her for a witch, and to escape their hostilities she moved to nearby Saint-Julien-de-Maurienne; but the ghostly events repeated themselves there, and so did the persecution. The *curé* and the village doctor took an interest, and journalists appeared in large numbers. The cure himself saw a coffee-pot fly through the air and execute strange manoeuvres before spilling its contents. An English newspaper man, Freddy Russell, was hit on the head by a saucepan. Finally Teresa was moved to hospital, where she was found to be suffering from an identifiable disease as well as the gift of mediumship, and the manifestations ceased.

Such is the frenzy of scepticism that Jean-Louis Chardans, a journalist who wrote a book on various kinds of fraud in connection with the supernatural, suggested that Teresa had cleverly fabricated these events in order to excite pity and obtain financial aid. Yet phenomena of this kind are among the commonest of paranormal occurrences throughout the world.[10] From London comes the report of a spirit that used to barricade itself inside the bedroom of a Mr and Mrs Howells, who were obliged to call in the police to get rid of it. In October-November 1952 a series of visitations took place at the home of the mayor of Neudorf (Bruchsal, Baden-Württemberg) and were investigated by Professor Hans Bender of the Freiburg Institute of Parapsychology. The mayor, Notheis by name, recorded 116 unauthorized movements of objects in the space of thirty-two days, not to mention a rain of nails that took place in an upper room in the presence of five people: the nails came from a cupboard on the ground floor, where they were kept locked up, and the shower descended no less than sixteen times in forty-five minutes. All this used to happen when the mayor's young son Bernhard was at home, and especially when he was asleep in bed.

Adolescence, of course, is an arduous period of transition towards a new psychosomatic equilibrium, and is often accompanied by turmoil and open or repressed aggression. Retarded physical development likewise involves disequilibrium and may, for similar reasons, be conducive to mediumship. A

166

pertinent example comes from the Greek island of Thasos, where the house of a Mr Yannakis was plagued by falling stones and the violent displacement and breakage of crockery. The police could find no cause for this, and Yannakis was taken to court for spreading false and alarmist rumours. However, he appealed to the president of the Greek Society for Psychical Research, General Tanagras of the army medical corps, who arranged an experiment in the presence of the local magistrate and police and a journalist: this showed (after a wait of some hours) that the household objects did move about of their own accord in the presence of a feeble-minded maid.

A major in the French gendarmerie, Emile Tizané, has spent twenty five years collating evidence from police and court archives of what he calls 'the unknown presence in the causeless crime.'[11] He emphasizes that the evidence stands without contradiction in the official record, that it was drawn up immediately after the events and that the witnesses were mostly disbelievers in the supernatural. This, however, has not sufficed to protect Tizané from an attitude of scepticism and mockery, even on the part of some professional students of paranormal events.

In 1958 Drs. J.G. Pratt and W.G. Roll, who both formerly contributed to Professor Rhine's studies, were able to investigate a series of poltergeist occurrences at the home of a Mr Hermann at Seaford, Long Island, who had a twelve-year-old son called Jimmy. Pieces of furniture and ornaments moved of their own accord, bottles uncorked themselves and spilt their contents, and so on. Observations were also carried on by a police officer named Tozzi, an electrical engineer, a building expert and others. They were all agreed that the phenomena were not due to normal causes, yet Pratt and Roll finally abstained from drawing a definite conclusion.[12] Many students of paranormal events play for safety in this way, like Robert Amadou, who writes: 'It would be rash to assert that there are no genuine paranormal physical phenomena, but we must accept that their existence has not as yet been proved.' So much for Tizané's official records![13]

One way in which the sceptic professional, or the professional sceptic, defends his integrity as a scientist and protects himself against sniping from his colleagues is to insist on tests being carried out under laboratory conditions; but in the kind of case we are dealing with, this requirement is

167

probably illusory. We must choose, in effect between the defeatism of M. Amadou and the empiricism of Major Tizané, who does not set up to be a scientist but has made a factual compilation of the utmost value.

### A doubtful vocation

In the library of the Girolamini monastery at Naples there is an eighteenth-century manuscript describing the strange events which happened when 'Don Carlo Ulcano, knight of the city of Sorrento and nobleman of the city of Naples' sought admission as a novice. The corridors were filled at night with a deafening din; stones rained from the ceiling of cells and of the chapel during Mass; friars' habits were mischievously sewn together, and dignitaries felt tugs at their vestments. All this was regarded as a machination of the Devil, bent on frustrating Don Carlo's vocation; but as prayer and exorcism proved fruitless, the monks reluctantly decided to send him away with all the honour due to his rank. As soon as they did so, the manifestations ceased.

Monsignor Antonio Bellucci, an archaeologist and the present librarian of the monastery, believes that the pranks were deliberately organized by Don Carlo himself; but is seems at least possible that he was a telekinetic medium like the others described in this chapter. Perhaps his vocation was not a true one and his inner doubts and conflicts found expression in this way, which would be consistent with Fodor's theory. But we may add to this the possible operation of a collective psyche. As Sir William Mackenzie suggests, mediums may act as catalysts of the psychic energies of a whole group of people; and we may imagine Carlo acting, unknown to himself, as an 'accumulator' of all the grudges and discontents that must have existed in the monastic community as in any other. From this point of view the medium is indeed possessed by a super-entity with something devilish about it, which enjoys a transient yet fairly stable existence as the emanation of many subconscious minds, but if far from being identical with the Devil himself.

The works by Fathers J.H. Crehan, Herbert Thurston, A. Gatterer and R. Santilli make it clear enough that many cases of 'diabolical' possession can be interpreted in this relatively naturalistic light. Fr. Santilli, for instance, states that: 'No one on the Catholic side of the argument today has any difficulty in admitting that mediumship has nothing supernatural about it, and that the psychic and psycho-sensorial phenomena in question are due to the subject finding himself in a dynamic state of an unusual kind. This does not mean that, as faith and theology tell us, there may not also be some intervention on the part of superhuman beings. This is a matter to be examined in each separate instance without regard to sentiment, superstition or religious ignorance, which often sees diabolic possession or interference in cases that are due to the operation of natural forces, as yet undiscovered or known only to scientists.'

## The stones of Sienna

So far, the 'rebellious objects' we have considered were an expression of individual or group anxiety or psychological disturbance; but there are cases which do not appear to be due to a subjective cause of this kind, like the mysterious rain of stones thirty years ago at Sienna, in a traditionally 'haunted' spot near the Botanical Gardens. According to the story confirmed to me by eye-witnesses and by those directly involved, over a period of years small boys who ventured into the area by night (and who are now respectable citizens) were regularly greeted by volleys of stones, and no one was ever able to find that these had been thrown by human beings. The boys organized regular patrols to find their assailants, but the attack always came from a different quarter, as though the stones had human intelligence. Outside the area they fell more gently, or made their way into people's pockets. Once they rained exclusively on the head of a single youth, who was wearing a military helmet.

In cases like this the haunting seems to be a function of the place itself rather than of anybody's subconscious, although it probably cannot take place unless there is a medium at hand. This brings us back to the notion of the 'psychic residuum' and of special localities which enable, or oblige, the medium to apprehend past events. As we saw in Chapter 12, some mediums (whether or not they are aware of being such) can identify with the mysterious records or traces of the past and thus re-live old passions and conflicts. May not some cases of haunting and physical disturbances be symbolic expressions of long-forgotten agitations of the mind? This is of course mere speculation, but it may be mentioned that the 'ghost' of the Sienna Botanical Gardens is reputed to be a monk who commited suicide in a nearby house.

## Invisible persecutors

Yet there are other cases of haunting which still defy classification. In 1954, at Maiano in the Udine province, the bicycles and motor-scooters in Arturo Riva's garage began, one by one, to rise into the air or go for a short run and return to their proper places. Tools would disappear and turn up in unlikely spots, cans would overturn and spill oil round about, and so on. All this happened in daylight and before many witnesses. It aroused much interest in the press throughout Italy, and also among scientific investigators. Riva endured the confusion for two and a half months; he got rid of an assistant who he thought might be an unconscious medium, but as that did not work he left the neighbourhood.

The new tenants wished to use the shed to keep vegetables in, but (as Dr A Ronchi relates in the Bulletin of the Italian Society for Parapsychology), 'a load of potatoes they had left there suddenly flew all over the place, hitting the walls and ceiling.' Whatever the explanation of these amply attested events, they appear to show that the occult forces have a taste for persecution. This is not always fully brought out in press accounts, as reporters prefer to stress the bizarre or comic aspects. I may, however, quote the case of a peasant family at Catena di Villorba (Treviso province) who, in January 1963, were forced by turbulent 'spirits' to leave a comfortable farm where they had lived in peace for years. For three months they had put up with an extraordinary series of violent events: volleys of stones, broken lamps and windows, blows of the hand or fist delivered in broad daylight and leaving visible marks. These facts were confirmed to me by the people themselves and by witnesses. When they decided they could stand it no longer, the family of five moved to a single room in the house of some friends, where they lived in discomfort but unmolested. When I heard the story they were still there, and their own home was empty and abandoned.

Still grimmer cases of persecution by poltergeists are described by Hereward Carrington and Father Thurston, but we may leave the unpleasant subject at this point. If the entities responsible are in fact more or less autonomous creations of the human psyche, individual or collective, it must be admitted that they behave at times with extraordinary and apparently motiveless malignancy. We may judge from this how much remains to be discovered about psychic phenomena, and how much prudence is called for in our approach to hypotheses concerning them, however plausible.

# CHAPTER 17

The pranks of spiritualism

*Mediumistic games*

As we have seen, inanimate objects may associate themselves with the subconscious mind in such a way as to express in symbolic form the latter's rebellious, mischievous or self-persecuting tendencies. We now turn our attention to objects which fulfil, as it were, the role of playmates and help to satisfy the universal taste for small surprises of an intriguing nature. These are common enough in mediumistic sessions, such as those held at Brussels in 1920 in the home of Monsieur H. Poutet, an insurance agent. The sessions were witnessed by Professor William Mackenzie and were organized by a lawyer named A.T., who was himself the medium: he did not go into a complete trance, but appeared at times to be in a state of reverie. M. Poutet was gifted with a preternatural faculty of rapid calculation, which was doubled, as will be seen, with the powers of 'Stasie', this being the name of the spirit-personage evoked at the sessions. All that was known of Stasie's identity was that she was not, according to her own statement, the soul of a departed human being.

The experiments took place with the aid of a table used for rapping, some packs of cards and a small roulette wheel. On one occasion a cat which happened to be in the room was used to indicate replies by strokes with its paw. In one of the games, a certain Madame S. was invited by Stasie to choose a card and hide it. Instead of saying at once which card it was, Stasie caused the medium to write down a number of fifteen digits and requested that it should be multiplied by another number composed of the numerical values of the first and last letters of a word at the top of p. 350 of a book lying on the table and previously selected for a different purpose. The letters were the twelfth and fifth of the alphabet, so that the multiplier was 125. When the product was obtained by M.

Poutet it was 'translated' back into letters and spelt the phrase 'knave of clubs', which was the card Mne. S. had chosen. It will thus be seen that Stasie, in addition to knowing the right card in the first place, had (1) translated its name into a number of some seventeen digits; (2) factorized the number into 125 and a number of fifteen digits which she dictated to the medium; and (3) located, in a closed book, the letters corresponding to 12 and 5.

Stasie, who 'appeared' regularly at M. Poutet's sessions over a period of years, executed hundreds of *tôurs de force* of this kind. It is significant, however, that although she had previously displayed her powers in other directions through the mediumship of A.T., she did not show off her mathematical abilities until M. Poutet, himself a lightning calculator, joined the circle. Her other feats were in the realm of precognition, telekinesis (moving objects at a distance), thought-reading and influencing people's actions without their knowledge. One night she invited those present to shuffle and cut a pack of cards repeatedly for the space of an hour and a half, and made the knave of clubs come up every time. Performances such as these may seem trivial and even wasteful of extraordinary powers, but, as Professor Mackenzie remarks, there is more to it than that: 'Stasie never talked philosophy, but by means of four simple psychophysical operations she confronted the observer with some of the most enigmatic aspects of reality, as if challenging him to find out the deep significance of the most commonplace events.'

Who or what was Stasie? Mackenzie emphasizes that, while speaking as though she was a real person, he does not mean thereby to express any judgement as to her 'substance', and he uses for greater precision such terms as 'entity' and 'existence', But one can hardly dispute the real, independent existence on some plane of reality — of a being with what he calls a 'live, autonomous psyche' and a character essentially different from that of the participants in the séance, though possibly borrowing traits from some of them; a character, moreover, which appeared to preserve its identity for several years.

Thus we are brought back from mathematical parlour-games to the enigmatic fact that the human psyche is apparently capable of creating not only ideas but independent psychic entities with a certain power of duration, whose life may

173

perhaps be compared with that of parasitic plants.[1]

## Table-turning

In the nineteenth century a prominent place in spiritualistic literature was occupied by the behaviour of tables which rise in the air or spun about or delivered more or less foggy answers to anxious enquirers. Elizabeth d'Espérance was one of the mediums who had most to do with these manifestations, and she described how a strong man exerted all his efforts, but unsuccessfully, to prevent a small table moving about; on another occasion, the table danced to the tune of the Star-Spangled Banner but resolutely ignored God Save the Queen. Other mediums who appeared to cause tables, chairs, lamps etc. to dance about were Daniel Home, Stanislawa Tomczyk, Eusapia Paladino, Miss Goligher and Rudi Schneider. Since the early part of this century phenomena of this kind have given place to others, though they have not entirely ceased to occur. Mackenzie records that: 'At Warsaw,[2] in a red light that was quite strong enough for me to distinguish people and objects, I saw a heavy laboratory table rise almost to the ceiling and then break with a crash into several pieces; two of those present were hurt by the falling fragments. Infrared photography showed no sign of the fluidic or ectoplasmic arms that one reads of so often in mediumistic literature . . . But the table must have been lifted up by *something*.'

What in fact does move objects in this way; and, if it is the human psyche, how does it produce physical effects?[3] To put the question thus implies a dichotomy which would be removed if we suppose, with Teilhard de Chardin, that 'every microphysical unit must be endowed with an infinitely small or infinitely diffused psychic element.' Whately Carington takes a similar view as to the explanation of telekinetic phenomena, which many besides Mackenzie have described: for example Myers, de Rochas, Aksakoff, Ochorowicz, Flammarion, Crawford, Lombroso, Morselli, Bergson and the Curies (Pierre and Marie). Upton Sinclair records an occasion on which Einstein caused a table to rise in the air in the absence of a medium.[4] Even more interesting than such events is the phenomena known as 'apport', i.e. the sudden appearance of an object from far away. This is analogous to a rain of stones, nails etc., but with the difference that the object

174

appears instantaneously. Plants and flowers were evoked in this way by Elizabeth d'Espérance under the control of 'Yolande', who figured in several of her séances. Stanislawa Tomczyk, a medium studied by Professor Ochorowicz, produced similar results in the form of a wooden ashtray which appeared from upstairs just as the professor was lighting a cigarette, or his hat which was suddenly on his head instead of on a peg in the next room. Ochorowicz, it may be added, was not aiming at manifestations of this kind but was himself more interested in telekinesis.[5]

Such phenomena seem to have become rarer and, for whatever reason, are treated nowadays with indifference or hostility. One aspect on which scepticism fastens is that of fraudulent mediums, which is a less simple topic than it appears. As Servadio remarks, there may be frequent interference, at one and the same séance, between authentic phenomena and others involving automatic imitation. The medium, it must be remembered, is in a state of trance akin to dreaming, so that the conscious mind is more or less inactive. Dreams, on the other hand, tend towards wish-fulfilment: with ordinary people this remains in the mind, but in the case of mediums or some somnambulists the fulfillment may take place in the objective world. A medium may, and occasionally does, commit unconscious fraud at the automatic, somnambulistic level. At the same time, many celebrated mediums have also been guilty of conscious fraud for reasons of prestige: one may mention Daniel Home, Eusapia Paladino, Mrs Duncan, Linda Gazzero, Erto and Florence Cook.

During the last century an interest in mediumistic phenomena went hand in hand with an interest in illusionism, and celebrated magicians such as Robert Houdin, Cazeneuve and John Henry Anderson (or, more recently, Houdini, Julius Zancig, Robert Heller and Harry Kellar) endeavoured to the utmost of their powers to devise methods of counterfeiting spiritualistic and paranormal results. Some magicians actually palmed themselves off as mediums: e.g. Ira and William Davenport of Buffalo, N.Y., who were unmasked several times but made a fortune out of their deception. Instances like these encouraged those who perferred to believe that mediumship was nothing but a fake; yet anyone acquainted with true manifestations in this field as well as illusory ones has no trouble in distinguishing between the two. There is, after all, an essential difference between the mediumistic state, in which consciousness is reduced to a minimum, and the alertness of a conjurer whose art depends on split-second timing and the skilful diversion of his audience's attention.

To show that psychokinetic effects, though they may have become rarer, are certainly not extinct, I will describe a session which I attended in October 1963 in a handsome villa outside Treviso, through the courtesy of Dr Cino Boccazzi and in the company of several friends of his. (I can furnish to any reader who is interested details of other séances organized by this group). At 11.30 p.m. six of us were sitting in the dark around a massive table on which a display of 'rapping' had taken place: it had been as trivial as such performances often are, and I confessed to the company that I felt tired and bored. My words seemed to act as a signal. The table suddenly rose so that one of its legs grazed my head; one of the women screamed, and my chair, with myself on it, glided backwards four or five feet. The master of ceremonies turned on the light and we saw the table resuming its position; the hair of the lady who screamed was, to all appearances, being pulled back by an invisible force. We broke up the session at once.

Two hours later the medium and I were driving back to Treviso in our host's car, and I was brooding rather resentfully on the character of the spirit-presence, which had chosen to assume the name of Giuseppe Verdi. Suddenly I saw a small white object dancing in the glare of the headlights, and a moment later a pebble weighing an ounce and a half came hurtling through the windscreen (but without breaking it) and hit me painfully in the forehead.

The medium, I may add, was a quiet, well-mannered professional man, not especially striking to look at but with piercing eyes. There is certainly nothing in mediumship which marks out its practitioners to the ordinary eye: in the past fifteen years, this unassuming man had caused the movement of enough objects, large and small, to fill a volume with documentation. Extraordinary facts of this sort had been confirmed to me by a judge, a well-known restaurant owner, and other respectable townsfolk: I had checked and rechecked their stories in every possible way, and collected a mass of written evidence.

Outside Treviso is a small cemetery dating back to Napoleonic times, and likely in the near future to be swept away as the city expands. Whenever the medium and his friends went there it was the scene of strange events. Once, in the evening, a gravestone was wafted through the air to the visitor's feet, and on another occasion Prince T.F. found on one of the graves some papers that he had locked up in his safe at home. Late one night an electric torch from one of their homes came gleaming through the air to meet them on a country road. Another member of the group had his spectacles whisked off his nose, and found them again inside his car, which was locked and protected by an anti-theft device.

One day the friends had been for a short drive and stopped in a square adorned with flower-beds, with a shell-shaped fountain in the centre. One of them threw a few pebbles into the fountain, after which they moved off in the car. They had hardly started when they heard the pebbles rattling against the bodywork. They stopped and made sure there was no one about, and then threw some more pebbles into the fountain, marking one with a Star of David pattern. This time all the pebbles except the marked one came straight back, and all of them were wet. Back in Treviso, they were about to get out of the car when the marked pebble, also wet, appeared for a moment above the bonnet, shot through the windscreen with a sharp crack and rested on the driver's chest. The stones of Treviso, it will be seen, are not too different in behaviour from those of Sienna, described in a previous chapter.

*Glimpses of a wider universe*

The events we have been describing are inexplicable on traditional premises, e.g. that the laws of the physical world are absolute and unalterable, that science as we know it has for its province the whole of reality, and that the physical and mental universes are completely distinct. But if we were to abandon these premises, many things that appear strange would be intelligible and our view of the universe might well be more adequate than the simplistic one typified by Haeckel and other scientists of the past two hundred years.

Modern science is already approaching a truer view of reality, for instance in the admission that 'natural laws' may have statistical rather than absolute validity, i.e. that they are matters of probability rather than of certainty. This applies

177

to the microphysical universe of particles as well as to the macrocosmic phenomena of physics, physiochemistry and biology. Nature, in short, obeys wider laws than those of the sensory universe, and unknown forces prevail in exceptional cases. Ideas of this type range from the finalism and neo-finalism of the 'vitalists' to the synchronism of Jung and Pauli, while in biology the 'probabilistic' school of thought is represented by Ralph Lillie and Edmund Sinnott.[6]

Further, it is coming to be realized that 'scientific' reality is only one sector of the whole — a thin film overlying true reality, as Jacques Bergier puts it. Modern physics, as we know, fights shy of the deterministic premises of naive empiricism and, with the aid of mathematics, advances more and more towards an abstract as opposed to a common-sense view of reality.

It is this line of thought which appears most helpful to our present purposes. Tyrrell, for instance, is convinced that para-normal phenomena 'are not isolated facts unlinked with other natural phenomena, nor do they infringe the physical laws of the universe': they demonstrate 'the existence of a life and a universe beyond those with which science is concerned.'[7] Luigi Fantappiè, who has tried to relate paranormal phenomena to a physio-mathematical view of the world, says: 'It appears clear that reality is not wholly comprised in the space-time of the universe that we know through our senses: to describe it fully we must have recourse to a wider scheme.' Fantappiè himself, after devising a mathematical model of the universe somewhat more complex than that suggested by Sitter (cf. Chapter 4), undertook the task of defining math-ematically all the categories of 'possible worlds', not as mere abstractions but as universes that may exist — one perhaps included within another — in an inexhaustible variety of forms within a single organic unity.

As Fantappiè says, 'What appears inexplicable in one uni-verse may have a logic of its own in another world, associated with a wider range of transformations and degrees of freedom.' To illustrate this he takes the example of a hydrogen atom, which in his notation represents universe No. 1 in category B. From time to time a photon (unit of luminous energy) im-pinges on the atom and causes it to jump from one level of energy to another. This event would be unintelligible to an observer in the tiny atomic universe, since its cause comes

178

from outside, but it is merely the manifestation of a wider or more complex reality. This may stand as an analogy for the physical world as we know it and the paranormal world with its extra 'degree of freedom' — a world, for instance, in which a stone can traverse the windscreen of a car without breaking it.

What range of freedom do human beings enjoy? A very limited one on the space-time plane of ordinary consciousness, but considerably more as far as the secret and transcendent self is concerned. By virtue of this spiritual self, Fantappiè maintains, we belong to the whole gamut of possible universes and are, at least potentially, free to move from one to the other.

This imaginative view is diametrically opposed to that of the 'physicalists' and particularly the mathematician Wassermann,[8] who considers that paranormal phenomena are to be explained exclusively with the language and methods of physics: his theory presupposes the existence of a so-called 'Psi field' about which he discourses at length without defining it in 'operational' terms,[9] as might reasonable be expected from who regards mental experiences as epiphenomena. However, not all physicists take this empire-building view of their own science, and among those who have opposed Wassermann are Maby and Bertalanffy.[10]

It is indeed the modern progress of physics, and especially the study of the events and phenomena of the sub-atomic world, that have caused eminent scientists to postulate a non-physical world as the basis of the physical one. This applies to such men as Dirac, Broglie, Jordan and D.L. Lawden. In a recent work the latter speaks of the 'psychic conduct' of elementary particles, i.e. the fact that they behave in a way contrary to mechanistic laws.[11] This is reminiscent of Teilhard de Chardin and of the view put forward in 1945 by the biologist Ralph S. Lillie, that the influence of the psychic factor on physical events is a universal phenomenon and is to be explained by a conscious 'selection of probabilities' inherent in microphysical events — a theory which has found much response among parapsychologists.

Thus the gulf between soul and matter appears less profound than it formerly did. We cannot foresee the result of the present fermentation of new ideas, but at all events it tends to undermine the over-simplified common-sense view which refuses to admit that a stone or a table can move without physical cause. Paranormal phenomena, which are trivial on the one hand yet extraordinary on the other, are valuable because they force us to review the premises of what has hitherto passed for irrefragable knowledge. The rest, perhaps, will come of its own accord in due course, when the antinomy between soul and matter is finally resolved and the dispute between different modes of explanation is seen to be a dispute in words only.

# CHAPTER 18

---

## Magic without ritual

*Obedient objects*

Arriving punctually at 3.30, Gustavo Adolfo Rol took his seat in a leather armchair in the foyer of a big hotel in the centre of Turin. Awaiting him, besides myself, were the film director Federico Fellini, Professor P. from Arco and Dr M., the chief physician of a clinic in the same city. I was sitting opposite Rol, who began talking with animation about the film *Eight and a Half*; then, changing the subject, he asked Fellini if he might play a trick on him — just a 'piece of nonsense' — provided he had a spare pair of shoes at the hotel. Fellini replied that he had, and Rol asked him to get up and walk about the foyer. As he returned to the sofa on which he and the other two were sitting, he began to walk a little awkwardly. He sat down, took off his right shoe and found part of the heel had been cut off. Dr Rol, who sat smiling at him, held the missing portion in his hand.

A few hours later, at the home of two young ladies who were cousins of Dr Rol, the latter gave an extended demonstration of other 'pieces of nonsense', this time with unused packs of cards which, handled by his guests, performed all kinds of tricks at his bidding. This time eleven of us were present, including Fellini and Dr M. As an instance, Dr Rol — who was sitting several yards away from me, at the other end of a long table — told me to spread out a pack of 52 cards fanwise, which I did: the cards were all face down. Then he told me to put them together and spread them out once more. This took barely three seconds, but to our amazement the cards this time were alternately face up and face down — an arrangement which it would have taken several minutes to effect in the ordinary way.

In another 'experiment', Dr M. was asked to go into the next room and shuffle the pack thoroughly, after which he

181

returned and dealt out the first few cards on the table, face down. When we turned them up we found on each occasion that certain cards designated by Dr Rol, which had played a significant part in previous experiments, appeared in positions which he had indicated beforehand. Unlike an ordinary drawing-room conjuror, Dr Rol at no time touched the cards himself. The performance was in fact one of pure 'magic', without the aid of any ritual or anything resembling a mediumistic trance; in fact, Dr Rol continued to chat with his usual animation while the tricks were going on. For practical purposes there was no essential difference between them and the arithmetical diversions of 'Stasie', described in the previous chapter, although the latter were due to a collective effort of the unconscious mind, while in Rol's case there was a single operator in a state of complete lucidity. But one may suspect that he too was aided by the psychical resources of the assembled company, especially those with whom he was most frequently in contact.

### Magic and modern research

The phenomenon of 'obedient objects' has been recognized by researchers and subjected to quantitative tests. The term 'magic', which smacks of superstition, is of course banned, and investigators prefer to speak of psychokinesis (the affecting of material objects by mental force), or PK for short. The 'Psi factor' (after the first letter of the Greek word psyche) is a term coined by Thouless and Weisner to cover both action at a distance and paranormal perception.

One of the first investigators in this field was Professor Rhine of Duke University, North Carolina (the coiner of the term 'extra-sensory perception'), who suspected that the 'luck' of certain gamblers might be due to a power, unconscious or otherwise, to influence the fall of cards or the throw of dice. He got his wife Louisa to throw dice repeatedly while concentrating in an effort to influence the result, but the outcome was negative, i.e. the scores were no different than was to be expected from pure chance. To satisfy the professor on this point, Mrs Rhine had to throw the dice no fewer than nine hundred times. Later, however, Rhine experimented with other subjects and concluded that his theory was justified, though the power in question varied considerably from one person to another. Others have reached the same conclusion, e.g. Forwald, who used dice made of different materials such as wood, steel and plastic. The subject was told to concentrate on influencing one material and not the others, and the outcome showed that he or she was able to do so.[1]

As experiments multiplied, further safeguards were devised such as a special apparatus to prevent the fall of the dice being influenced manually by the thrower. Chevalier and De Cressac, in the sixth of a series of tests, measured the deviation from the vertical of a steel ball dropped by automatic means into a glass tube full of liquid paraffin. The subject endeavoured to deflect its fall in a direction stated beforehand, and the deflection, however minimal, was measured by means of an optical apparatus that projected an enlarged shadow of the ball on to a screen. The data published by these investigators appear to bear out Rhine's theory.[2] More complicated tests have been performed by Hardy at the *Institut Métapsychique International* in Paris, but with inconclusive or negative results. Aimé Michel is at work on an ultra-sensitive electronic apparatus. Scientists do not agree in the evaluation of all these tests, but they seem, *inter alia*, to show that the degree of success depends on the subject's interest and enthusiasm and tends to fall off as he becomes mentally tired. Interest and optimism are of course characteristic of gamblers in real life, and it is understandable that laboratory tests, where boredom and weariness are apt to set in, should give less striking results.

### The man who always won

From the neuro-physiological point of view we may conjecture that gamblers' successes are less due to conscious will-power than to the emotive factor associated with the hypothalamic centres. Psychoanalysis teaches us that the will is only really effective when backed by instincts and impulses that are rooted in the subconscious. If Rhine is to be believed we may all be gifted with magic powers, but only in relation to things that interest us on every level and mobilize all the resources of our being.

Charles Brigg Karrer, who was born in poverty in Korea, died at an early age in the USA leaving a fortune of $18,500,000 which he had acquired neither by trade nor by dishonest means, but simply by always winning at gambling games of all kinds. As a boy he went with his parents to America; then they settled in India, and later he returned to the US. Cards, racehorses, lottery numbers and roulette all obeyed his bidding, and he became an unwelcome figure in clubs and casinos. Several attempts were made on his life, one with dynamite; he was accused of fraud, but acquitted for lack of evidence. Insurance companies refused to cover gambling establishments against the 'Brigg Karrer risk', and the latter were forced to pay him to stay away, which he did reluctantly as he preferred to 'earn' his money.[3]

Gamblers who appear to possess phenomenal luck — though in a lesser degree than Brigg Karrer — are not uncommon, and a close check is kept on them by casino managers. They do not play a 'system', but are boundlessly confident of winning. If the science of psychology can throw off some of its present inhibitions it may give a name to the quality of 'success-proneness', which does not depend simply on the kind of techniques recommended by Samuel Smiles, Dale Carnegie or Mark Caine. Whatever its roots are, and they are certainly mysterious, its existence is recognized in military and other circles where men are chosen for dangerous responsibilities.[4] A kind of PK factor may be discerned in the careers of those who are brilliantly successful in politics, business or love, and a whole field of social parapsychology is here waiting to be explored.

Many more examples could be cited of the operation of the PK factor in games of chance. When Pope Pius XII died, many people in Rome, Turin and Milan won lottery prizes on the basis of numbers corresponding to that event; and on 24 August 1962 there were spectacular wins at Naples for a similar reason, this time connected with the Irpinia earthquake. Lombroso and others have collected many instances of this kind.

### Sovereign powers of the mind

Events like these cannot be due to mere chance, and we are driven either to adopt Jung's 'synchronic' theory or to seek a causal one in terms of parapsychology. In some cases it may be a matter of precognition, but we are inclined to think that the phenomenon is generally due to the operation

184

of several wills concentrated on a particular result and both desirous and confident of achieving it.

Dr Antonio Mendicini, a neuropsychiatrist, relates that once at Palermo, when the weekly draw was taking place, an enthusiastic crowd began shouting the desired numbers — 6, 22 and 26 — and, sure enough, these were drawn by the blindfolded child that was performing the operation. Turning to other aspects of PK, Professor Riccardo Salvadori relates that a Greek girl, Clio Georgiou, demonstrated her ability to deflect a compass needle in the Physics laboratory of Athens University, observed by Professor Tanagras and three of his colleagues; a year or two later she repeated this feat in the presence of Professor Tanagras and Lidio Cipriani, an anthropologist of Florence University. On the first occasion she made the needle oscillate and stop at will, and on the second she made it rotate on its own axis. This took place in broad daylight, 'with no possibility of fraud', and the compass was protected by a double glass case. Mediums such as Kluski and Elizabeth d'Espérance showed similar powers in their time.

Some years ago a French electronic engineer, A. Dusailly, performed an experiment in the presence of several scientists, with a PK subject and a lamp cut off from any source of current. The subject was told to 'think of nothing', and then, by will-power, to light the lamp, which he was able to do for a brief moment. To explain this we may perhaps recall Lillie's theory that the human mind is capable of 'selecting' from among the inherently unforeseeable possibilities latent in individual subatomic particles. The ability to stop a motor functioning some distance away may be explained on similar lines.

Major Attilio Gatti, a geographer and anthropologist, relates that while on a trip in Mozambique he encountered three witch doctors who asked for a lift in his land-rover, which he refused. The next thing he knew, three tyres burst and the engine failed for no discoverable reason. He changed his mind and took the men on, whereupon they assured him there would be no further trouble, which was indeed the case.[5]

In the case of conscious PK subjects, as with the lightning calculators described in Chapter 8, there appears to be a harmonious collaboration between the two levels of consciousness that are usually thought of as opposed to each other. This cannot be regarded as a 'regressive' phenomenon, since it is the conscious mind that has the upper hand; and we may regard subjects of this kind as representing a higher degree of evolution than ordinary mediums, though still belonging to a stage of transition with all the difficulties that that involves. The matter is complicated, however, by the fact that in some subjects the threshold of vigilance may be lowered for a longer or shorter period without their being aware of it, so that it is hard to tell where the medium ends and where the PK subject or 'magician' begins.

In what category, for instance, should we place Eileen Garrett? Besides her mediumistic powers, she relates that when her daughter had gone out of doors, and although she did not know her whereabouts, she was able to 'will' her to bring home flowers of a certain kind and colour; and she expresses her firm conviction that the conscious mind can influence other people's behaviour as well as physical phenomena.

There are many precedents for this. Goethe discovered as a young man that he had extraordinary powers: when out for a walk he would sometimes feel an overwhelming desire to meet the girl or woman who was at that time his lady-love, and before long she would turn up, having felt an inexplicable impulse to leave home and wander to that very spot. The poet himself related instances of this kind to several friends, in letters and conversation.[6]

We have thus moved from the topic of obedient objects to that of people conforming to occult instructions: one may speak of mental powers in this context, but we do not know what they are or how they work. Schopenhauer used the term 'magic expression of the will', and W.W. Atkinson in our day speaks of 'mental magic'. At all events it is not purely a matter of the conscious mind. The latter exercises a directing role, but an external one: the real work is done by the inner, secret self, which accumulates transcendent powers and occasionally places them at the disposal of the conscious self. The latter can say what it wants, but cannot take a hand in the process of getting it. When the PK subject throws the dice he formulates a desire or directive in his own mind, but he cannot say how it is realized. Thus the full credit should never be given to the conscious mind, even in the rare cases when it is able to make the subconscious obey it.

Cases in which the psyche is fully integrated under the command of the conscious mind are generally informed by one of two 'magic' forces (as Ringger calls them):[7] love and hate. Bozzano reports many well-documented instances of subjects who were able to afflict their enemies, at a distance, with hallucinations or panic; and Atkinson tells of a black-smith who persecuted a man living two miles away by ham-mering on his anvil late at night and 'willing' that the other should hear the noise and be upset by it.[8]

John P. Harrington of the Smithsonian Institution describes mind-battles between the medicine men of rival Indian tribes in California: the challenger would stand at a given point and endeavour to make his way across level ground to a fixed line, while his opponent would try to prevent him by sheer will-power. Not all the challengers succeeded, and even those who did showed signs of extreme exhaustion.

This field of enquiry is a wide one and is still plagued by superstition, like all subjects that are neglected by science. However, a 'mind over matter' experiment was tried some years ago by physiologists from the University of Manitoba and psy-chiatrists from the University of Montreal, who took three hundred mice and inflicted on each of them an identical wound by removing a small portion of skin. The mice were kept in three cages, a hundred in each. Twice a day for sixteen days running a professional 'healer' took the first cage and held it in his hand for a few minutes; the second cage was treated in the same way, but by people chosen at random; the third cage was left alone. At the end of the test, the wound had healed considerably more in the case of the first lot of mice, a result which Ringger would perhaps put down to 'love'.

In 1953 Richard da Silva, a British doctor living in Cey-lon, read a paper to a congress of microbiologists at Rome on the development of two identical cultures of typhoid bacilli. At the moment of seeding these were precisely alike, but after twenty-four hours in the same environmental conditions one covered an area three times as large as the other. Dr da Silva declared that this was because he had spent half an hour mentally encouraging the growth of the one and discouraging the other. It is not hard to imagine how the congress received

187

this; and yet the idea is not without precedent. In 1947 a French physician, Dr Paul Vasse, and his wife Christiane carried out an experiment under the auspices of the *Institut métapsychique international* by planting wheat seeds in two identical rectangular containers. For a quarter of an hour a day Dr Vasse or his wife would stand a few feet away from each crop, uttering kindly remarks to the one and harsh words to the other, and accompanying these with appropriate thoughts and visualizations of the result. Sure enough, one flourished and the other was stunted.[9] In a further series of experiments Paul and Christiane Vasse were able, at the suggestion of Dr Rhine, to induce plants to grow in a direction or at an angle selected by themselves. It is not for nothing that in Anglo-Saxon countries people who are successful with gardens are described as having a 'green thumb'.

In the Tay mountains in Viet-Nam contests used to be held between sorcerers each of whom tried, by will-power, to make his own mango-tree flourish and to stunt his rival's,[10] and elsewhere in the Orient people are reputed to be able to blast a fully-grown tree by looking at it. This may be an exaggeration, but we should not dismiss it out of hand. If the mental power of individuals can produce such effects as in the Vasse experiments, how about the collective focussing of love or hatred? Dr Franklin Loehr, a Presbyterian minister at Los Angeles, got a hundred and fifty of his parishioners to pray for the well-being of a particular set of plants and the blighting of others, and these prayers were answered with striking effect — more so in the case of the 'hate' prayers than of the loving ones, for the blighted plants did not recover when the experiment was tried in reverse.[11]

We do not know whether mankind will ever regain command of the magic arts on which it turned its back more than two centuries ago. For the time being they live a shadowy existence, alluded to in cautious terms by the observers of strange phenomena connected with mice or wheat-shoots or the fall of dice, but not recognized as a biological force of universal application. Yet anyone who does not see magic in this light and realize, with Schopenhauer, its potential importance to every human being is bound to write it off as something primitive, irrational and morbid. This attitude is still all too common, and as long as it persists the possessors of exceptional powers will be inclined to hide them.

None the less, here is another example to prove that they are real. Federico Fellini (who told the story to myself and to Simone di San Clemente) was walking one day in a park with Dr Rol when they saw a baby in a perambulator and its nurse dozing on a bench beside it. A hornet started to buzz around the baby, and Fellini was about to brush it away, but Dr Rol anticipated him: he pointed his finger imperiously at the insect, which fell to the ground lifeless. Fellini himself comments: 'Perhaps I ought not to have divulged this story, but it is time people woke up to the stranger aspects of reality. As a rule they will only believe in the common mysteries, not in unusual ones. There is plenty of evidence, but they aren't willing to receive it. We are all idolaters of science, prisoners of reason, and we have forgotten the existence of faculties that belong to a higher sphere than reason itself.'

# PART VI

## The diffusion of mind

# CHAPTER 19

## Our dumb friends

*Canine intelligence*

This is the story of Hector, a seemingly ordinary terrier which belonged to W.H. Mante, first officer on board a Dutch merchant vessel, the *Simaloer*. One day in April 1922 Hector was accidentally left behind at Vancouver when the *Simaloer* sailed for Japan. Out of five ships still at the quay, it happened that the *Hanley* was loading for Yokohama, and on the morning of April 20 her first officer Harold Kildall noticed a dog that he had never seen before, running from one ship to the other as though inspecting them. Then he lost sight of the animal, but once the *Hanley* had sailed they found Hector ensconced on the threshold of the captain's cabin: The ship's company were kind to him, but he showed no special affection except to Kildall, whose rank was the same as his master's. He behaved like a true sea-dog, however, running to the galley at meal-times and, every now and then, turning up on the bridge to cast a knowing look at the compass. Eighteen days out from Vancouver the Japanese coast hove in sight. When the *Hanley* moored at Yokohama, Hector became wildly excited and barked furiously at a small boat belonging to a merchant vessel at the same wharf. This was the *Simaloer*, and one of the two men in the boat was none other than Hector's master.

These facts were published in the *Reader's Digest* by Commander Kenneth Dodson, who personally questioned the officers of both ships. In the ordinary way, when a dog succeeds in rejoining its master hundreds of miles away we speak of 'instinct' and 'orientation', but this hardly suffices to explain Hector's choosing the very ship which was bound for Japan — and in any case how did he know that was the *Simaloer's* destination?

A railway worker, Elvio Barlettani, had a 'travelling dog'

193

named Lampo (Lightning), so described because of its passion for rail journeys and apparent mastery of timetables. It used to go on long and complicated trips, changing at the right places and evading the attentions of unfriendly guards, and always returning punctually to Campiglia Marittima near Leghorn in time to accompany its master's children to school. The dog became a celebrity and was seen on television, and its master wrote a book describing its feats.

No doubt we tend to underrate the intelligence of animals, but is 'intelligence' the right word to describe the behaviour of Hector and Lampo? If we really believe that Lampo understood timetables, we must also suppose that he could tell the time by the clock! We should heed the opinion of Olivier Quéant, who observes that the great mistake we make in trying to fathom the supernatural is to reason like human beings. Since we are men we cannot avoid doing this, but we should at least realize that our thoughts do not apply to what is neither material nor physical.

The behaviour of animals belongs essentially to the subconscious level, drawing upon the resources of the secret universe of which we know so little. If we accept that the 'psi' factor may operate to some extent in animals as it does between human beings, we may be less surprised by such stories as the following.

In 1940 a government official at Summersville, West Virginia, found a wounded pigeon in his backyard and gave it to his twelve-year-old son as a pet. That winter the boy was taken to hospital at Philippi, some sixty miles away, for an operation. One night, during a snowstorm. he heard a gentle flapping at the window: the nurse opened it, and the pigeon flew in. A few days later his parents came to the hospital and were astonished to see the pigeon there. It had disappeared from home a few days after the boy was taken away, so it could not simply have followed the ambulance.[1] We know of course, that migratory birds perform prodigies of orientation on the way to sunnier climes, but how could the pigeon have known where to look for its young master? Dogs, as is frequently reported, travel long distances in a similar way to find their owners, and we must agree with Remy Chauvin that this can hardly be due to their olfactory or other senses.

The mystery of animal orientation is observed in many species. Butterflies travel long distances, even against a headwind, to find their mates, and larvae inside trees bore their way to the surface by the shortest route. The Soviet chaolar Vasiliev speaks of 'biological radiocommunication'. The anthropologist Lidio Cipriani recalls the fact that vultures will appear from over the horizon as soon as one of their species has sighted a corpse: he believes that this cannot be due to sight or smell alone, and puts it down to 'telepsychism', a kind of super-organic, super-individual power. This is similar to the 'psi factor', with the difference that on this theory it is the normal direct basis of communication within the animal kingdom.

The story has been told[2] of a merchant vessel from Marseilles whose crew took on a dozen cats at Istanbul, where the ship called occasionally; they treated them kindly, but on the next visit the captain had the animals put ashore and returned to their owners. Over a year later, when the ship was en route for Istanbul, the cats assembled on the wharf at the very place where she was due to come alongside. This happened on the eve of the ship's arrival, for which there was no regular schedule. It is impossible, or rather meaningless, to explain behaviour of this kind by talking of 'instinct'. What it involves is telepathy, clairvoyance and/or precognition; there must have been, as Cipriani would argue, some communication at the unconscious level between the cats individually and the ship's crew.

Animal precognition is exemplified by the story, quoted in Bozzano's work, of a 'strike' by the famous St. Bernard dogs in February 1939, when for the first time on record they refused to go for their morning walk. An hour later a storm broke, and the path where the monks would have been with the dogs was engulfed by an avalanche. One may imagine that the dogs, by some kind of instinct, foresaw the storm, but St. Bernards are not afraid of storms; the avalanche, on the other hand, could not have been predicted by anyone.

There are some, nevertheless, who insist on believing that animals are aware by sensory means of impending fires, earthquakes or avalanches, or that ESP is at best the exception and not the rule. However, the 'psi factor' is amply documented

195

in other spheres and seems to offer a simpler and more probable explanation in this field also, as is confirmed by the evidence of psychobiology.

At Cervinia (Breuil, in the Val d'Aosta) there is a ceramic bas-relief of a dog named Bleck, a mongrel that used to accompany the guides and mountaineers and, as Enzo Grazzini relates, had extraordinary powers of 'foreseeing' avalanches, storms and other changes in the mountain weather. It also showed other forms of intuition. One day, when an officer in the Alpine troops lost his life in a mountaineering contest, the dog, which was then at Breuil, turned its nose towards the snowy peak and gave a long, melancholy howl. In summer 1933, when two students and a guide fell to their death on the Linceul, Bleck left his sleeping-place and howled for a great part of the night.

Ringger suggests that there exists between domestic animals and their masters a state of psychological interdependence similar to that between small children and their parents, or the 'telepathic cordon' between mother and baby, to use Ehrenwald's language. The special link between men and dogs, celebrated in literature from Homer to Jack London, is a kind of psychic symbiosis that has made the canine world a necessary appendange of humanity.

Hans Christian Andersen related to his friends the story of a dog named Amour which was left in his keeping by its owner, who had to go to Italy for his health. It underwent periodic fits of depression and these were found to coincide with especially dangerous crises in its master's illness (he was consumptive). One night Andersen, who had just gone to sleep, was awakened by the dog licking his hand. It began to howl and then lay down in a strange attitude, with all four legs extended. This was at half past eleven, and sure enough it proved that the dog's master had died at that moment.

We may suppose that the psi factor is especially powerful in animals owing to the very limited role that intellect plays in their case, and that it is intensified by their love and devotion towards human beings. A similar case, reported by Bozzano, is that of a greyhound named Wamar that belonged to Captain Maris Galli of Turin. The Captain was serving in the Abyssinian war, and one day in June 1936 Wamar showed signs of great agitation, roaming about the house and howling miserably. In the evening he lay down at the foot of his master's bed, barking feebly from time to time and refusing to eat any food. He got up once or twice to scratch at the wardrobe, and lay down again shivering. All efforts by the family and the veterinary surgeon were in vain, and in a few days he died — of starvation, physically speaking, but in reality of grief. Captain Galli, it turned out, had been seriously wounded on the day Wamar first showed distress, and had died that same evening.

Cases of this kind are numerous, and Dr Geley has remarked on the unforgettable sensation of hearing a dog howl in fore-knowledge of an approaching death.[3] Animals have a great capacity for love, though some would deny that they have a soul or a psyche — Descartes is said to have thrown a cat out of the window to prove his point that they were insentient beings.[4] Certainly animals are inferior to us in terms of conscious reasoning, but their psyche has depths that are largely hidden from us, save for occasional man-ifestations that we interpret in an anthropomorphic way. May not Boris Noyer be right when he says that we should do better to investigate the psyche in all its forms than to build space-ships and go hunting about the universe for new worlds and supermen?

*Animal somnambulists*

As is well known, dogs appear to have dreams like human beings, and they make restless movements in their sleep as if re-living the day's adventures. But, as with human beings, their dreams may have still stranger effects.

The neuro-psychiatrist Nandor Fodor had a dog with two curious habits: it would 'play' the piano whenever it got a chance, and appeared to have a hatred of books, which it would tear to pieces and even attempt to devour. This became such a nuisance that Dr Fodor gave the dog away. One night, some time later, he heard a noise of scratching at his bed-room door, then of paws running about and finally of the piano as his dog used to play it. Yet the piano was closed and there was nobody in the house except Dr Fodor, his wife and small daughter. Reporting the incident to the American Society for Psychical Research, Dr Fodor suggested that the dog might have been dreaming with intensity of his lost home. The noises were unquestionably objective; Fodor was wide awake when he heard them, and had never suffered from hallucinations. He therefore concluded that the dog, in its sleep, had projected its 'oneiric body', a kind of phantom which had actually visited the house.

A curious story of apparent telepathy in animals is that of two Airedale terriers, Snooker and Napper, who lived in neighbouring houses and used to go off roaming together. One night Snooker awoke in great distress and refused to be comforted, and next day it was learnt that Napper had been run over by a lorry and killed. Snooker, who had till then been extremely venturesome, showed for the rest of his life a terror of wheeled traffic. The conclusion drawn by Mrs Mabel Robinson is that he must have been accompanying Napper 'in spirit' when the latter, to whom he was devoted, met with his fatal accident.[5]

Clairvoyance, as we know, may involve identification; but it would perhaps be more accurate to suppose that identification is the primordial basis of consciousness in all its forms. The novelist Rider Haggard, whose powers of precognition were mentioned in Chapter 5, once dreamt that he saw a setter of his named Bob lying half-dead among some reeds. He began himself to cry out as though in a nightmare, but in a voice resembling that of a wounded animal. Next morning Bob was found to be missing; a search was made and his body was fished out of a pond a mile or two from the house. His skull was smashed and his paws broken, as though he had been hit by a train.[6]

### Special affinities between men and animals

According to Maeterlinck, human beings and animals live on the same plane in an undefined element, governed not by intelligence alone but by a psychic power independent of the brain, a 'diffusion of mind' which may be thought of as the psychic substratum of the universe. This power, we may suppose, is strongest in people who show exceptional ability to influence the vegetable creation or to communicate with animals. Frederica Hauffe belonged to this category, and according to Aimé Michel the calculator Lidoreau had an extraordinary affinity with birds. The clairvoyante I.R., whom we have mentioned before, possessed powers of this kind as a child, though not when she grew up. Birds would flock around her, a horse would kneel of its own accord to enable her to mount, and a dog of the quietest disposition once bit her mother's hand when she struck the child. The young medium used sometimes to go to sleep lying face downwards on a large bough, clasping it with her hands so as not to fall off, and she was always awakened by a crowd of sparrows fluttering around and perching on her head and body; some even got into her pockets.

Bozzano speaks of a sub-normal boy who, from the age of two, used to go into the garden daily for a long 'talk' with the birds, whose twittering grew shrill and animated when he appeared; if for any reason he did not, there was a disappointed hush. He grew to be a man and died of consumption at thirty: his mental backwardness persisted and, for this reason perhaps, so did his power to communicate with birds. Saints, of course, have also had this power, no doubt because of their child-like simplicity and love. Animal tamers, on the other hand, are apt to prefer the way of fear, but there have been exceptions like Vladimir Leonidovich Durov in Russia and Sergeant Maimone, the trainer of a celebrated dog named Dox.[7] It is curious that Professor Tocquet, an eminent student of paranormal phenomena, should deny the existence of a psychic symbiosis between humans and animals, though other experts regard this as an essential biological fact.[8]

The present author once knew a 'sensitive' of Russian origin, Mme S., who lived in a flat with her invalid husband and two dachshunds. People were constantly passing the door and going up or down the stairs, but the dogs barked only when visitors were coming to the flat itself — though they had no way of seeing beforehand that this was the case — and would sometimes 'announce' them as soon as they passed the outside gate. Their owner's comment was simply: 'Dogs know such a lot — if only they could talk! But we understand each other pretty well.' We may certainly agree that dogs know a great deal, if by this we mean the kind of subconscious knowledge that is the subject of the present chapter. To revert to Cipriani's view, previously suggested by Mackenzie, there is between animals and humans what the latter calls a 'direct polypsychic interference' whereby animals can at times escape from their biological limitations and apprehend events at a distance without physical aid of any kind.

Professor Koehler, a specialist in animal psychology, had a

parrot which used to cry out 'Goodbye!' to any visitor who was just leaving. Many tried to deceive it by moving towards the door, putting on their coat etc., but the parrot was never fooled.[9] Whether we call this kind of intuition 'intelligence' is a matter of terminology. It is true, of course, that some animals do possess a degree of intelligence of the conscious, individual kind. This applies, as experiment has shown, to dolphins and octopuses, bees and various other species; but we are apt, in our anthropocentric way, to believe in animal intelligence only in the case of creatures that can behave like human beings. From this point of view the prize might go to an Indian bird of the crow family (*gracula religiosa*) which, it appears, gave an impressive display of human-style 'conversation' some years ago on BBC television.

### Other animal skills

In a sense, the anthropomorphic feats of animals are less interesting than the extra-individual powers they sometimes display. Sixty or seventy years ago much attention was aroused by the 'calculating horses' of Elberfeld in Germany, which were trained by Karl Krall to perform extraordinary feats. There were four stallions named Zarif, Mohamed, Hänschen and Hans 'the wise' (who, in spite of his nickname, disembowelled himself trying to get at a mare that had been imprudently left in an adjoining stable). The stallions were observed by a large number of scientists, among the first being Professor William Mackenzie and Roberto Assagioli. Mohamed, whose mathematical gifts were the most pronounced, extracted numerical roots of the third and higher powers almost instantaneously, giving the answer by striking the ground with his hoof an appropriate number of times. According to Maeterlinck, cube roots were a kind of relaxation to him after more exacting 'conversational' sessions. Although give the answer with alacrity as soon as the problem had been chalked up, first beating out the units with his right hoof and then the tens with his left. There was no sign of a pause for consideration: it was as though the answer sprang forth at once from some invisible intelligence.

Dogs have been among the most famous 'animal prodigies': one of the best-known, Rolf, was picked up as a stray by Frau Moeckel of Mannheim. This animal learnt the rudiments

200

of arithmetic as his mistress taught them to her little girl, but he branched out in other directions as well. A code was devised for him to answer questions, and such dialogues took place as: 'What are you?' — 'Part of the Original Soul.' — 'What am I?' — 'Also a part.' — 'Where did you hear about the Original Soul?' — 'I don't remember.' Lumpi, a descendant of Rolf's, used to answer questions in a similar way. 'Do you like riding in a car?' — 'No, too fast.' — 'How do you come to be so clever?' — 'I don't know.' — 'Would you like to be human?' — 'Better a dog, more spoilt.'

Similar displays have been given by canine prodigies in Italy, including Bonnie and Dana, a Scotch terrier and a poodle owned by Emanuele Gino Del Mar, and Peg, a poodle belonging to Signora Giordano Corridori. These animals (all bitches) replied to questions by arranging cards bearing letters of the alphabet; some of their performances were given in public. On one occasion, in a surgeon's house, Bonnie was asked: 'What do you think of these men?' — 'Dunces.' — Do you know what that means?' — 'Ignorant.' —What does "ignorant" mean?' — They don't know anything.' Peg, when asked what she thought of cats, replied: 'Dogs better'. — 'And men?' — 'Not much good.'

Answers like these are too human to reflect the animal's own mind, and it is an elementary mistake to think of beasts as possessing human minds in animal bodies. Communication between humans and animals, as we have seen, belongs to the subconscious level and not that of the intellect. As for the calculating horses, any arithmetical training they had — for instance, Mohamed had learnt that five is the square root of twenty-five — could not possibly account for their more spectacular calculations, such as extracting the fifth root of a long number written on the blackboard, the answer being unknown to the audience themselves. These can only be due to a mysterious supranormal intelligence manifesting itself through the animal in question, in the same way as in the case of human mediums. (The same may be said of Lady, a mare at Richmond, Virginia, which gave telepathic and clairvoyant displays and answered questions by striking her hoof against a sort of alphabetical keyboard).[10] In fact, the conclusion that seems to impose itself, and that we have already hinted at, is that all animals are potential mediums, living as they do in a kind of dream-consciousness. Dr Ochorowicz, following Cuvier, remarks that an animal's waking state has much in common with human somnambulism; and Maeterlinck observes that animals, having no notion of space or time as such, live in a kind of perpetual sleep. This being so, it is natural to agree with Mackenzie that the animal prodigies we have described are 'four-footed ouija boards' — with the important difference that they are alive and therefore have biophysical reactions of their own.

Animals, then, like mediums, are the instruments of a transcendent psyche, which is best explained by the theory of association or polypsychism. A medium at a séance, as we have seen, generally reflects the faculties and tendencies of the participants, though he or she may also achieve results that go beyond these. In the same way an animal reflects the known and latent faculties of the human beings it is in contact with, and it does so the more faithfully because its own individuality is little developed. The polypsychic entities that speak through animal prodigies have their roots in the human beings and animals concerned, and they may also be part of the diffusion of mind of which we have spoken. When Rolf talked about the Original Soul he was, in our opinion, not voicing his own theosophical ideas but rather those of somebody close to him, and the same may be said of Lumpi's and Peg's repartee. As for the discriminating dachshunds of Mme S., she was herself a clairvoyante and probably they shared her gifts. To say this is not to disparage animals in any way, but rather to excite admiration for their mysterious power to assimilate our known and unknown faculties. There is, in short, a common background shared by different animal and human individualities, and animals, like children and perhaps for the same reason, enjoy fuller access to it than mentally mature adults.

## Are animals subject to remote control?

This brings us back to a consideration of the mystery of instinct. According to modern theories, the main directives of animal behaviour are transmitted genetically through the properties of two essential constituents of cell plasm, viz. ribonucleic and deoxyribonucleic acid; certain peptides (small proteic molecules) have also recently been spoken of as transmitters of information. But some forms of behaviour, even of a normal kind, are insufficiently explained on this basis.

An example may be taken from the extensive documentation accumulated by Cipriani. As is well known, birds look after their offspring carefully until they are old enough to fly by themselves, and then push them out of the nest for good. Cipriani constructed special nests in which the parent birds could feed their chicks but were unable to push them out — whereupon they killed them off by feeding them poisonous berries and insects. This expedient could not be the result of instinct, and one is inclined to imagine a mysterious 'something' external to the individual and telling it what to do in emergency. In Mackenzie's view animals enjoy an 'infused knowledge' that guides them infallibly and is often superior to human cognition. We may call this instinct if we like; at all events it is a form of knowledge that does not belong to the individual but to something much wider. Clearly a single bird, or any number of birds, could not by their own efforts hit on such an exceptional and abnormal course of action as to kill their progeny, not to mention the botanical and entomological knowledge involved.

On another occasion Cipriani was encamped on the left bank of the Zambezi near a vast herd of zebra. These animals go about in their thousands under a single leader; by day a particular one is always on the watch, but at night the 'guard' is relieved every twenty minutes, and this without any special sign such as neighing or the beat of hoofs. If the watchman dozes, another comes forward and replaces him at once, as if impelled by the working of a collective psyche.

The notion of a group psyche seems indeed to offer the best approach to a mystery that the vague term 'instinct' and the hypotheses of biochemistry do not suffice to explain. Nor do theories based on the sensorial acuteness of animals, since this is not applicable to a state of drowsiness, which does on the other hand favour the supernormal activity the subconscious. We are certainly concerned here with intelligence, but not of an individual kind.

## The collective mind of the termitarium

Zebras are not the only species which obey such directives, but the phenomenon is most obvious in the case of social insects, such as termites. The construction of a termitarium presupposes not only technical and architectonic powers but also organizing qualities — the division of labour and the co-ordination of different specialities — which we cannot attribute to the tiny brain of a single insect. The same may be said of the skills displayed by ants, bees, spiders and certain wasps; and it should be recalled that an ant's nervous system consists of a mere 250 cells.

Maeterlinck advanced the view that a termitarium possesses a collective 'soul' and a single (non-individual) memory embodying all the knowledge acquired by the species since its creation. Mackenzie similarly holds that a collective soul may, in certain circumstances, come into existence as between organisms of one or more species, enabling the group to perform supranormal activities. He maintains that 'Any group of living organisms is enveloped in a common psychic field from which its members may receive knowledge and impulses conducive to its preservation, directly and independently of the senses.' This collective psyche manifests itself in different aspects and degrees, providing general and specific directives for the subordination of individual interests to those of the group. Mackenzie adds that 'the whole phenomenology of instinct in living beings is essentially of a mediumistic character' — with the difference that it is not sporadic, but a permanent and universal device of Nature to further her biological ends. Similar concepts may be found among psychobiologists and vitalists and in the work of Teilhard de Chardin.

## The path of evolution

The conscious intelligence of mankind is a major evolutionary triumph, but it would be of no value without the invisible soil from which it draws nourishment, as a tree's roots absorb lymph from the earth. Modern man, is intoxicated with pride at having evolved an autonomous intellect capable of rejecting the directives of the universal psyche or 'diffused mind', as we have called it; but he should remember that responsibility carries with it the risk of dangerous error. Atten-

204

tion must be paid to the roots as well as the foliage, the ocean as well as the wave. As Cipriani writes, the price we pay for reason is the imperfection of our free acts. Through the unconscious, the individual transcends his own narrow limitations and participates fully in the life of the species. The intellect, as Alexis Carrel observed, cannot compensate for the loss of instinct. According to Maeterlinck, intelligence is a form of lethargy, imprisoning us in a narrow corner of space and time; if evolution had taken a different course and given priority to the subliminal, we might be able through intuition or immanent knowledge to share the secrets of 'what is perhaps an all-knowing universe.'

Perhaps indeed man's evolution is in a transitory state. The conscious intellect has evidently come to stay, and therefore presumably to perfect itself; but what we must hope and strive for is a greater degree of harmony and co-ordination between intellect and will on the one hand and, on the other, those buried riches of the mind that for the present appear to lie outside our control.

# CHAPTER 20

## The present state of science

As we have pointed out, the phenomena described in this book are not recognized by official science, which, as Henri Poincaré put it, is interested in the 'measurable': recurring events which can be observed at will and reproduced in prescribed conditions, so that their qualitative aspects can be translated into quantitative or numerical terms. Science has achieved brilliant results on this basis, especially in physics, but at the cost of neglecting refractory phenomena and especially those of the paranormal sphere, which are comparatively rare and difficult to observe. (One reason for their rarity in some cases is that they are associated with transitory phases of human evolution.) As Professor Gardner Murphy puts it, they are transpersonal, transtemporal and transspatial, or rather ultra-physical — whatever future science may make of our present distinctions between physical and psychical factors.[1]

The fact that paranormal phenomena do not lend themselves to investigation on customary lines, and have therefore been ignored, does not mean that science must continue to ignore them in the future. Unfortunately, however, we are fettered by a nineteenth-century conception of reality whose inadequacy is shown up by the latest developments in physics and biology. This conception is a materialistic and mechanistic one, imbued with positivism and a monistic philosophy of the physical world, so that belief in paranormal phenomena is simply put down to ignorance, superstition or mental backwardness. Rhine's attempt to subject some of these phenomena to statistical methods has been powerless to shake official scepticism. Dr George R. Price, a chemist at Minnesota University, declared in an article in *Science* on 6 August 1955 that he would not believe in Professor Rhine's ESP tests unless they were conducted in the presence of twelve sceptics and on conditions which he specified in detail.

Conservatism of this sort cannot stand out indefinitely against present trends in science; but it has to be noted that observers of paranormal phenomena are themselves divided into two camps. At first sight these appear to consist of methodological purists and others who are less rigorous, but the real criterion is whether or not they accept physical monism. It is no use admitting in theory that there may be non-physical forces or phenomena outside the categories of space and time, if one continues to accept the constraint of a method of investigation that presupposes a world consisting of matter and energy and regards the objectivization of phenomena as its principal goal.

The purists — to call them so for convenience — are essentially defeatist and retrograde, seeking to narrow the range of science at a time when broader horizons appear to be opening. It would be interesting to know the unconscious motives of this attitude, which often seems to be due to laziness or a kind of snobbery. Sir Julian Huxley tells us that paranormal cognition is inexplicable within the framework of any scientific theory, and Robert Amadou, as we saw, declares that no paranormal phenomenon with physical effects has ever been scientifically proved.[2] A similar attitude was displayed by Professor L.G. Voronin of Moscow University when he declared to Professor Leonid L. Vasiliev that 'a fact that cannot be reproduced does not belong to science, and therefore telepathy is not a scientific problem.' (*Science et Vie*, Jan.-Feb. 1964).

Some purists, while accepting Rhine's statistical method, refuse to be convinced by the most elaborate and closely safeguarded observation of 'spontaneous' paranormal phenomena, many of which could not possibly be reproduced in laboratories. In taking this line they reveal themselves as devotees of a particular technique rather than of science as such, whose task is to advance human knowledge by every available means. Such people arbitrarily dismiss more than eighty years of research in the 'metapsychical' field (to use the term coined by Richet in 1913), and begin the history of this branch of knowledge in the 1930s, with the rise of the American school of parapsychology founded on quantitative investigation. It is extraordinary that at the Royaumont symposium in 1956, many former adherents of the metapsychic school referred to it disparagingly as 'pre-scientific', despite the eminence of its leaders and the impressiveness of their results and theories. Scientists of the younger generation, it is true, lacked experience of some of the most striking mediumistic phenomena, but their *parti pris* of reactionary scepticism was none the less shocking on that account.

It should be made clear that the division between the two camps of which we have spoken is not absolute; there are shades in between, and each of them includes people of different mentality and academic background. None the less, their opposition is a regular feature of national and international meetings[3] and congresses, and is reflected in official publications. In a review of Amadou's book already quoted, Professor C.J. Ducasse remarks that on the latter's criteria science could never have proved the existence of earthquakes, eclipses or volcanic eruptions.[4] François Masse, former editor of the *Revue métapsychique*, observes that parapsychology is one aspect of metapsychics, viz. what Richet called *métapsychique subjective* (as it involves no physical phenomena). He goes on to remark that parapsychologists generally disbelieve in the reality of physical paranormal phenomena, whereas most of the *métapsychistes* regard it as possible, probable or definitely proven. For some years past, it is true, there have been very few human subjects in whom these phenomena could be observed, and consequently few are on record. It is a question therefore whether or not we should trust the evidence of a previous generation; but, this author continues, 'many of us think that our predecessors were in no way inferior to us from the methodological point of view, and that it is folly to reject their conclusions simply because we do not like them.'[5]

It is noteworthy that many of the strongest protests against purism in this field come from eminent physicists and chemico-physicists, such as Professor Maurice Gex, lecturer in the philosophy of science at Lausanne University, who writes: 'The exclusion of the historical method would be a grave disservice to parapsychology. A complex "psi" phenomenon must be described in full historical detail in order to record characteristics which may be essential though they elude statistical investigation . . . The methods applied to an object of study must be determined by that object itself... Parapsychology must not neglect any method on false grounds of scientific austerity.'[6] Many eminent scientists have said the same — Giorgio Piccardi, Nicola Pende, Raphaël Sanzio Bastiani, Giovanni Schepis, Francesco Egidi and others, not to mention the writer Aldous Huxley. Cecil J. Maby, the British physicist, has protested against the assumption in parapsychological circles that the phenomena of life, the mind and the soul can be discussed in mechanistic and materialistic terms or can be localized, defined, measured and analysed in the same way as physical objects and events.

## The 'fetish' of repeatability

Professor Ludwig von Bertalanffy of California University — a distinguished member of the school of thought which believes in a unitary conception of the universe — has observed that: 'Up to now the unification of science was envisaged as a reduction of all science to physics and all phenomena to physical ones, in accordance with the philosophical trend of modern logical empiricism. But it is impossible to base a unitary conception of the world on the prospect of such a reduction, which is certainly remote and probably illusory.' The notion that it is for physics to impose its laws and methods on the other sciences is an outdated preconception — what Francis Bacon called an *idolon mentis* — that is already being refuted by chemico-physics and biology. Some fetishes have already been rejected, and others will follow them. Relativistic physics have destroyed the common-sense idea of absolute space and time, and the Cartesian principle of universal causality has given way to probabilism. Once it was believed that science could pursue its ends with perfect objectivity; now it is realized that every observation and deduction involves an irreducible margin of subjectivity, so that the experimenter is part of the experiment. Finally, it was once assumed that phenomena could be observed and repeated at will, as is usual in physics; but it has been found that some events which appear strictly determined cannot be so repeated, as the variables on which they depend are too many and too fugitive to be controllable.

Chemico-physics, for instance, is concerned with phenomena inherent in evolving systems dependent on a huge number of variables that are not all known, much less observable, so that the phenomena can never be exactly repeated;

and it follows that this science must work out its own methodology, independent of that of physics. Similar considerations apply to biology and parapsychology. Who, for instance, could repeat at will a successful séance or display of clairvoyance, when the experiment might be ruined by hostility or mistrust on the part of the investigator or any of the audience? Servadio and Tocquet have commented on the inhibitions to which mediums and 'sensitives' are liable;[7] but apart from this negative factor, positive ones are requisite if the necessary emotional tension is to be achieved, and this is hardly feasible in the laboratory.[8] It is not surprising that the performance of mediums varies in quality according to who is conducting the test: Eileen Garrett, as we saw in Chapter 6, made some pertinent remarks on the disappointing results of the experiments to which she was subjected to by Professor Rhine. The Elberfeld horses were temperamental too: according to Maeterlinck, if they did not like a scientist's beard or his morose expression they would return silly answers to the simplest questions for hours or even days, a reaction probably due to inhibition rather than mischief.

To refuse to adapt methods to phenomena is an error all too frequent in human history: it was stigmatized by Galileo, who wrote to Federico Cesi: 'We must not expect Nature to conform to what we would think the best disposition, but must suit our own minds to what she has done.' Ironically, it is the present-day champions of Galileo's memory who insist on the universal applicability of the methods of physics. They forget that astronomy itself is one of the sciences completely outside human control; yet today we know more about the heavens than about earth, and no one denies the existence of novae and supernovae because they come into view sporadically and cannot be reproduced in laboratories.

The study of paranormal phenomena may be of immense importance in causing other sciences to adopt new points of view and wider horizons; but it must advance boldly and not allow itself to be trammelled by 'official' methods that cannot solve its problems. Some university chairs have been established,[9] but the road ahead is long and difficult. If the new science were to remain subject to methodological taboos, it would have no future except as a hunting-ground for fools and charlatans.

# Notes

CHAPTER 1

1. Erich Fromm, *The Forgotten Language*, New York 1952.
2. Cf. William Oliver Stevens, *The Mystery of Dreams*, 1950;
G. Zorab, *Proscopie: het raadsel der toekomst*, The Hague,
1953; W.H.C. Tenhaeff, *Oorlogsvoorspellingen* (War Proph-
ecies), The Hague, 1948; Louisa Rhine, *Hidden Channels of
the Mind*, 1962; Raymond de Becker, *The Understanding of
Dreams*, 1968.
3. E.g. Calpurnia's dream announcing Caesar's death, or the
vision of Caesar that appeared to Brutus before Philippi. The
emperor Julian the Apostate, having dreamt that he was to
die 'in Thrace', avoided that province all his life, but died in
a village of the same name. The Bible, Homer, Aeschylus and
Virgil record many stories of premonitory dreams.
4. As will be seen later in the book, lottery wins of this kind
may involve a psychokinetic element as well as, or instead of,
a precognitive one.•
5. R. Trintzius, *La Magie a-t-elle raison?*, 1942.
6. See M. Verneuil, *Dictionnaire pratique des sciences occul-
tes*, Monaco, Les Documents d'art, p.429.
7. S.P.R. *Journal*, vol. L, No. 2, April 1956.
8. *Tomorrow*, vol. 4, No. 2, winter 1952-3.
9. Treatises of oneiromancy were written by Aristotle and,
centuries later, by Artemidorus of Daldis (2nd century A.D.).
The Pythagoreans used propitiatory practices to obtain inspired dreams, and Plato describes such methods in Book IX
of the Republic. Sick persons who frequented the temples of
Aesculapius and Serapis performed rituals in the hope of
being instructed in dreams how to cure themselves; the practice survives in modern Buddhism.
10. The word *daimon* in post-Homeric times did not suggest
anything diabolic, but a kind of being intermediate between
gods and men.
11. V. Tweedale, *Ghosts I have Seen*, 1919.
12. C.G. Jung, *Seelenprobleme der Gegenwart*, Zurich, 1946.
13. F.H. Myers, *Human Personality and its Survival of Bodily
Death*, 1903.
14. Cf. Charles Baudouin, *Introduction à l'analyse des rêves*,

Geneva, 1945. – Freud believed in telepathic dreams but denied the possibility of precognitive ones; his followers have shown increasing readiness to accept paranormal phenomena.

15. Cf. N. Kleitman, *Sleep and Wakefulness,* Chicago, 1939; Edwin Diamond, *The Science of Dreams,* 1962, and works there quoted.

16. Cf. Dr A.J. Kerner's life of Fredereike Hauffe, 'the Seeress of Prevorst', (1845) which quotes her as saying during a trance: 'My brain knows nothing, it is my spirit that speaks; and if my waking brain could know what my spirit says, I should die.' Dr Pagenstecher in his account of María Reyes de Z. similarly infers the existence of a special consciousness operating in the state of 'lethargy'.

17. J. Huizinga, *Incertitudes* (translated from Dutch), Paris, 1946; and cf. Jung, op. cit.

18. Jung, op. cit.

19. Quoted in H. Hoffding, *Outlines of Psychology* (translated from Danish), 1891.

20. *Nos pouvoirs inconnus,* 1964.

21. Baudouin remarks that 'dreams express themselves in images, like poetry'. We may notice that in telepathic or precognitive dreams the emotive 'charge' may be greater than the actual content of the dream justifies: e.g. a tub overturning is not terrifying in itself. In interpreting dreams it is necessary to pay attention to their general atmosphere as well as what appears to be the specific message.

22. *L'hôte inconnu,* 1917.

23. Professor Cyril Burt in his preface to *The Infinite Hive* (1964) suggests that a 'universe of psychic forces' may well exist alongside the universe of matter and energy. Eminent physicists and biologists have taken a similar view.

## CHAPTER 2

1. As Myers writes (op, cit.), we are united with others by our minds but separated by our bodies. The notion of a single, indivisible human consciousness has been advanced by Jung and by parapsychologists including Réne Warcollier, Gardner Murphy and Tenhaeff.

2. R. Tocquet writes in *Les Pouvoirs secrets de l'homme* (1963), p. 119, that theories of the kind put forward by Jung, William James, Bergson and Marcel 'are, alas, purely verbal, and it is hard to see how they could be verified by experience.'

But their heuristic value surely consists in giving a meaning to facts that would otherwise be unintelligible.

3. B. Noyer, 'Réflexions sur l'inconnu', in *Soleil*, No. 5-6, 1963.

4. In a letter to Charlotte von Knobloch (1762) and in *Dreams of a Spirit-Seer, Illustrated by Dreams of Metaphysics* (German original 1763), Kant discusses the content of Swedenborg's visions but does not dispute their authenticity.

5. Some authors, particularly in English-speaking countries, use the psychiatric term 'dissociation', which has clear pathological implications; but Gardner Murphy disputes these, e.g. in *Revue métapsychique*, No. 24, 1953.

6. R. Trintzius, op. cit., p. 23.

7. Charpignon, *Physiologie, médicine et métapsychique du magnétisme*, 1848.

8. H. Thurston, S.J., *The Physical Phenomena of Mysticism*, 1952.

9. Interesting data on the powers of Mixtec priests are given in *Extra-sensory Perception* (Pyramid Books), in an account by Susy Smith of the expedition by Dr and Mrs Gordon Wasson.

10. Maurice Bouisson, *Magic, its Rites and History*, 1960.

11. *Journal of Parapsychology*, vol. 21, No. 4, Dec. 1957. In more recent years the US Air Force has taken an increasing interest in ESP, and the Russians have set up eight research laboratories on telepathy and connected subjects.

12. V. Turvey, *The Beginnings of Seership*, 1911.

13. Cayce exercised his powers for thirty-five years, treating over 30,000 cases. In 1931 the Association for Research and Enlightenment was set up for the purpose of observing his activity.

14. Max Kroenig, *Gibt es ein Fortleben nach dem Tode?*, quoted by Moufang in *Magier, Mächte und Mysterien*, Heidelberg.

15. Neurophysiologists generally hold that the intellectual faculties are associated with the cerebral cortex (the most recent part of the brain from the evolutionary point of view) and the 'associative areas', while more ancient and fundamental powers, including probably those of a paranormal kind, are connected with the thalamic and hypothalamic centres of the diencephalon, the medulla oblongata etc. There would appear to be a kind of antagonism between the two seats of consciousness, which would explain why mediums and 'sensitives'

have to be in a state of trance or semi-trance to exercise their special faculties.

16. Cf. Teilhard de Chardin, *The Phenomenon of Man*, 1959, and P. Leroy, *Pierre Teilhard de Chardin tel que je l'ai connu*, 1958.

## CHAPTER 3

1. This is the 'somnambulistic' stage of a hypnotic trance, during which paranormal powers come into operation while the subject becomes less sensitive to external stimuli, e.g. physical pain.

2. This was the case with 'Delta', a medium studied by Tenhaeff: see Chapter 10 below.

3. J.R. Buchanan in *Journal of Man*, 1849, vol. I; W. Denton, *The Soul of Things, or psychometric researches and discoveries*, 3 vols., New York, 1863-73.

4. On the basis of a few archaeological fragments Elizabeth Denton described Cicero's house, the destruction of Pompeii and the tombs of the Pharohs at Thebes (Luxor): cf. W. and E. Denton, *Nature's Secrets, or Psychometric Researches*, 1863.

5. As Whately Carington remarks (*Telepathy*, 1945) the proof of the pudding is in the eating: hypotheses must be judged by facts.

6. G. Pagenstecher, *Past Events Seership*, New York, 1923.

7. *The Shadow Land*. op. cit.

8. P. Devaux, *L'avenir fantastique*, 1942; G.W. Lambert in *Journal* of the S.P.R., No. 683, March 1955 ( and ibid., July-Oct. 1953); Serge Hutin, 'A propos du cas du Trianon', in *Revue Métapsychique*, Nos. 24 and 26, 1953. [Translator's note: also Lucille Iremonger, *The Ghosts of Versailles*, 1957].

9. Op. cit.

10. *Tomorrow*, March-April, 1955.

11. Pagenstecher, op. cit.

## CHAPTER 4

1. Maeterlinck, *Le temps enseveli*, 1908.

2. As Tyrrell observes (*The Personality of Man*, 1947), the faculty of seeing in the dark is part of the hallucinatory state.

3. 'If one can imagine a pattern, originating in some mind, extending to a large number of percipients, then all those percipients might be telepathically impressed to see the same

scene.' (Tyrrell, op. cit., pp. 66-7).

4. *Revue métapsychique,* 1921, pp. 380-3. The first message was forwarded to Dr Geley and Dr Jules Roche about two months before it was confirmed by events.

5. *Neue Wissenschaft,* Oct. 1956, and *Tomorrow,* Nov. 1955.

6. R.G. Trilles, *Les Pygmées de la forêt équatoriale,* 1932.

7. Eileen Garrett, *My Life as a Search for the Meaning of Mediumship,* 1939.

8. We do not believe, however, that this could be achieved by everyone. Dunne was evidently a 'sensitive', as shown by the number of his precognitive dreams.

9. P. Forthuny was not only clairvoyant but a poet and dramatist. He once wrote: 'When I become aware of a future event the knowledge explodes in my mind with such force that I lose all control over my ideas.'

10. Cf. C.H. Hinton, *What is the Fourth Dimension?* (1887), quoted by Dunne, op. cit.

11. J. Huizinga, op. cit.

12. Another view put forward in this connection is that precognition involves thinking with out 'future brain': see the Dutch physicist J.M.J. Kooy in *Journal of Parapsychology,* No. 4, Dec. 1957. This idea is based on the fact of our continuity through time: the 'future brain' must contain a record of everything that is going to happen to us.

13. G. Zorab (of the Hague) in *Parapsychological Supplement to Minerva Medica,* vol. 50, No. 38.

14. As Planck observes, 'Seen from the outside, the human will is casually determined; seen from within, it is free.' Similar paradoxes occur in physical science. Physicists have discovered that the microcosmic world cannot be explained on the principles of Bacon and Descartes, and it would be surprising if the same were not true to some extent in the field of psychology and parapsychology, where the variables are so much more numerous and intangible.

*CHAPTER 5*

1. *Le Temps enseveli,* op. cit.

2. *Journal of the American S.P.R.,* No. 3, July 1956.

3. Op. cit.

4. Charles Richet, *L'avenir et la prémonition,* 1931.

5. On the night of 22 November 1963 Signora A.P., a doctor's wife in Florence, dreamt she saw the President walking along

in broad daylight beside a wall; then some ivy growing on the wall hid his face, and she awoke with a feeling of distress. The ivy is significant as a parasite which sucks the vital juices from plants. Details of the dream have been furnished by Prof. William Mackenzie.

6. Cf. A. Mackenzie, *Frontiers of the Unknown*, 1968, pp. 50 ff. [Translator's note].

7. Dunne had numerous precognitive dreams of the explosion of Mont Pelée (1902), in which 40,000 died, and also of a railway disaster on 14 April 1913 near the Forth Bridge. Dr Prince had a nightmare in which two trains collided at the mouth of a tunnel; the event took place a few hours later, some sixty miles away, with many details resembling those of the dream.

8. *Journal of the American S.P.R.*, No. 4, Oct. 1956.

9. As Maeterlinck observes, of the former class people will avoid disaster by falling ill, changing their plans, losing their way etc.: a love-affair or a lawsuit, a moment's laziness or forgetfulness will ensure that they tread the path of safety. The others, *per contra*, are sure to board a train that is going to be derailed, or enter a house that catches fire, or walk under a tower that is about to collapse; and if they fall in love with a woman she is certain to be the wrong one. Modern psychologists recognize that accident-proneness is related to conflicts in the subconscious, guilt-complexes and self-punishing tendencies. For 'success-proneness', cf. Chapter 18 below.

10. e.g. the plane crash at Warsaw on 14 July 1924 in which Dr Geley, the only passenger, was killed: the accident was predicted several times, notably by P. Forthuny who informed Geley himself, but neither of them had reason to surmise that he was the victim.

11. *Neue Wissenschaft*, Jan. 1954.

12. *Planète*, No. 6, pp. 101 ff.

13. Cf. Jean Suyeux in *Science et Vie*, Feb. 1962.

*CHAPTER 6*

1. See the latter's *Des esprits et leurs manifestations fluidiques*, quoted by Trintzuis, op. cit.

2. Latter from Chopin to Grzymala, 28 July 1894.

3. *Métagnomie, télépsychie, diapsychie* (Boirac); *cryptesthésie* (Richet); telaesthesia (Myers); telemnesia (Hislop). None of these terms have had much success in common speech.

4. According to Tyrrell (*The Nature of Human Personality*, 1954), telepathy, clairvoyance, psychometry and precognition all represent an enlargement of our nature beyond its normal bounds.

5' Ossowiecki, when studied by Dr Geley in 1923 at the *Institut métapsychique international,* stated that in his own case the onset of a semi-trance was marked by a sensation of warmth in his head and cold in his hands. 'After that I soon have little consciousness of my surroundings, and begin to see, hear, feel and say whatever I am asked to reveal.'

6. Neurophysiological studies of this subject are in their infancy; however, the opinion of Dr Francis Lefébure (*Expériences initiatiques*, 1956, vol. II, p. 57) that mediumistic faculties are connected with functional characteristics of the medulla oblongata seems to be confirmed by Franke and Koopman, though others take a different view.

According to Dr Orlando Camaseno in the Argentine, the electro-encephalograph of a medium in a trance is not unlike that of a light sleep, with normal frequencies and reductions of voltage. Prof. Umberto di Giacomo in Rome reports on amplification of the alpha rhythm with no increase of frequency.

7. Raoul de Fleurière, a medium studied by Tocquet, states that in the condition of trance he does not feel as though his conscious self has ceased to exist, but as though it and the unconscious were simultaneous occupants of his being on two different planes: the conscious mind above, in a state of relative passivity, and the unconscious below, in lively operation.

8. Lévy-Bruhl, *Les fonctions mentales dans les sociétés inférieures*, 1912. The author associates this condition more especially with primitive peoples.

9. 'There are two profoundly different ways of knowing a thing: by going round about it and by penetrating into it. The former depends on the angle of vision we choose and the symbols by which we express ourselves; with the second, there is no angle of vision and no symbols. The first is relative, the second — where possible at all — is absolute.' (Bergson, *Introduction to Metaphysics*, 1913).

10. This 'unknown' was also the object of enquiry by Plato and Aristotle. In the *Phaedrus* Plato admits that a kind of intuitive knowledge, superior to that of discursive reason, is granted by divine favour to certain men and women: it op-

erates in a kind of eclipse of reason or fit of delirium, this term however not implying madness but something akin to religious or poetic exaltation or the transport of love. Aristotle held that the clairvoyance of sibyls and prophetesses was a natural faculty and not a disease of the mind.

11. Among the best-known are harmine or telepathine, mescaline (extracted from the peyotl cactus), psilocybin (from a Mexican fungus) and the synthetic substance LSD (lysergic acid diethylamide).

12. Moufang, op. cit.

13. Prof B. Riess of Hunter College, New York, as reported by Rhine, carried out 1,850 tests with Zener cards with a girl who achieved an average of 18.24 successes out of a possible 25, and on one occasion actually scored full marks; but the authors stress that this was an exceptional case.

Tests appear to show that better scores are obtained by subjects who believe in ESP ('sheep') than by sceptics ('goats'), and that results also depend on their state of mind and health, age, sympathy with the experimenter, the possible use of drugs etc. Fatigue always sets in after a time and has a negative effect. See also Sophie de Trabek in *Initiation et science*, Sep.-Dec. 1959.

14. Cf. G. Spencer Brown, *Probability and Scientific Inference*, 1957.

15. Similar views have been expressed by Giovanni Schepis, who points out that emotion may well be a valid component of ESP and telepathy in general, and F. Egidi, who writes: 'Rhine's experiments were intended to convince official scientists, but have not in fact much altered their view of parapsychology. Moreover, subjects like Linzmayer and Pearce, who got full marks with Zener cards, do not seem to have any other paranormal gifts of note, while, on the other hand, the most famous clairvoyants do not work with Zener cards.' (Bollettino della S.I.P., July-Dec. 1957).


*CHAPTER 7*

1. Paramahansa Yogananda, *Autobiography of a Yogi,* New York, 1946.

2. Cf. Chapter 4, note 3.

3. Alexandra David-Neel, *With Mystics and Magicians in Tibet,* 1931. This author describes telepathic messages sent 'on the wind' by sages to their disciples, by means of intense concen-

tration and a prior attunement of minds which can be improved by training.

4. However, inter-mental contacts paly an important part in infancy, and Ehrenwald speaks of a 'telepathic cordon' between mother and child. Some scholars hold that this accounts for the rapidity with which young children acquire the gift of language and other skills.

5. W. Tudor Pole, *The Silent Road*, 1960.

6. Liselle Reymond, *My Life with a Brahman Family*, 1958.

7. W. Franklin Prince, *The Case of Patience Worth*, New York, 1964; also Ruby Yeatman in *Light*, Dec. 1956.

8. *Pittura e disegni metapsichici*, Milan, 1954. Some of the instances in the text are quoted from this work.

9. Op. cit. (Chapter 1, note 20).

10. Ramacharaka, *Raja Yoga*, 1917.

CHAPTER 8

1. Aimé Michel, 'Les jeunes prodiges', in *Science et vie*, No. 357, June 1962.

2. E.g. the young organist Jean-Claude Pennetier, referred to by A. Michel, op. cit.

3. The philologist Alfredo Trombetti (1866-1929) was born of illiterate parents but taught himself French and German in childhood. At twelve he knew Latin, Greek and Hebrew, and when adult his score of languages mounted to over a hundred. To learn e.g. Persian took him only a few weeks.

4. For mathematical prodigies cf. Myers, op. cit. Inaudi was the subject of an article by Binet in *Revue philosophique*, 1896. See also Robert Tocquet, *Le calcul mental à la portée de tous*, 1960.

5. The first of the three stages known collectively as *samyana*, which lead to the acstatic condition of *samadhi* as described in a later chapter.

6. As Prof. Mackenzie pointed out in an interview, mathematical prodigies like Inaudi are to be distinguished from paranormal calculators who perceive results by intuition. But the distinction is somewhat theoretical, as many have exemplified both faculties, including Inaudi himself.

7. In 1961 Dagbert gave an exhibition in a Calais theatre to an audience of 1,300, the results being checked by an expert mathematician using a computer. Dagbert's speed beat the computer's by ninety-five seconds. (*Bollettino di Informazione*

*per i Centri Meccanografici*, Milan, Dec. 1961).
8. See Aimé Michel in *Planète*, No. 17, July-Aug. 1964, p. 141.
9. David Aurel, *La cybernétique et l'homme*, 1964, especially Chapter III, and references there to the congress held at Teddington near London, Oct, 1958.
10. Like mediums and clairvoyants, mathematical prodigies have often suffered from physical or nervous defects; but they also include such genuises as Euler, Gauss, Arago and Ampère. Similarly, from Socrates onwards many great men have had mediumistic gifts: Gothe, Lincoln, Napoleon, Byron, Tennyson, Victor Hugo, Mark Twain, Einstein, Jung and scholars like De Sanctis, Dunne, F. Morton Prince and Gabriel Marcel.
   The notion that there is something pathological about mediums goes back to the epoch of strenuous séances which left their mark on the subjects' personality and nervous system. It is upheld at the present day by many scientists, including Binet, A. Assailly and Chauvin, while a more objective view is taken by, among others, Martiny, Urban and Hagenbuckner.
11. B. Vives, 'Les mathématicians n'en font qu'à leur tête', in *Science et vie*, 1962'

CHAPTER 9
1. Cf. J. Lhermitte, *Les Mécanismes du cerveau*, 1949, and an article on bilocation by the same author in *La Tour Saint-Jacques*, No. 6-7, 1956.
2. *Revue métapsychique,* No. 5, 1930.
3. S. Muldoon and H. Carrington, *The Projection of the Astral Body*, 1965; Gabriel Delanne, *Les apparitions matérialisées des vivants et des morts*, 1911; also papers by Hornell Hart and J.H.M. Whiteman in Proceedings of the S.P.R., May 1956.
4. See *Planète*, No. 9, where Chauvin writes: 'Not having had its revolution, psychiatry is too often merely a conjectural science.'
5. Warcollier was director of the *Institut métapsychique international* and spent nearly fifty years investigating paranormal phenomena, especially telepathy and thought transmission.
6. *Planète*, No. 15, p. 25.
7. Mircea Eliade, *Shamanism: archaic techniques of ecstasy*, 1964.
8. L. Massignon, *Al Hallaj, martyr mystique de l'Islam*, 1922.

9. G. Casaril, *Rabbi Siméon Bar Yochai*, 1961.
10. J.C. Chatterji, *La philosophie ésotérique de l'Inde*, Brussels, 1898.
11. Ramacharaka, op. cit.
12. W.T. Stace, *Religion and the Modern Mind*, New York, 1952.
13. Op. cit.
14. Maryse Choisy's tests, carried out in 1952, showed different results corresponding to the three stages of *dharana*, *dhyana* and *samadhi*. Drs Das and Gustaut presented a paper in 1955 according to which the EEG of a yogi in a state of *samadhi* appeared as an anomalous but not a pathological line, which could be taken as indicating intense excitement of the cerebral cortex together with bodily lethargy.
15. G. Bernanos, *Diary of a Country Priest*, 1936.

*CHAPTER 10*
1. A report by a special group of Italian and French journalists was published simultaneously in *Scienza e Vita* and *Science et vie*, July 1964.
2. Romaios, *Cultes populaires de la Thrace*, Institut français d'Athènes, Cahiers d'hellénisme, I (1949); Jeanne and Georges Roux, *Grèce*, 1957; and articles by Marianthi Diamantoglou in *Revue métapsychique*, 1952 and 1953.
3. Harry Price, *Confessions of a Ghost-Hunter*, 1936.
4. Olivier Leroy, *Les hommes salamandres*, 1931.
5. P. Devaux, *Les fantômes devant la science*, 1954.
6. Cf. Herbert Thurston, S.J., op. cit. in Chapter 2, note 8. Like other Catholic authors, Fr. Thurston does not regard the exceptional gifts of so many great mystics as 'charismatic' and therefore marks of sanctity: the requirement for canonization is, first and foremost, the practice of heroic virtue.
7. Cf. the preceding note.
8. Moufang, op. cit.
9. The photographs, taken at three different stages and from different positions, showed the yogi in a horizontal position about a yard off the ground, his hand lightly resting on a stick.
10. *Presse médicale*, No. 83, 14 Oct. 1936.
11. For anabiosis see L. Talamonti in *Scienza e Vita,* June 1956, and J. Filliozat, *Magie et médecine,* 1943. The results of Dr Brosse's second visit to India were published by Harvard

University.

12. Among mediums who emitted light during séances were Daniel Home, Eusapia Paladino, Stainton Moses, Erto and Don Luisito (on whom see Chapter 14 below); also a woman at Pirano on whom Prof. Protti of Padua made a film in 1934.

Scent: various yogis and Western mediums, including Stainton Moses and 'Margery' (Mrs. Crandon),

Elongation of the body: Home and others.

Fasting: Molly Fancher, Therese Neumann and Marie Fuertner.

As Fr. Thurston's book shows, many mystics also displayed these gifts.

13. About forty years ago Jules Romains of the *Académie française* showed by experiment that some 'sensitives' can develop extra-retinal vision in certain circumstances, the faculty being located in various parts of the body but usually in the tips of the fingers. His evidence was ignored by academic science, but recently the same gift has been found to exist in Rose Kuleshova, a Russian girl from Nizhni Tagil, and in Patricia Stanley, whose case was studied by Prof. Richard Youtz at Barnard College, New York. The literature on extra-retinal vision goes back to 1785. Cf. L. Talamonti in *Scienza e Vita*, March 1963.

CHAPTER 11.

1. *Tomorrow*, vol. I, No. 2, winter 1952-3.

2. Cf. Podmore and Sidgwick, *Phantasms of the Living*, 1923, and studies by Louisa Rhine. An exhaustive study of hallucinations was made by the British S.P.R. in 1951.

3. James H. Hislop observes that 'Other things being equal, the deeper the trance, the better are the phenomena.' The principle also works in reverse: with María Reyes de Z., the more searching questions were put to her the deeper her trance became, to the extent of resembling actual lethargy.

CHAPTER 12

1. F. Lefébure, op. cit., 1959.

2. *Revue spirite*, 1929.

3. See note 1 above. Lefébure mentions the practices of holding the breath, shaking the head rhythmically in a certain way, repeating mystic syllables (mantras) and concentrating mentally on centres of energy.

4. See Whiteman in *Proceedings of the S.P.R.*, May 1956. The report adopts a position similar to that of Myers and denominated the Revised Etheric Object Hypothesis: it postulates a kind of double which can be evoked at will and possesses a real existence in the psychic universe, but can also manifest itself in the physical universe and move along the time-scale.

5. *Proceedings of the S.P.R.*, Vol. XIV, pp. 343-7, quoted in H. Carrington, *The Psychic World*, 1938.

6. Olivier Leroy, *La raison primitive*, 1927; also *Almanach des missions*, 1907.

7. This corresponds to the Egyptian *Ka*, the *simulacrum* of the Romans and the 'subtle body' or *linga-sharira* of Hinduism.

8. Alexandra David-Neel, op. cit., speaking of phantasms created by living persons, says: 'The apparition may be identical in form to its author, and in that case it may be thought of, if we choose, as an ethereal double; but sometimes there are several apparitions, so that it is hard to ascribe them to a single double; and in other cases the apparitions, whether one or many, do not resemble their author.'

## CHAPTER 13

1. N. Naegeli-Osjord in *Neue Wissenschaft*, No. 2, Aug.-Sept. 1957.

2. Cf. W. Stuart in *Light*, March 1957.

3. Many psychiatrists deny the existence of genuine hallucinations as opposed to purely subjective and pathological ones. Among those who recognize the former are Tenhaeff, Urban, Hagenbuckner, Naegeli-Osjord, Disertori and Assagiolo.

As for communications with the 'beyond', we may bear in mind Tyrrell's remark (op. cit. in Chapter 6, note 4) that death does not take us into a different world, but merely into a different mode of knowing and perceiving.

4. Some mediums have spoken similarly, e.g. Eileen Garrett: 'Since thought is the fundamental process of creation, and nothing that has once appeared in the world is ever lost, it may be that those who lived before us have imprinted a living record of themselves on the ether of our cosmos, and that such forms can be brought back to life by those who desire to do so and have some special link with the past.'

5. One reason for supposing that ghosts, whatever their true nature, cannot materialize without human help is the fact that their appearance involves a loss of nervous and thermic energy

on the part of mediums and others; cf. the article cited in note 10 below.

6. For the Millvale ghost see *Harper's Magazine*, 1938.

7. *Tomorrow*, vol. I, No. 2, winter 1952-3.

8. Myers was convinced that a ghost was not to be identified with the entire personality of a dead individual: he wrote (op. cit.) that 'if the relationship between a ghost and the after-life of the surviving self is similar to that between a dream and reality, then spectral manifestations can only represent a vague memory or instinct of the kind that gives an obscure individuality to our commonest dreams.' Myers believed firmly in survival, but not in anthropomorphic terms. He also made the interesting suggestion that some ghosts behave like subjects under post-hypnotic suggestion.

9. There is an interesting parallel between modern ideas of the pluralism or stratification of personality and ancient religious or philosophical notions, e.g. the threefold Hebrew distinction between 'breath of life' (*nishmat*), soul (*ruach*) and the 'spirit of the bones' which remains attached to the body after death, and can be compared with the 'psychic residue' (cf. note 15 below) of which ghosts are made. In Buddhist doctrine, again, the self is a pure illusion and personality is the effect of a non-permanent psychic aggregation. We have more than one consciousness, and the desire to live inheres in only one part of our being. (Alexandra David-Neel, op.cit.).

10. *Tomorrow*, vol. I, No. 3, 1953: article on the Rockland County ghost, using material from Eileen Garrett's files.

11. S.P.R. *Journal*, 1911. Lieutenant Sutton's ghost appeared several times to his parents: he had been killed in a quarrel with fellow-officers, but the military authorities published a version of suicide. After some months the body was exhumed at the family's request, and the details of his wounds etc. as described by the ghost proved to be accurate.

12. In this case too a young man was falsely supposed to have committed suicide. His ghost appeared several times to his former employer, who did not even know he was dead, urging him not to believe the official story.

13. G. Delanne, *Les apparitions des vivants et des morts*, 1911.

14. Sir A. Conan Doyle, *The Edge of the Unknown*, 1930.

15. R. Guénon, *Le règne de la quantité et les signes des temps*, 1945: Chap. 27, 'Résidus psychiques'.

16. Prof. K. Hagenbuckner quotes a somewhat similar case in

*Tijdschrift voor Parapsychologie*, Jan.-March 1959. A small girl used to converse with an unknown invisible playmate who, from her description, was evidently a brother of hers who had died at fifteen years of age, before she was born. However, she knew him as a child of seven or eight at most: her unconscious had chosen a 'vestige' of the past suited to her need for company of her own age.

## CHAPTER 14

1. See Chapter 10, note 3.
2. Claparède, *Théorie biologique du sommeil*, Geneva, 1905.
3. Th. Flournoy, *Nouvelles observations sur un cas de somnambulisme avec glossolalie*, Geneva, 1902.
4. The argument about ghosts and related paranormal events has been bedevilled by the misapprehension that they prove or disprove survival after death: prejudices on the latter point have, all too often, swayed people's opinion on the former.
5. This was the view of Richet, who first used the term 'ectoplasm' in this sense, and of Mme J.A. Bisson, author of *Les phénomènes dits de matérialisation*, 1914. Professor W. J. Crawford, in experiments with the medium Miss Goligher, believed that he had established that the medium underwent a loss of weight equivalent to the amount of ectoplasm generated. Modern views on the nature of this substance are less certain. It appears to assume many forms, from an invisible or semi-fluid consistency to that of a solid resembling protoplasm.
6. G. Geley, *L'ectoplasmie et la clairvoyance*, 1924.
7. Tocquet, in *Les pouvoirs secrets de l'homme* (op.cit., p. 446), writes: 'Like most mediums, Guzik was capable of resorting to crude deception when the atmosphere, or his own psycho-physiological state, was unfavourable to experiments. . . . Nevertheless he was a true medium with remarkable ectoplasmic and telekinetic faculties.'
8. Flournoy suggests in connection with the medium Hélène Smith that the personality may 'split' along predetermined lines, like a crystal. Many believe that the entities which manifest themselves at a séance are nothing but the medium's 'neurotic symptoms' or 'objectivized dreams': cf. Tenhaeff in *Tijdschrift voor Parapsychologie*, Nos. 2-3, 1957.
9. E.g. the entity 'Stasie' (Chapter 17 below), which manifested itself on numerous occasions over a period of years. The relevant literature is full of more or less mysterious beings

who appeared over long periods and sometimes to more than one spiritualist group — e.g. a certain 'Dr Bartoli', well known in Roman mediumistic circles.

10. See a letter from Thomas Mann to Alexander Imich, who wrote on the subject in *Tomorrow*, No. 3, spring 1953.

CHAPTER 15

1. E.L. Gardner, *Fairies*, 1966.

2. A. Conan Doyle, *The Coming of the Fairies*, 1922; Geoffrey Hodson, *Fairies at Work and Play*, 1925, and *Kingdom of Fairies,* quoted in Conan Doyle, op. cit.; Rudolf Schwartz, *Die Geisterwelt ist nicht verschlossen,* Preetz (Schleswig-Holstein), 1949; Anne Osmont in *Initiation et Science*, 1949.

3. Norbert Okolowicz, *Compte-rendu des séances faites avec le médium Franek Kluski,* Warsaw, 1928, quoted in Tocquet, op.cit.

4. Preface to Jean-René Legrand, *Méditations cabbalistiques,* 1955.

5. Serge Hutin, 'Du nouveau sur le cas du Trianon', in *Revue métapsychique*, Nov.-Dec. 1953.

6. *Journal of the S.P.R.*, July-Oct. 1955.

7. In lectures given at Canterbury and elsewhere some years ago, Lord Dowding maintained that fairies were small winged creatures, male or female, about a foot tall, and that he had friends who saw and talked with them. The belief in small supernatural beings of various kinds is of course found in many countries. It should be noted that superstition can also be a factor in the creation of 'life' by a collective psyche, i.e. the group will be capable of objectifying entities that they believe in.

8. Articles in *Tijdschrift voor Parapsychologie*, Nos. 1-5, 1955.

9. Hereward Carrington believed that the human psyche could create semi-material forms and that this might account for the evocation of demons in magic ceremonies etc. (On the other hand, he thought ghosts represented the actual personality of the dead). For a description of a recent séance at which diabolic entities were evoked see Francesco Waldner, *Mes aventures surnaturelles*, 1962, Chapter VIII.

10. In 1955 the Italian press reported the appearance of a diabolic entity at a death-bed at Sinopoli (Reggio Calabria), in the presence of many witnesses. Other cases of death-bed apparitions are described by E. Bozzano in *Le visioni dei*

*morenti*, 1953: one of these, recorded in 1902, was a female figure about three feet tall, wearing a peplum and a crown.
11. In the course of two years Dr Osis collected evidence from physicians and nurses on thousands of cases of death-bed hallucinations and visions, many being the 'ghosts' of dead husbands or wives.
12. However, Binet has shown that subjective hallucinatory images also seem to obey optical laws, e.g. if a hypnotized subject is made to look through a prism or lens or the wrong end of a pair of binoculars.
13. E.g. Jacques Bergier in *Nos pouvoirs inconnus*, p.40.
14. Article by Leif Aarstad in *Light*, Dec. 1957.

*CHAPTER 16*
1. Major A. Romier in *Light*, 1898, p. 65.
2. *International Psychic Gazette, 1925.*
3. Op. cit. in Chapter 13, note 16.
4. C.G. Jung and Wolfgang Pauli, *The Interpretation of Nature and the Psyche*, 1955, including Jung's monograph *Synchronicity: an Acausal Connecting Principle*. Pauli refers in this work to the Hersenberg principle of indeterminacy and to particles that appear to move against the time-stream.
5. Preface by Jung to English version of *I Ching*, 1951.
6. E. Tizané, *Sur la piste de l'hôte inconnu*, 1950.
7. *Annales des sciences psychiques*, 1911.
8. *The Haunted Mind*, New York, 1959.
9. Dr Alain Assailly was the first to point out that brief spells of haunting of this type are nearly always associated with the simultaneous presence of a person at the age of puberty and another undergoing the change of life. Cf. *Revue métapsychique*, July-Aug. 1964.
10. H. Thurston, *Ghosts and Poltergeists*, 1953; H. Carrington and N. Fodor, *Haunted People*, New York, 1951.
11. E. Tizané, 'Comment j'ai été conduit a m'intéresser aux hantises', in *Initiation et Science*, Jan.-Feb. 1955.
12. Pratt and Roll, 'The Seaford Disturbances', in *Journal of Parapsychology*, vol. 22, June 1958; see also *Tomorrow*, No. 3, 1958, and *Journal of the American S.P.R.*, No. 2, 1958.
13. *Revue métapsychique*, vol. I, No. 5, 1957 (letter to the editor).

## CHAPTER 17

1. Alexandra David-Neel relates (op.cit.) that she was originally sceptical of this, but changed her mind when she became acquainted with the power of certain sects in Tibet to bring maleficent beings to life and embody them in pictures or statues. It may be noted that a certain statuette was assigned symbolically to represent 'Stasie' from the outset of her manifestations.

2. Professor Mackenzie represented Italy at the Second International Metapsychic Congress at Warsaw, of which he was elected president. The account quoted was published in *Luce e Ombra*.

3. On the 'reality' of ghosts, Eileen Garrett wrote: 'I have seen thousands of apparitions of the dead that appeared most lifelike, and have received messages from them, but I still do not truly know where the messages come from.' Dr Philips Davis reports that the medium Daniel Home declared at the end of his life: 'No, a medium cannot believe in spirits: he is the one person who cannot.' Maria Reyes de Z. was not a believer in spiritualism, nor is Pasqualina Pezzola.

4. *Saturday Review*, 15 April 1958.

5. *Annales des sciences psychiques*, 1909.

6. Ralph S. Lillie, *General Biology and Philosophy of Organisms*, Chicago, 1945; Edmund W. Sinnott, *The Biology of the Spirit*, 1956.

7. *The Nature of Human Personality*, op. cit.

8. Wassermann, 'Field Theory of Parapsychology' contributed to a symposium on ESP organized in 1956 by the Ciba Foundation, London.

9. This term refers to the modern semantic doctrine that a concept must always be related to a clearly definable operation.

10. See Chapter 20 below.

11. See *Nature*, 25 April 1964.

## CHAPTER 18

1. *Journal of Parapsychology*, No. 26, 1962, p.112.

2. B. de Cressac and G. Chevalier, *Problème crucial: la métapsychique*, 1960.

3. *Psychia*, 1938, p. 210. —There may have been an element of precognition in Karrer's case, but it is unlikely that it would have assumed so precise and specialized a form.

4. During the second world war the Rockefeller Foundation financed an Institute of Personality Research with a team of psychologists under Dr Donald MacKenna, who applied this branch of investigation to the question of key military appointments.

5. Attilio Gatti, *Tom-Toms in the Night*, 1932.

6. Christian Lepinte, *Goethe et l'occultisme*, Strasbourg University, 1957, and Moufang, op. cit. Goethe described his experiences in this line to Eckermann.

7. P. Ringger, *Das Weltbild der Parapsychologie*, Olten, 1959, and article in *Neue Wissenschaft*, July 1957.

8. William Walker Atkinson, *The Secret of Mental Magic*, 1909.

9. *Revue métapsychique*, No. 2, 1948.

10. Paul Monet, *Entre deux feux: Français et Annamites*, 1928.

11. Franklin Loehr, *The Power of Prayer on Plants*, New York, 1959.

CHAPTER 19

1. Aimé Michel in *Science et vie*, No. 541, Oct. 1962.

2. By the French Consul-General at Istanbul, in 1952.

3. G. Geley, *De l'inconscient au conscient*, op. cit.

4. Cf. F. Boullier, *Histoire de la philosophie cartésienne*, 1868.

5. *Light*, 1926, p.608.

6. *Journal of the S.P.R.*, Oct. 1904.

7. Durov is said to have demonstrated to specialists his gift of telepathic communication with animals, and Sergeant Maimone claims similar powers: see Guglielmo Bonuzzi, *Gli animali si vogliono bene*, Bologna.

8. Tocquet, *Les pouvoirs secrets de l'homme*, op. cit., pp. 85-6: he believes that Durov's animals were controlled by cleverly concealed signs. A minority of observers hold the same opinion regarding the Elberfeld stallions. Tocquet's view contrasts with the pan-psychic theories advanced in his *La vie dans la matière et dans le cosmos*, 1950.

9. *Planète*, No. 7, p.48.

10. Marjorie Hessell Tiltman in *Light*, June 1957.

CHAPTER 20

1. *Proceedings of the S.P.R.*, vol. 50, Jan. 1953, p. 182.

2. *La Parapsychologie*, 1954; and seen above, Chapter 16,

note 13. In Oct. 1955 Amadou wrote, in the *Bulletin de parapsychologie de la tour Saint-Jacques,* 'there are other mysteries that science does not and cannot study.'

3. Such meetings were held at Utrecht in 1953, at Saint-Paul-de-Vence in 1954, at Cambridge in 1955 and at Florence in 1958.

4. *Journal of the S.P.R.,* 2 April 1955.

5. *Revue métapsychique,* No. 4, 1956.

6. From Prof. Gex's reply to a questionnaire in connection with the Florence congress (note 3 above).

2. E.g. Tocquet, op. cit., p. 109: 'What ordinary man could go to sleep in his own bed or engage in sexual activity under the observation of a dozen professors equipped with recording instruments? Yet metapsychical phenomena are far more delicate than these, and appear to require a favourable psychic climate.'

8. On the importance of 'sympathy', cf. the experiments with Zener cards by M. Anderson and R. White (*Journal of Parapsychology,* Sep. 1956 and June 1957), and article by J. Langdon-Davies in *Journal of the S.P.R.*, Sep. 1956.

9. Chairs or lectureships in parapsychology exist at Duke University, Durham, N.C.; Freiburg im Breisgau; Utrecht; Leningrad (under a different title); Buenos Aires (Universidad del Litoral); and Montevideo (Instituto Superior).